IMAGES
of America

FREDERICK COUNTY REVISITED

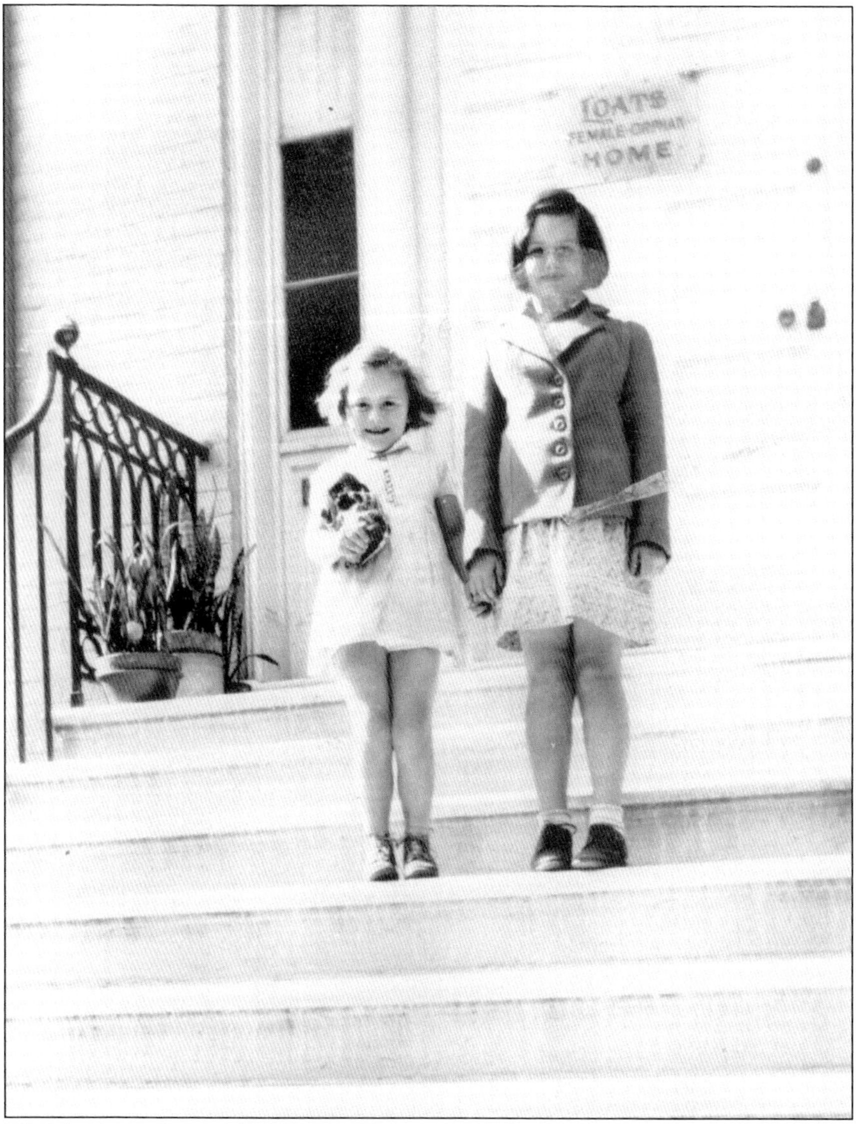

In his will, John Loats bequeathed his home on East Church Street in Frederick to the Evangelical Lutheran Church to be used as an orphanage. The Loats Female Orphan Asylum began accepting children in June 1882. On their first day in the home, sisters Audrey and Shirley Stallings got their photograph taken on the home's front steps. Over the years, more than 100 county girls called the building home until the orphanage closed in 1956. In 1959, it was purchased by the Historical Society of Frederick County to serve as its headquarters and house a museum and library. Today the facility welcomes thousands each year who wish to discover Frederick County's history.

ON THE COVER: From the 1880s to the early 1900s, Americans felt more and more removed from the natural world as the country rapidly industrialized. In response, some middle- and upper-class people turned to what would become known as therapeutic rusticity—escaping to the forest, mountains, or seaside to soothe their stressed minds. It seemed to have worked for these local fellows with the help of a block of ice, sandwiches, watermelon, and beer. (Historical Society of Frederick County.)

IMAGES
of America

FREDERICK COUNTY REVISITED

The Historical Society of Frederick County

ARCADIA
PUBLISHING

ISBN 978-0-7385-5258-3

Published by Arcadia Publishing
Charleston, South Carolina

Printed in the United States of America

Library of Congress Catalog Card Number: 2007922253

For all general information contact Arcadia Publishing at:
Telephone 843-853-2070
Fax 843-853-0044
E-mail sales@arcadiapublishing.com
For customer service and orders:
Toll-Free 1-888-313-2665

Visit us on the Internet at www.arcadiapublishing.com

Contents

ACKNOWLEDGMENTS

This book is the culmination of the efforts of a number of individuals. The Historical Society of Frederick County extends appreciation to staff members Julie Bryan, Heidi Campbell-Shoaf, Elizabeth Conn, Joyce Cooper, Duane Doxzen, Mark Hudson, Kluane LaBelle, Ron Marvin, Paula Riccobono, and Marie Washburn, and society library volunteers Jim Boston, Cassie DeCair, Paul Fogle, Frank Lesure, and Nancy Lesure for contributing research and captions for the book. Special acknowledgment in this regard goes to Heidi and Joyce, who went above and beyond in doing much more than their fair share. All gave up free time and otherwise found time in their busy schedules to participate in the project.

The Historical Society also thanks others who contributed to the book. The job of scanning and preparing the photographs for publication was completed by Bernie Becker, Duane Doxzen, and John Reynolds. Although he did not work directly on this project, David Maloney was of invaluable assistance through his recent efforts to scan the society's collection of glass-plate negatives onto digital media. Friendly assistance with the archival materials was offered by the society's library staff.

The society and project manager extends thanks to the staff at Arcadia Publishing and, specifically, Lauren Bobier, Southern publisher and editor, for making this and the two previous publication projects a pleasant experience.

The Historical Society acknowledges the many individuals and organizations that have contributed to the preservation of our county's history by donating historical images to the society's permanent collection and those who have enriched our understanding by contributing research. Our ability to share Frederick County's rich heritage is dependant on you.

Introduction

Frederick County, Maryland, was formed in 1748. By that time, the few Native Americans left in the area were quickly being displaced by an unending stream of settlers. Germans, English, Scots-Irish, and Africans—some slaves, some free—all poured into the county. They worked the rich Piedmont soil, captured the power of its creeks and rivers to turn their mill wheels, built homes and businesses, and put down lasting roots.

The county seat of Frederick grew to be the largest city in western Maryland, the second largest in the state. Other communities also sprouted up in all directions: New Market, Ridgeville, Woodsboro, Emmitsburg, Wolfsville, Middletown, Brunswick, Knoxville, and Point of Rocks, just to name a few. The Baltimore and Ohio (B&O) Railroad, Chesapeake and Ohio (C&O) Canal, National Road, and many other arteries of transportation and commerce were carved into the bedrock of the county, bringing still more people and with them their own customs and beliefs, as well as mores and pastimes, helping to form a distinctive community.

How do you fit 300 years of history into one book? T. J. C. Williams and Folger McKinsey tried in their seminal *History of Frederick County, Maryland*, first published in 1910. From 1819 to 1878, Fredericktonian Jacob Engelbrecht tried to capture important community events in his voluminous diary (published and available as *The Diary of Jacob Engelbrecht*). Well, the truth is you can't. Not even all the highlights.

This is the Historical Society of Frederick County's third collaboration with Arcadia Publishing to present images from Frederick County's past; *Frederick County* from Arcadia Publishing's Images of America series was published in 2005, and a book of the same name from Arcadia's Postcard History Series was published last year. The purpose of all these books is to provide interesting and informative images, accompanied by facts to make the reader want to learn more. By answering a few questions, we hope to raise many others.

All of the images included here are drawn from the Historical Society of Frederick County's extensive archival collection. This volume has benefited from a number of additions to the collection over the past few years, most notably the acquisition of the William O. Lee Jr. Collection. The Lee Collection of ephemera and photographs relating to the county's African American community has greatly deepened our understanding and ability to document that part of our heritage. The collection was generously donated in 2006 by the Lee family. A number of photographs from the collection are included in these pages.

Also of note is the inclusion of many images taken from the Historical Society's collection of glass-plate negatives. Many of these were created by the Byerly family at their studio in Frederick. A few have been published before. Others are from a collection of Emmitsburg glass-plate negatives donated by Paul and Rita Gordon.

We have tried to include images from throughout the county, from the mid-19th century to the mid-20th century. As with compiling the first Images of America book, one difficulty we encountered was the unavailability of many images from outside the city of Frederick. While the Historical Society's collection of historical photographs from the smaller towns and outlying areas of Frederick County continues to grow, the vast majority of quality images are related to Frederick. Hopefully this situation will improve through the society's dynamic efforts to locate such images and the growing willingness of individuals to share them.

Any pressure that we may have felt to include images of the historical "usual suspects," like Chief Justice Roger B. Taney and the Civil War, was greatly eased through the publication of the previous two Frederick County books. This time around, we were even freer to choose photographs that were simply visually interesting, even if their associated stories were "smaller." Nevertheless, the images in this book, and what they can tell us, are no less important to the understanding of our shared history, one that is mostly made up of such smaller stories.

A formidable effort was made to organize the images in the book into logical and useful chapters. Some images, like those with educational or religious themes, were relatively easy to categorize. Others were not. We also ended up with a number of images of people and places that did not neatly fit into other chapters. Rather than not include them we grouped them together for a final chapter.

You can't fit 300 years—or even the 170 since the advent of photography—of history into a single volume. But the Historical Society invites you to sit back, relax, and enjoy some of the fascinating, inspiring, and just plain odd images and stories that help form our community's history. We then encourage you to get up, get out, and dig deeper. To help you do just that, the Historical Society invites you to its museum, research library, the Roger B. Taney House, and the many public programs it presents throughout the year.

—Duane Doxzen
Book Project Manager

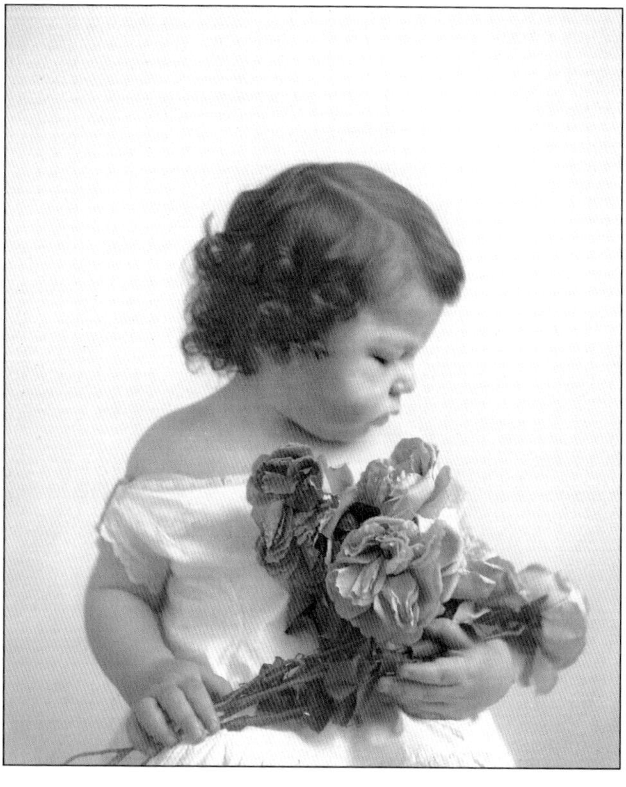

Charles Byerly took this photograph of his son John Francis Byerly about 1907. The Byerly family operated a photographic studio in Frederick from 1842 to 1915. Jacob Byerly, Frederick's first professional photographer, operated the studio until 1868, when he sold it to his son, John Davis Byerly. The latter Byerly passed it on to his own son, Charles Byerly, in 1899. Charles Byerly advertised in 1908 his "instantaneous portraits of children a successful specialty." Many of the best early local images extant can be attributed to the Byerlys. A number of their photographs appear in this book.

One

SCHOOL DAYS

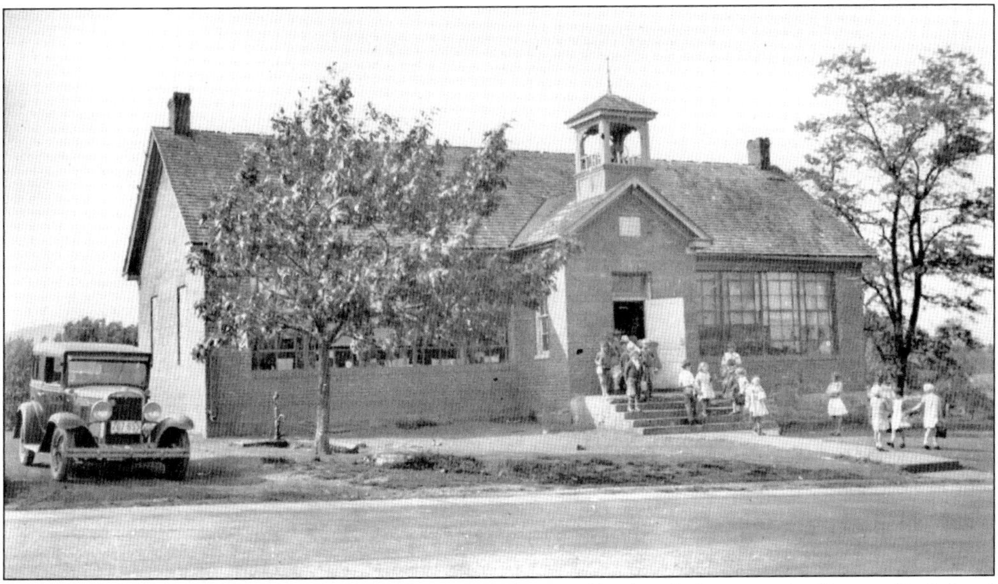

One of more than 100 small schools once scattered across Frederick County, the Feagaville School was constructed about 1900. Its two rooms, accommodating about 60 students in seven grades, originally were heated by wood and coal stoves. The hand pump in the yard provided water for drinking and for washing dirty hands and faces. The school building eventually became the Feagaville Community Center.

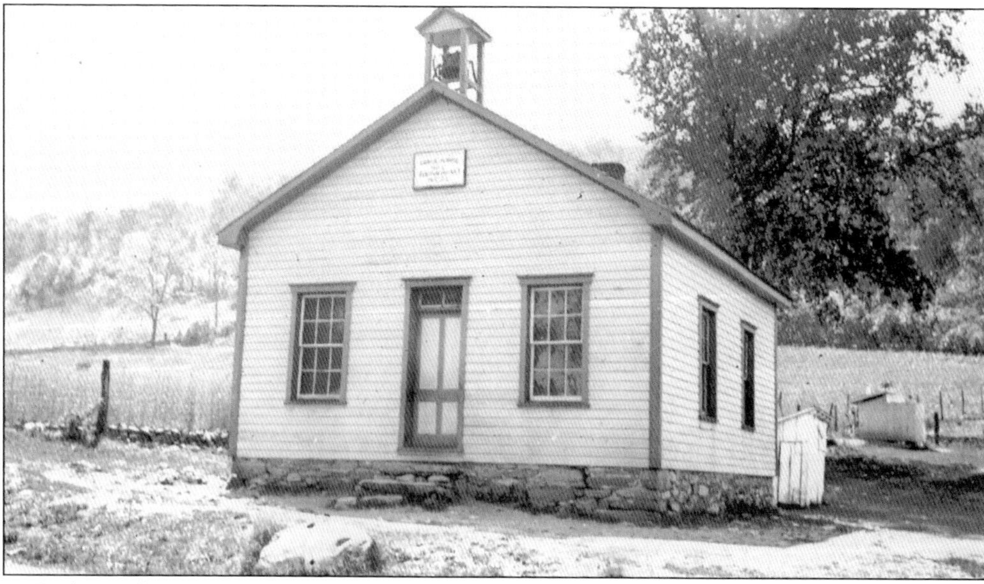

In Burkittsville, like other communities throughout the county, black and white students were educated separately until the 1950s and 1960s. The quarter acre of land on which this wood-frame one-room school stands was purchased by Frederick County's school commissioners in 1877. Located on the Gapland-Burkittsville Road near South Mountain, the Burkittsville Colored School remained in use until 1937, when the remaining 7 students joined the 19 attending the nearby Horsey Colored School.

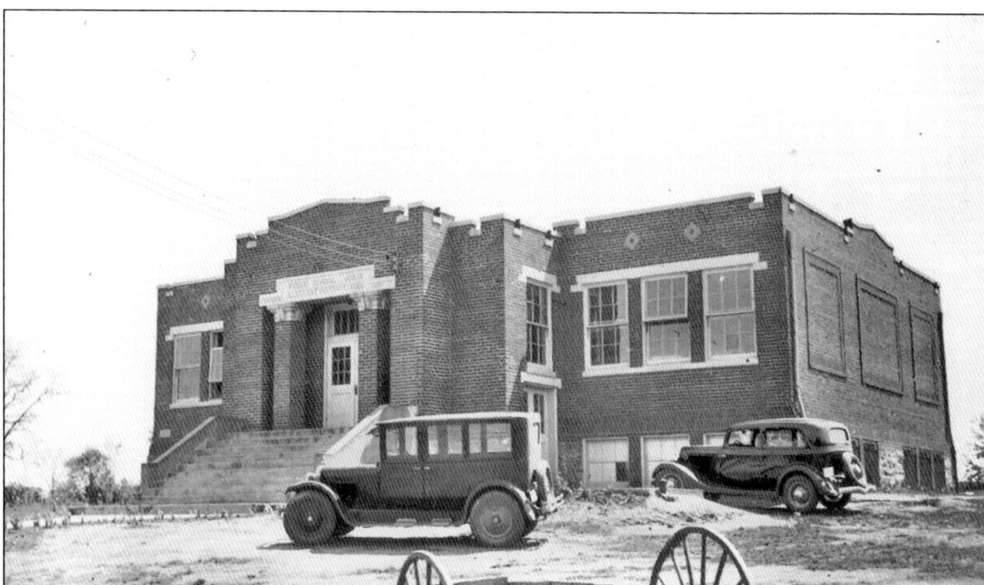

There was a lot of construction in Burkittsville in 1914. By May of that year, the Burkittsville Water Company had completed its installation of water pipes serving 20 homes in town fed by springs on South Mountain, and the school pictured here was complete up to the first floor. The school would serve the local community until 1968, but by then, the water system was long defunct.

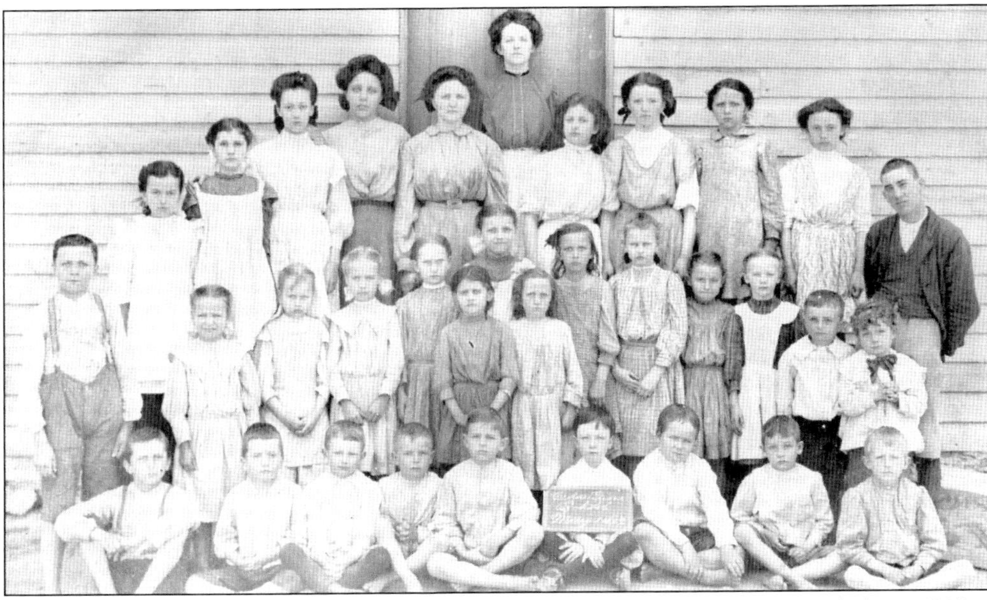

Cedar Grove School, located on the Woodsboro-Liberty Road, was constructed about 1887 to serve the Coppermine neighborhood of Frederick County. The teacher, shown here with her young charges in May 1902, was probably Ella Brant of Baltimore, who was appointed to the school in August 1901. A severe windstorm damaged the building in June 1931, possibly contributing to the school's closure and sale later that year.

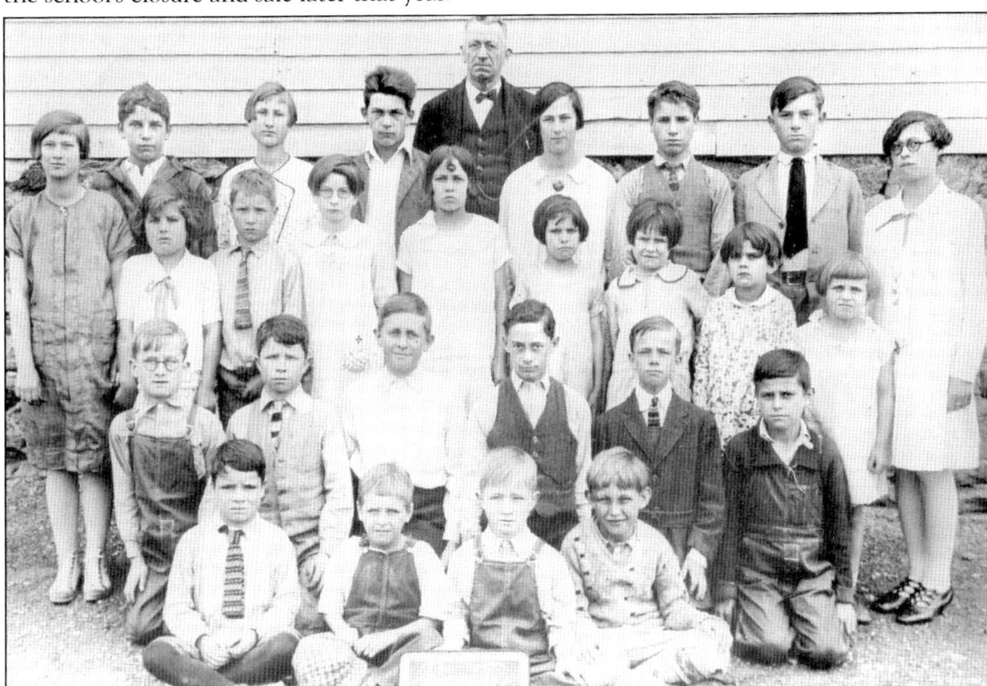

School consolidation throughout Frederick County brought about the closure of Pine Tree School at the end of the 1928–1929 school year. This picture likely shows the last group of students to attend the school, located on Daysville Road, three miles east of Walkersville.

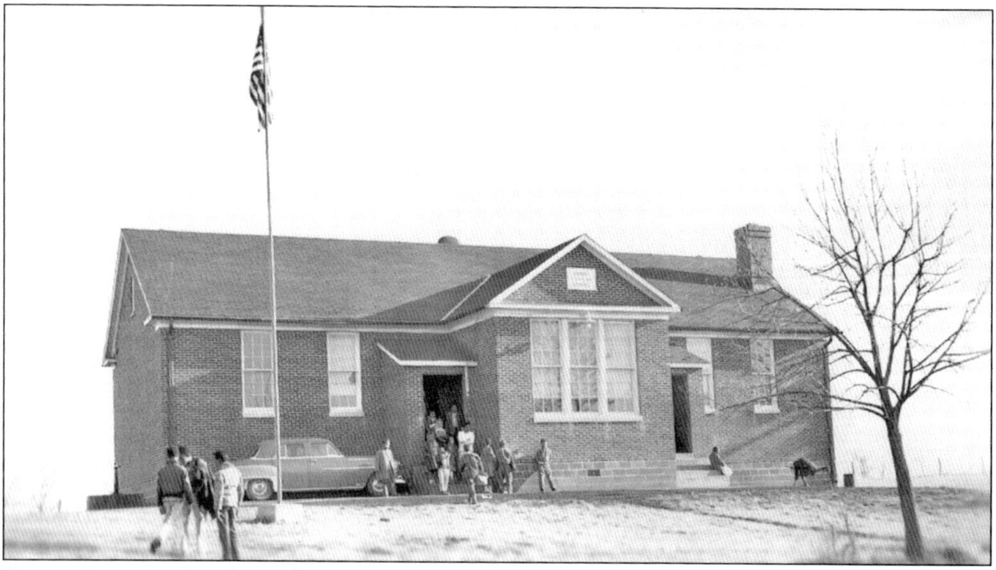

Originally opened in the early 1900s as the Pleasant View Colored School, the Doubs School was "the last of the segregated black schools in Frederick County" when it closed in 1965, according to the *Frederick News-Post*. The original school building was torn down, and the site became a parking lot for the building pictured here, which opened in 1949. The building now is a church.

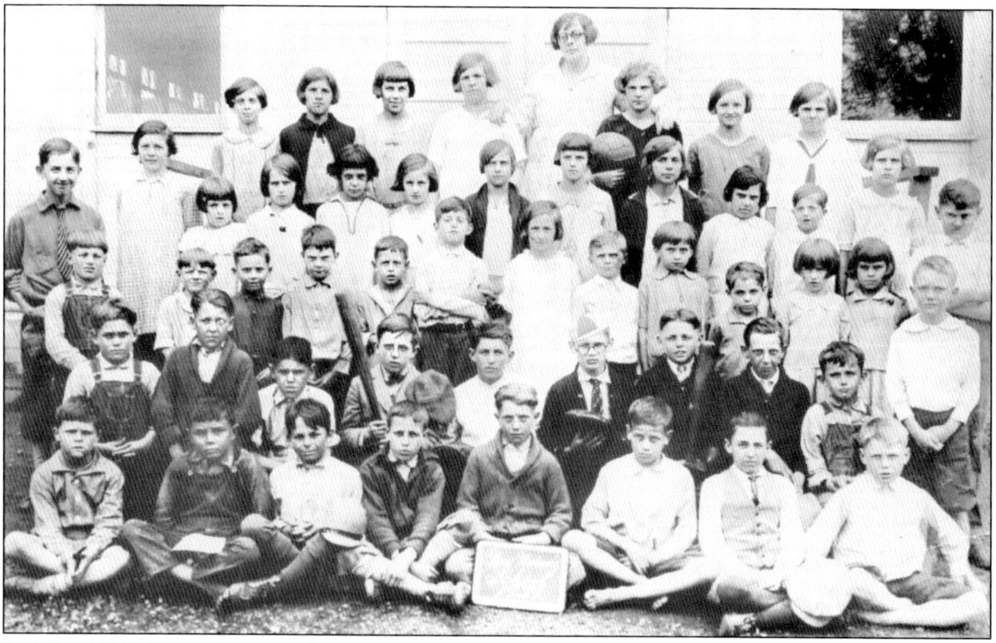

In May 1929, about the time this photograph was taken, six schools participated in a dodgeball tournament at the New Midway School, which these students attended. The Frederick County Board of Education, however, was planning a new six-room school to replace the building. By the next spring, the old school was sold to a private individual and the students were in their new classrooms.

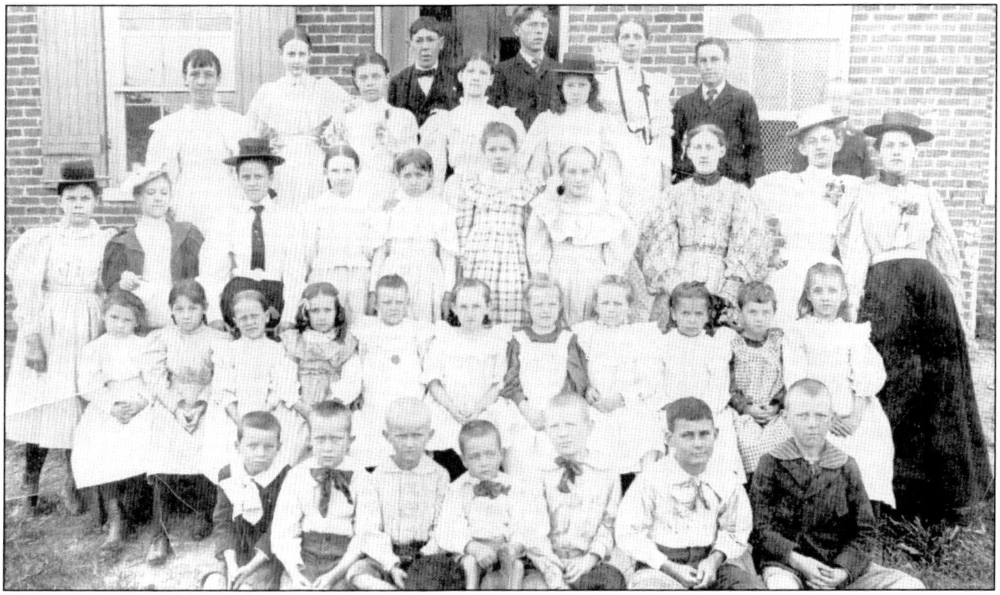

The students and teachers of the Adamstown Elementary and High School posed in front of their school building in 1896. The building, constructed in 1895 to replace an earlier structure, was soon outgrown, necessitating its enlargement in 1900 to four rooms—three for classes and one for the school's trustees.

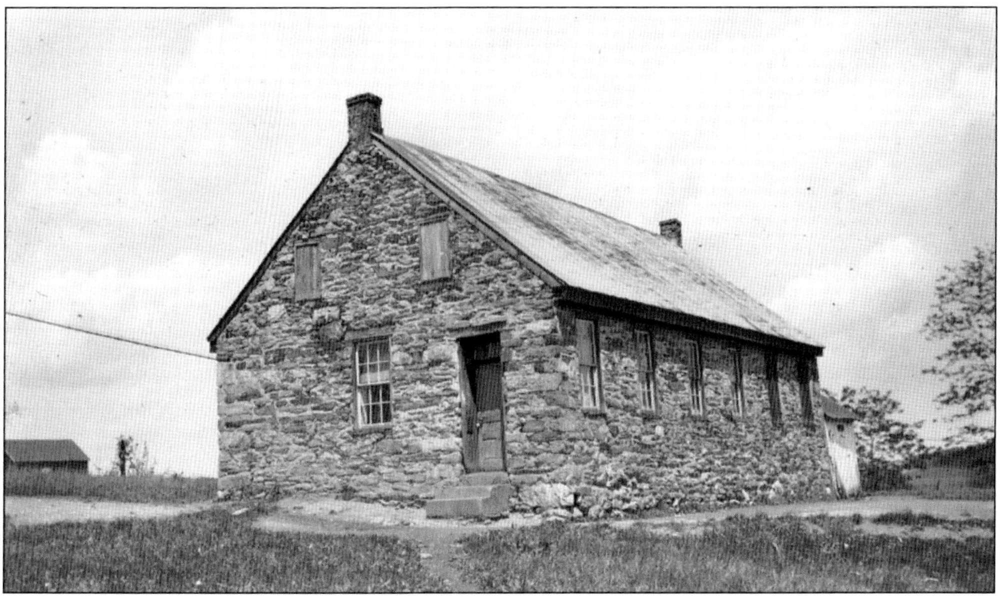

The first school for black children in New Market was a one-room log house converted to that use about 1850. The school building pictured here was built in 1868 for the community's white children but became a school for black students when a new whites-only facility was constructed across town. This school eventually was outgrown, and a larger one was built in 1939 that remained in operation until the desegregation of schools.

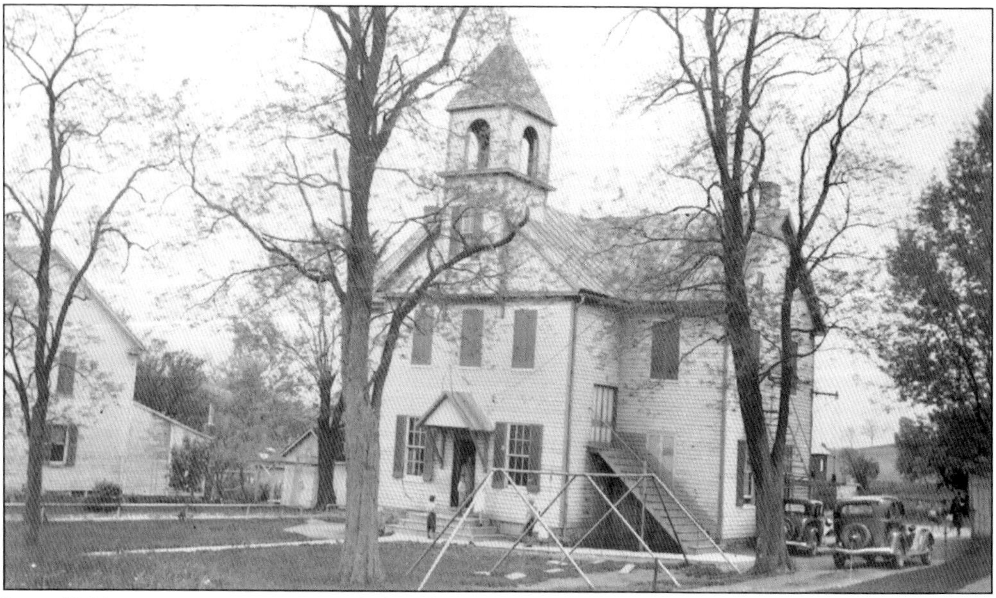

June 1936 was an exciting month for the graduates of the Unionville Elementary School. Commencement exercises—probably conducted in the school's second-floor auditorium—included prayer, readings, glee club songs, piano and violin solos, an address, and the presentation of certificates to the graduates. Decreasing enrollment and school consolidation culminated in the sale of the school property to a church in 1938.

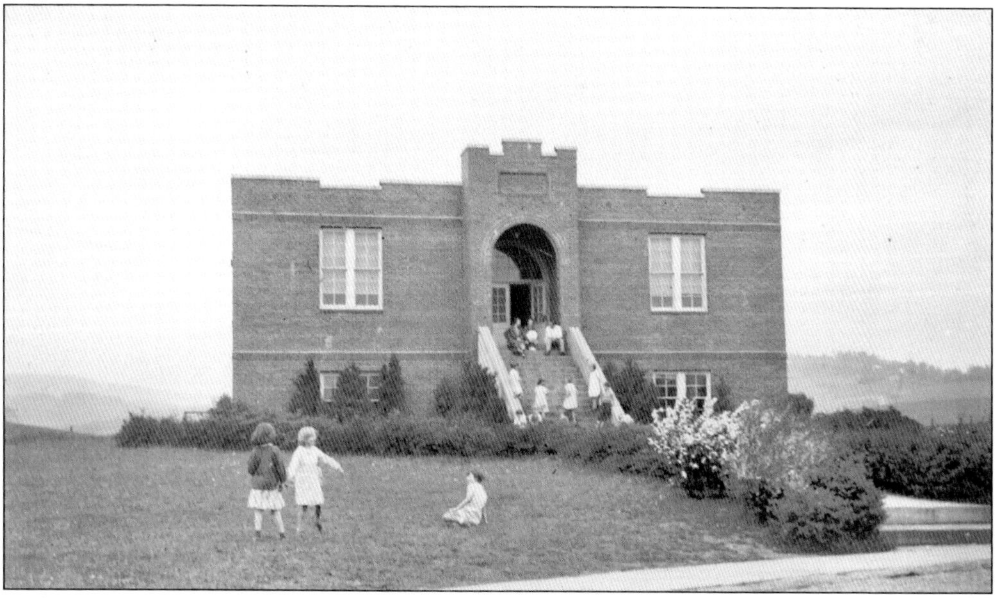

Built in 1927, the Myersville School included four classrooms on the second floor and an auditorium and boiler room on the first. In August 1933, the basement also included a kitchen, the scene of a fire that broke out when an overheated coal stove ignited a wallboard partition. Men working nearby doused the flames with water carried in buckets and dishpans before the Myersville Fire Company arrived on the scene.

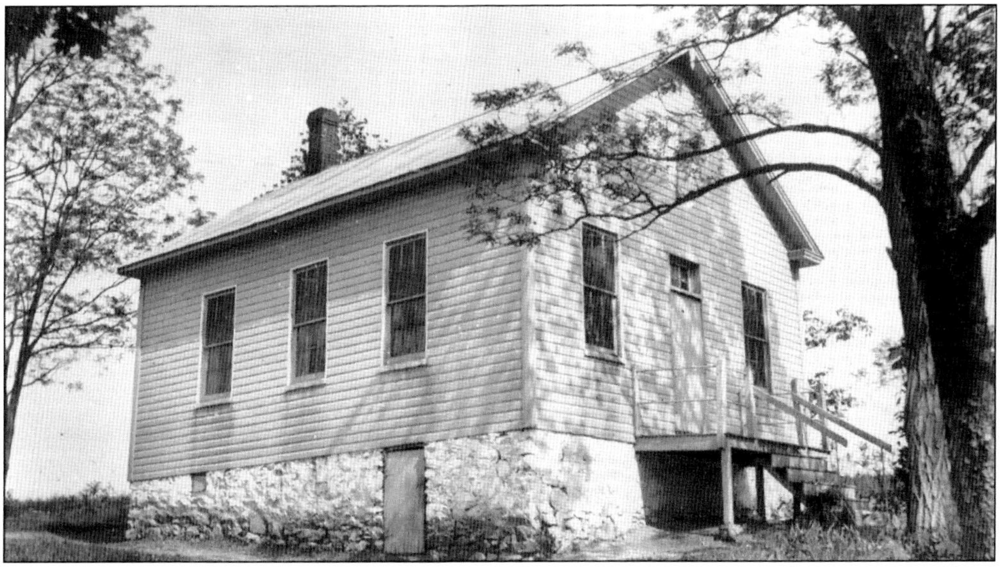

The Mount Pleasant Colored School stood along the road between Frederick and Libertytown on land purchased by the Frederick County School Board in 1896. The one-room frame elementary school was offered for sale in September 1939 as a part of the county's school consolidation process.

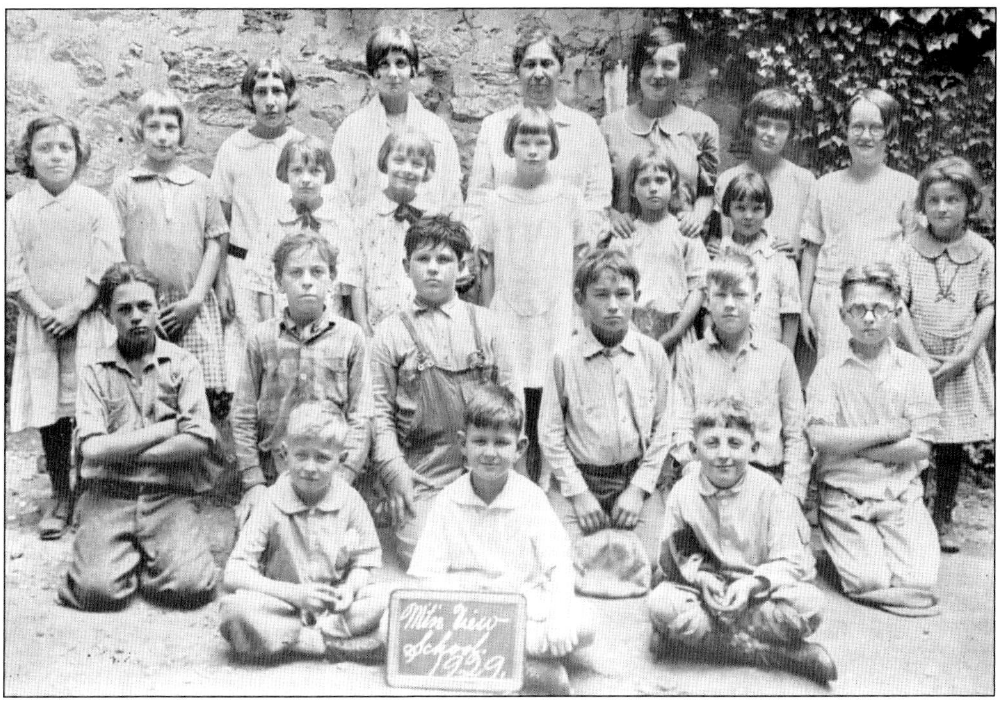

The Mountain View School, near Mount Pleasant, was in the news in 1922 over how it could provide hot lunches for its students, which had been shown to help student performance. At the time, providing hot midday meals was a new concept to Frederick County schools. We can wonder if these students benefited from the program. The school building would later be used for the Old German Baptist Church.

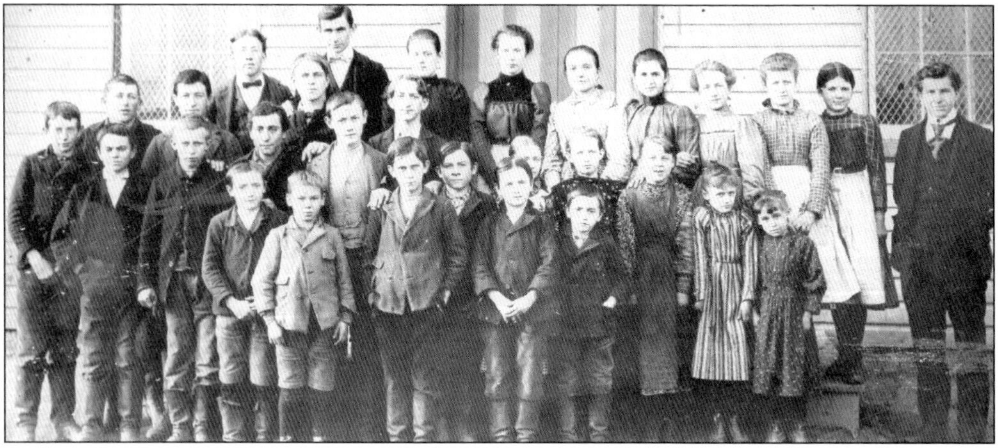

In 1866, land was surveyed for a school to be built at Woodville and called Friendship School. In 1913, teachers and members of the community raised $10 to build a library at the school; the local school board matched the $10 and also gave a bookcase. By 1928, the building pictured behind these smartly dressed students had been abandoned for a new school.

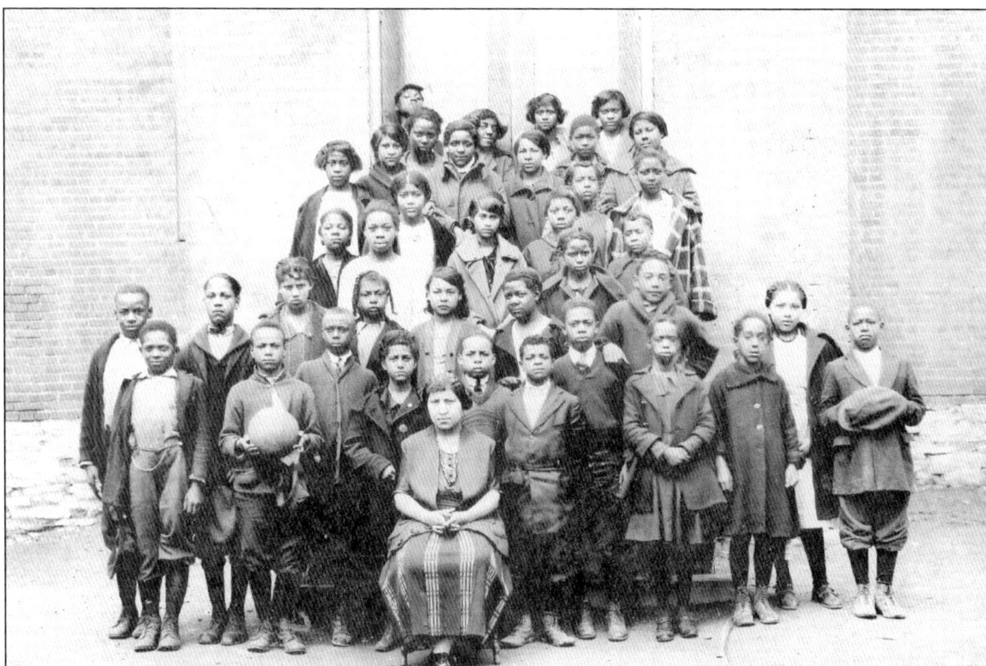

Lillian Proctor sits front and center of her pupils at the South Bentz Street Colored School in Frederick. Proctor served as the school's principal and only teacher. The school began at the end of the 19th century and closed in 1939, when the school's students were transferred to Lincoln High-Elementary School. The school property was sold and was one of 14 cleared to make way for the Lincoln Apartments complex.

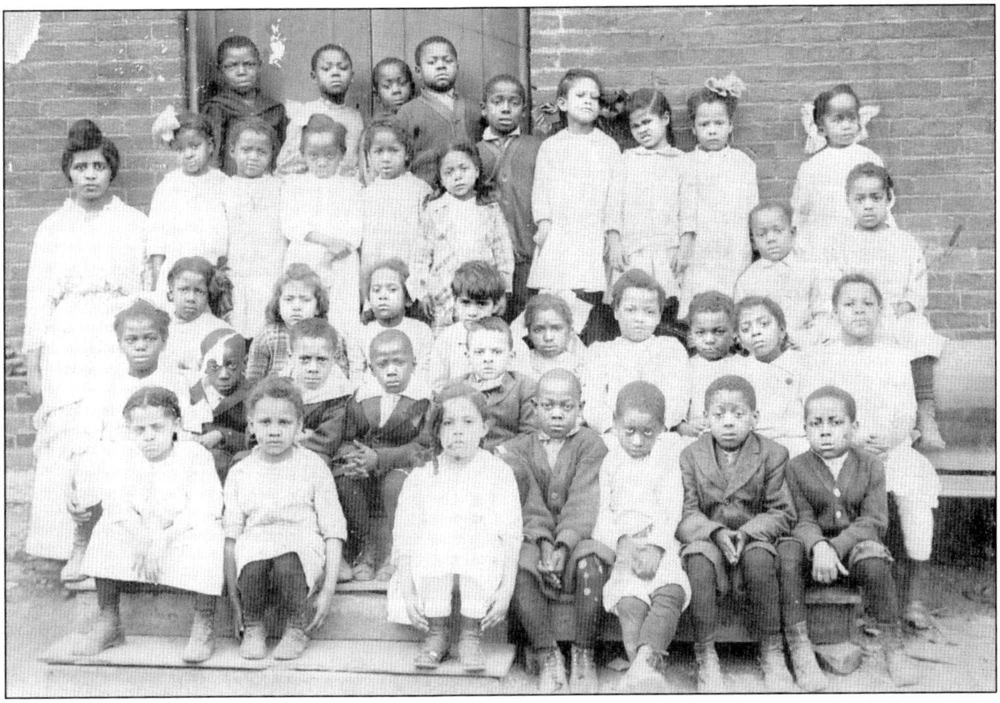

West Seventh Street Colored School's faculty and students posed for this photograph in the early 20th century. The school, located between Market and Bentz Streets, was one of the two elementary schools for black students in Frederick during the period of school segregation. The school building today houses the Fraternal Order of Police.

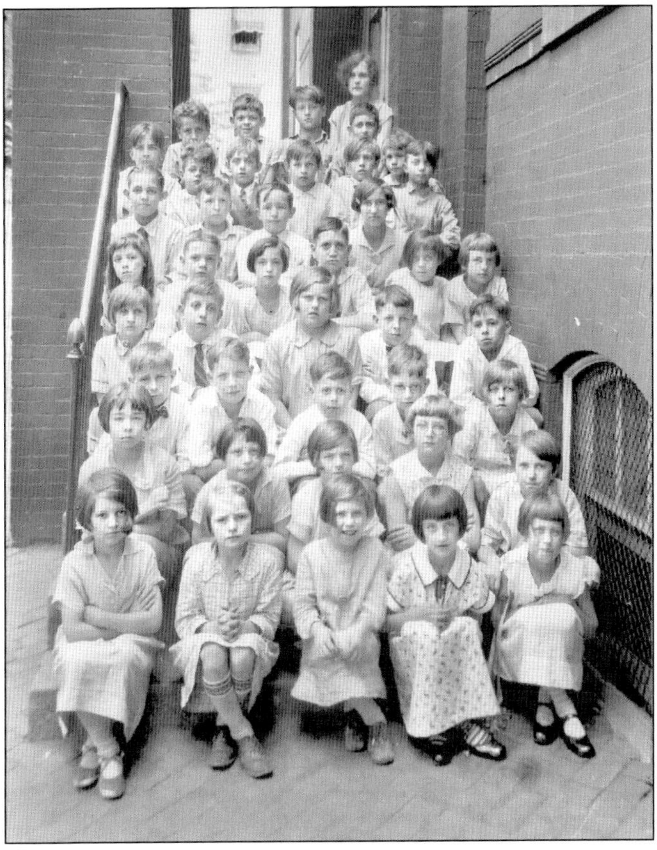

The 1928 enrollment at the North Market Street School in Frederick included 100 fourth-grade students taught by three teachers. The children in this fourth-grade class may have purchased their school supplies at a local drugstore, which sold tablets for a nickel and pencils two for a nickel. Underweight children at the school received two glasses of milk daily from a supply donated by local farmers.

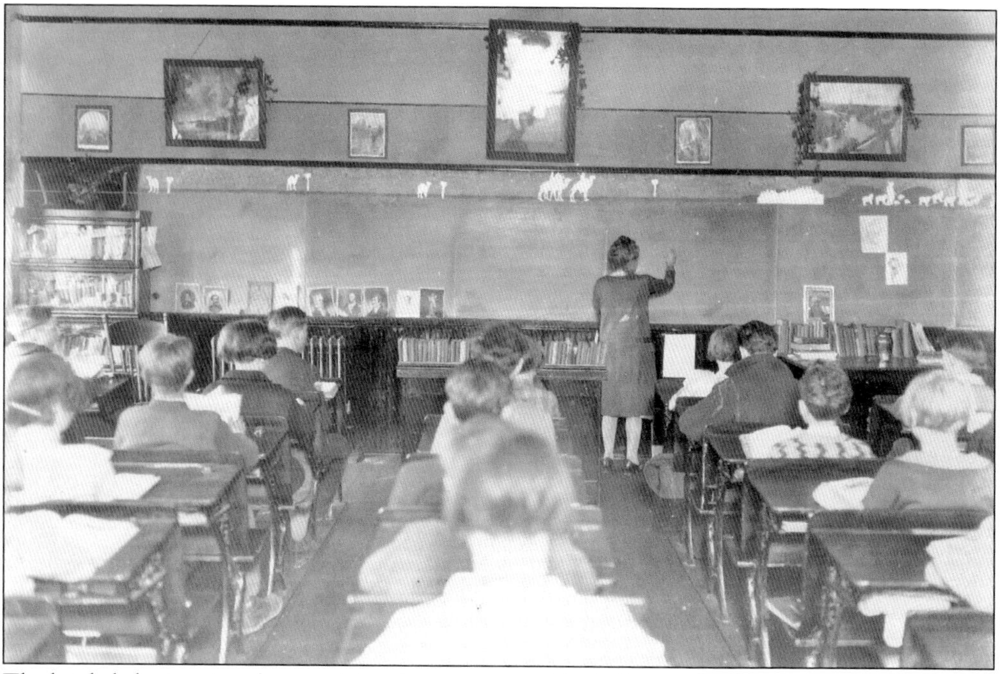

The brightly lit interior of Jeanne Kemp's classroom at North Frederick Elementary in 1960 (below) contrasts dramatically with the image taken about 30 years earlier in another Frederick County school. Only a generation separates the two, but many things had changed in the intervening years. In 1931, newspapers were reporting that state law raised the age for compulsory school attendance to 14, and in 1934, the total number of students enrolled in Frederick County schools was 10,400. By 1959, the number of elementary school students alone had surpassed 7,600 and the crush of the baby boom was keenly felt in the schools. When North Frederick Elementary opened in 1954, class size ranged from 35 to as many as 50 students per teacher and the search for more instructors drew people from various walks of life into the classroom.

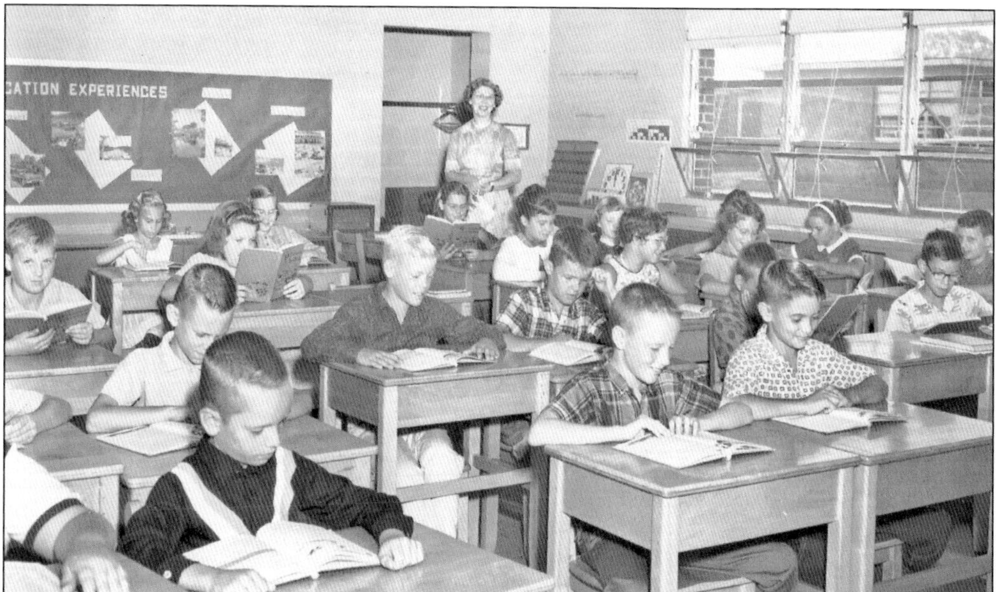

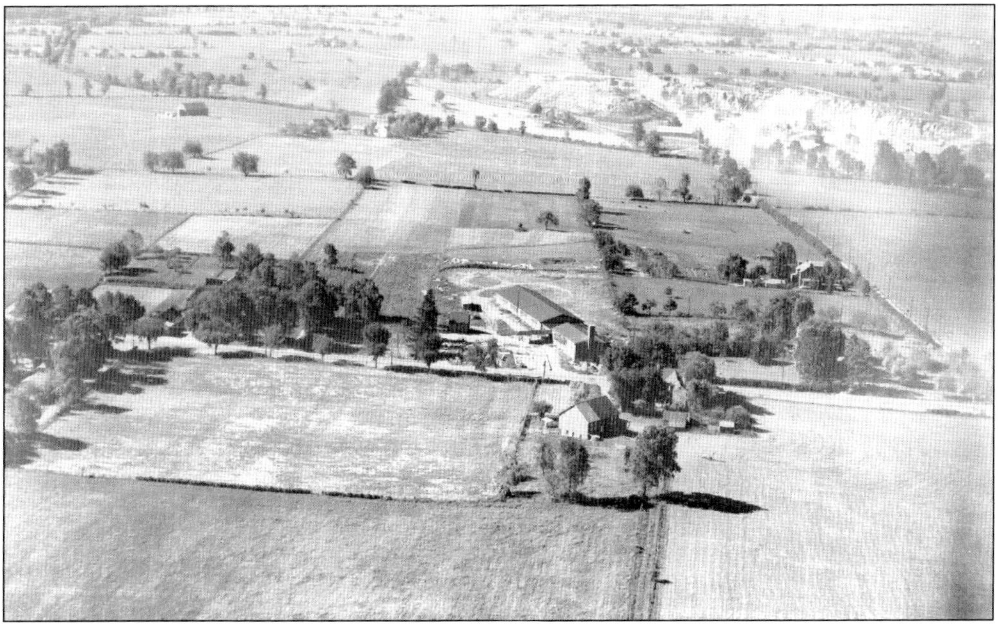

A 1952 aerial view of Frederick's east side shows a newly constructed East Frederick Elementary School surrounded by open farmland. After nearly 40 years and much development, traffic and noise pollution from the Frederick Airport, as well as aging facilities, were cited as reasons for the school to close in 1991. Spring Ridge Elementary was constructed nearby to replace the old school, which was eventually sold and demolished.

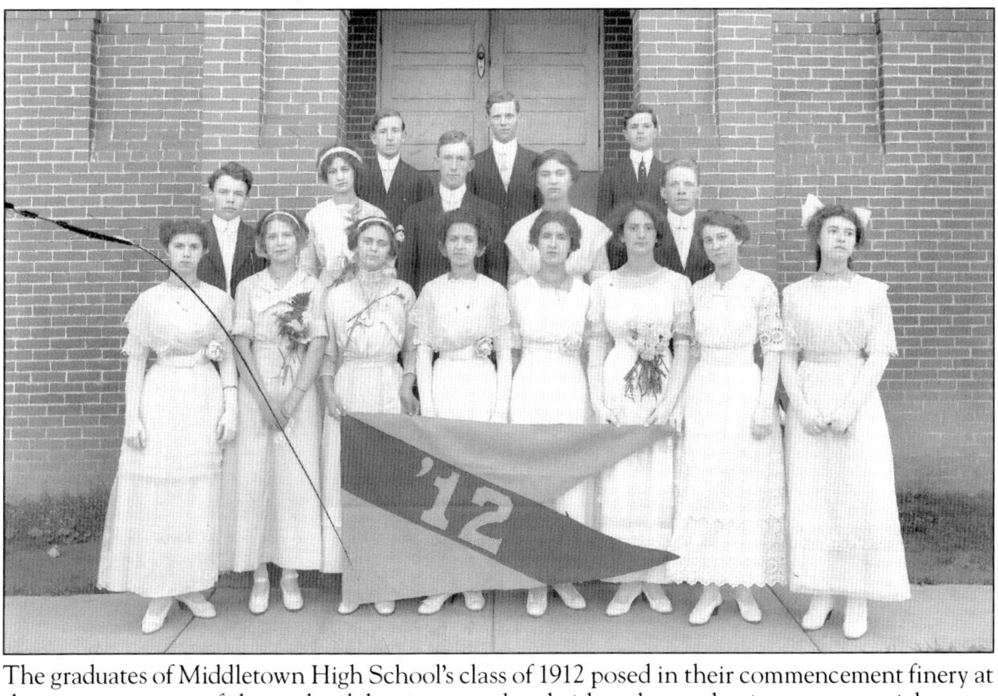

The graduates of Middletown High School's class of 1912 posed in their commencement finery at the main entrance of their school, having completed either the academic or commercial course offered them. They were among the 108 seniors who graduated from 10 of the county's 11 high schools that year.

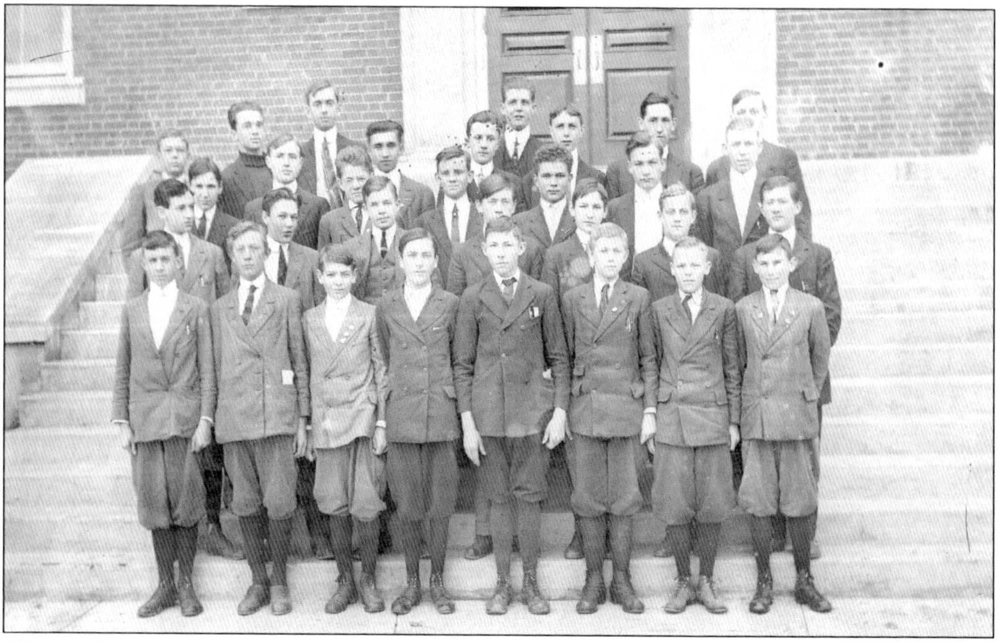

The ninth-grade class of Boys' High School in Frederick posed on the front steps of their school building on Elm Street in 1913. The same year, a student wrote that the school was located in a quiet part of town and enjoyed fresh air from the Catoctin Mountains; he also noted that the boys' separation from female students helped the young men concentrate on their lessons.

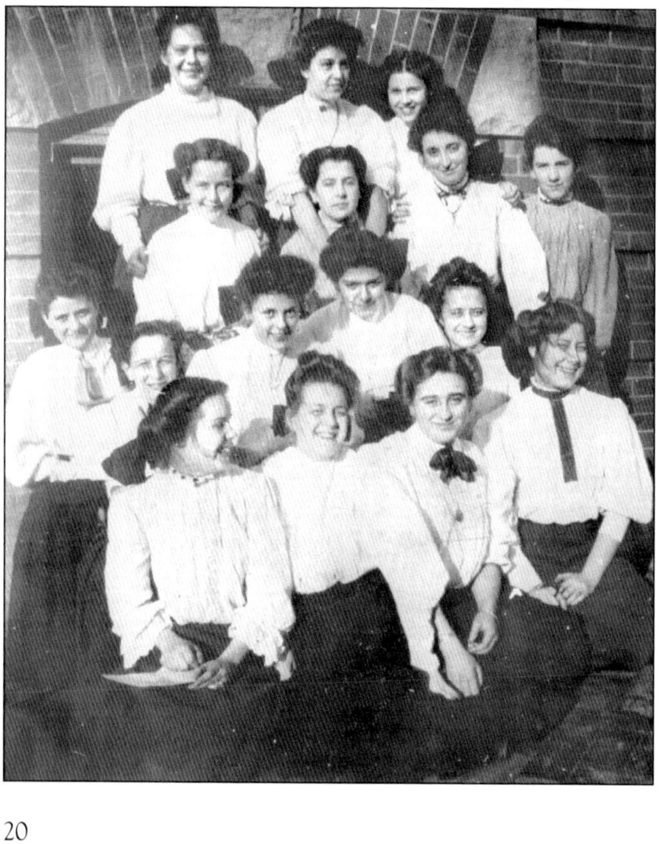

Perhaps these amused young ladies of the class of 1913 were anticipating their upcoming graduation from the Girls' High School on East Church Street in Frederick. Graduation activities ran from May 29 through June 6 and included a senior play—a comedy portraying school life—a banquet given by the junior class, a sermon to the class, an alumni banquet, and graduation exercises. Beatrice Geesey delivered the salutatory address that year.

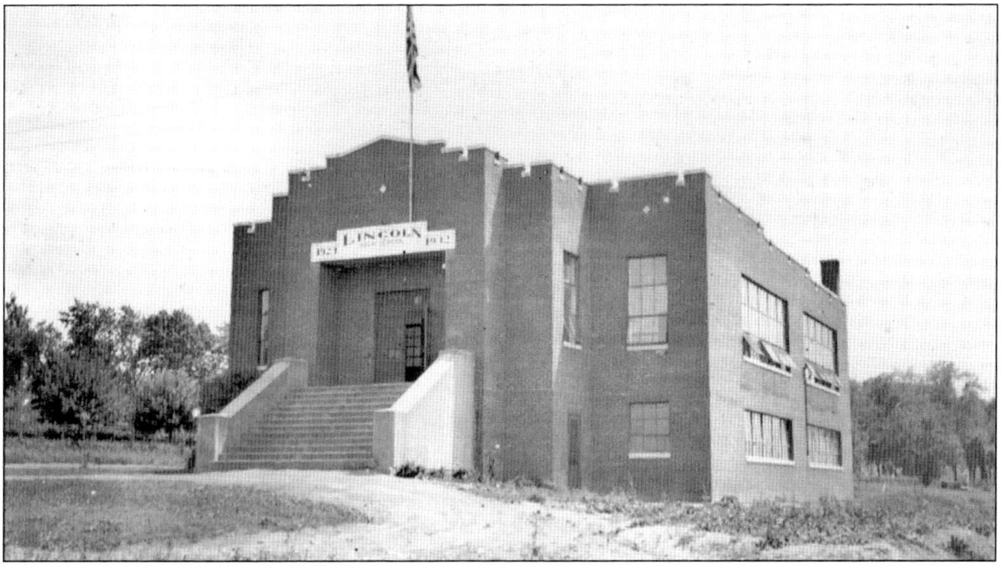

Lincoln High School, the county's first high school for black students, began with 35 students on West All Saints Street in 1920. By 1923, it relocated to a new facility on West Madison Street (above). It grew and expanded a great deal over the years. In 1958, its seventh graders were transferred to West Frederick as part of school desegregation. The high school finally ceased to exist in 1962, with the building becoming an integrated elementary school. Although the school lost its moniker for many years, the determination of former pupils to preserve the history of their alma mater led to the return of the name "Lincoln" to the school in 2006. Below, Lincoln's faculty and students posed for their picture on the steps of their new school in 1924. Faculty seated in the front row from left to right are Maurice Reid, Rose Armo Stepney, John Bruner, Mary Emily Taylor, and James A. Allen.

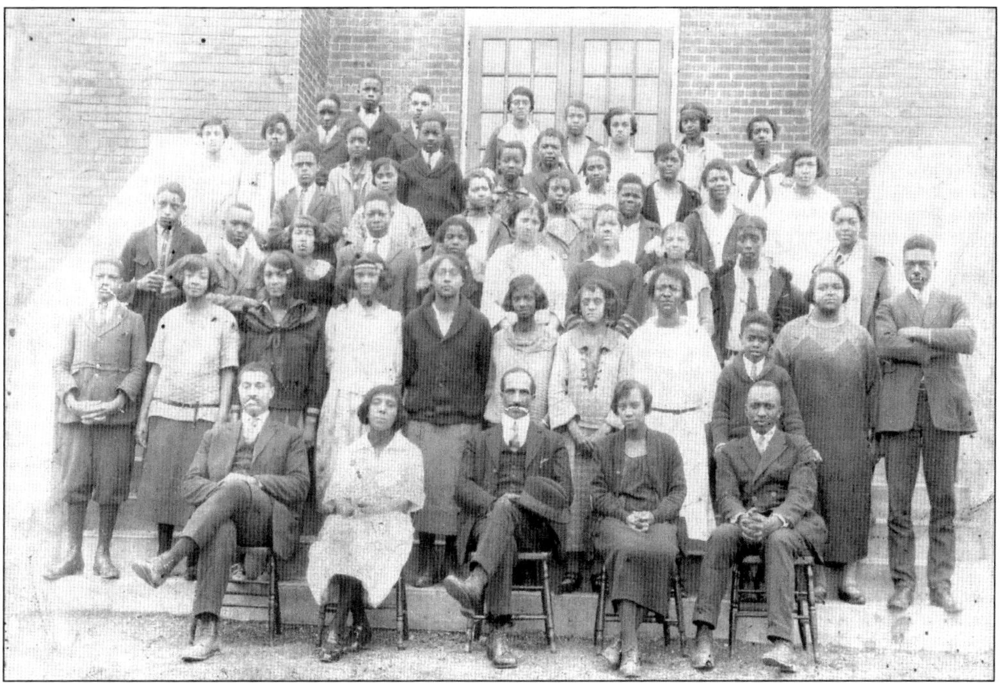

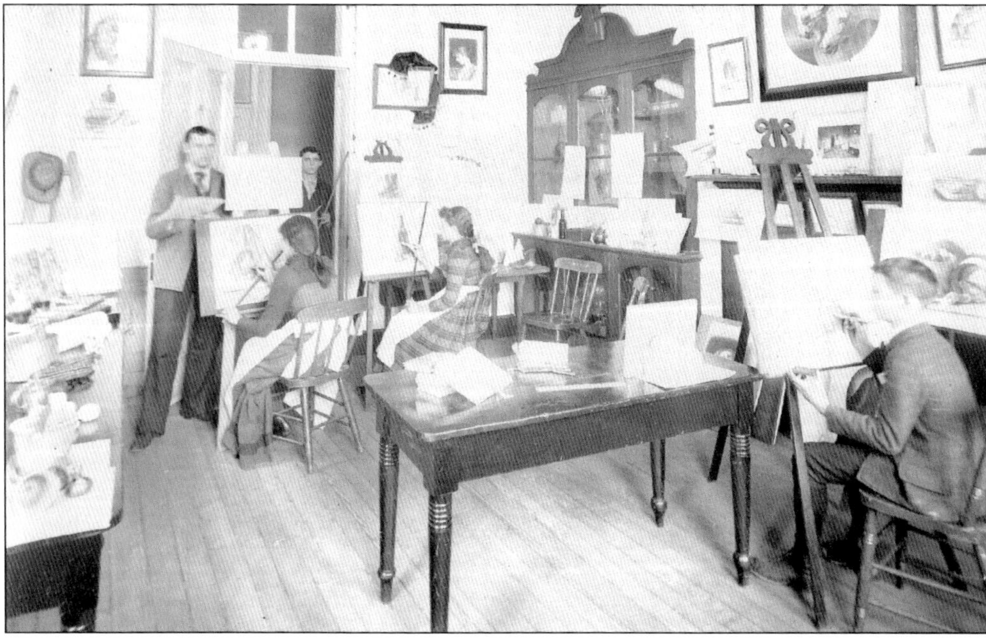

The Maryland School for the Deaf was established on Market Street in Frederick in 1868. By the early 20th century, in addition to academic studies, students were taught various trades and boys received military exercise training. They also had the opportunity to enjoy things like the art class pictured here about 1910.

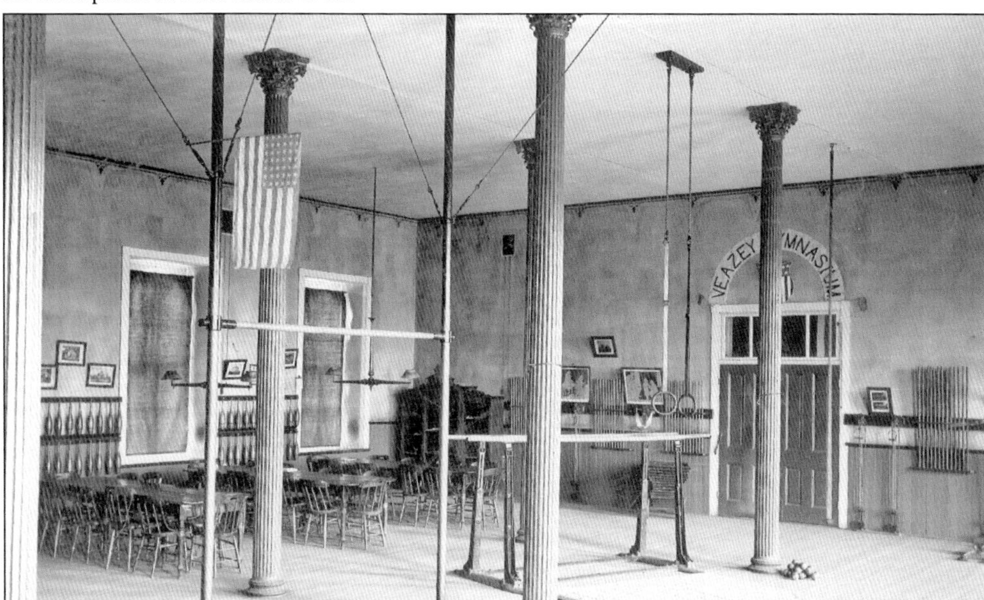

A Frederick newspaper reported in 1891 that J. W. L. Unsworth, a deaf photographer from Baltimore, visited the Maryland State School for the Deaf and took pictures of the Veazey Athletic Club and Gymnasium. The gym was constructed after the school's board of directors received $2,600 from the estate of Susannah Veazey, a deaf Baltimorean. In 1892, the school's "Veazey Deaf Eleven" football team played other local clubs and its Veazey baseball team defeated the Baltimore Orioles.

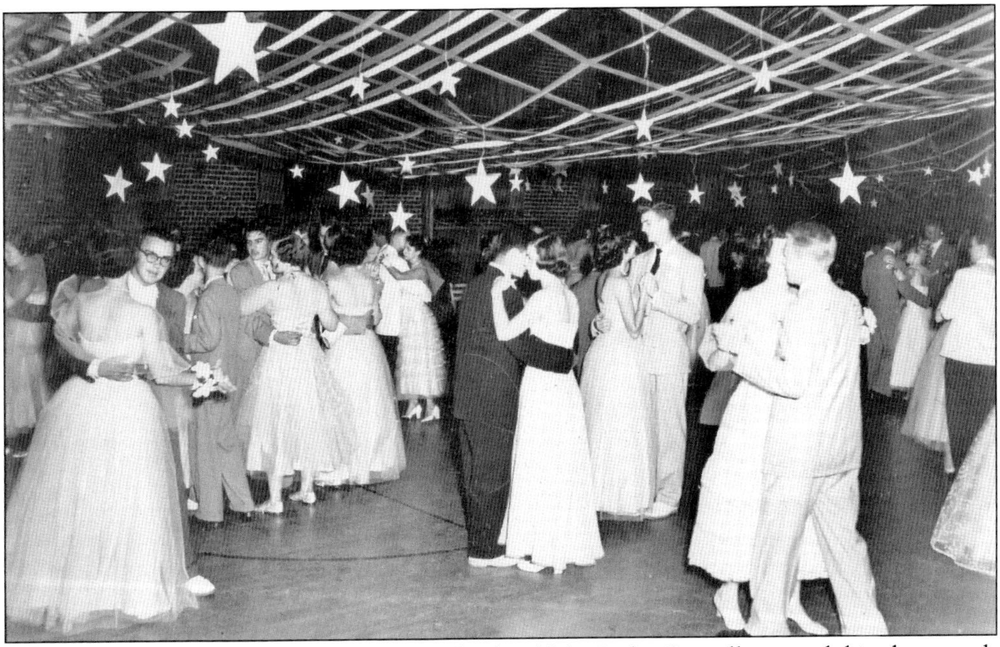

The spring formal is a celebrated ritual of high school life. Carlos Gosnell snapped this photograph at the Frederick High School Junior Prom on May 28, 1953. The class of 1954 danced to Dick Harp's Orchestra under stars and a papier-mâché blue moon, the dance's theme. During the band's intermission, Janiele Faust sang "Blue Moon." Barbara Bowles, Faust's accompanist, and Robert Falconer were deemed the best-looking couple.

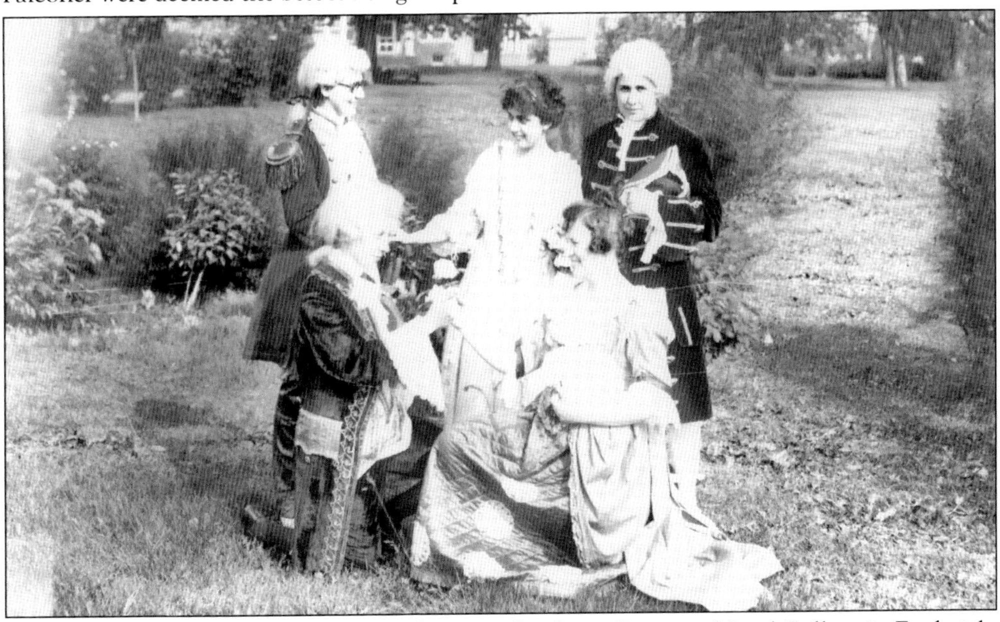

May Day celebrations were a festive tradition at the then all-women Hood College in Frederick. As in this c. 1900 photograph, a queen and "Prince Hood" were chosen each year. Prince Hood dressed in men's clothing and acted as the queen's escort for the day. Beginning in 1952, the escort became Princess Hood. In 1959, the May Day pageant was replaced altogether by the Festival of the Arts.

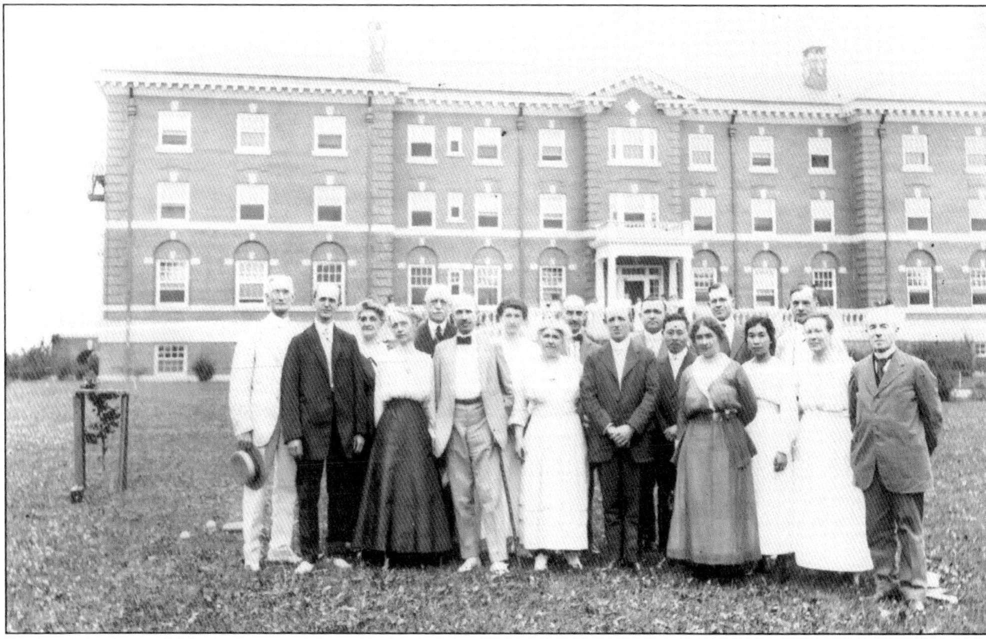

These Hood College faculty members are standing in front of Shriner Hall. Opened as a residence hall in 1915, it is one of the three original buildings on Hood's campus in Frederick. It has undergone changes since this photograph, most noticeably the addition of dormer windows to the roofline sometime before the early 1940s. Dr. Joseph Apple, president of Hood, is the man on the left in the white suit.

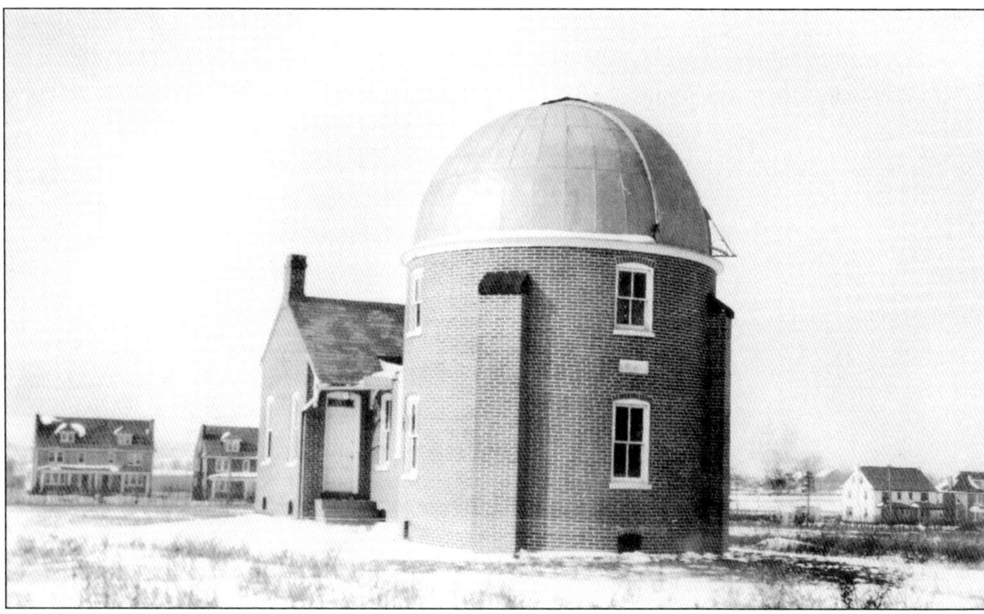

In 1924, construction of an observatory began at Hood College funded by a $35,000 bequest from M. Janet Williams. By the spring 1925 semester, students and guests were studying celestial bodies in the John H. Williams Observatory. Its nine-foot telescope, one of the largest in any women's college at the time, was built by Alvin Clark and Sons of Cambridge, Massachusetts, and was housed beneath a copper-covered revolving dome.

Two

The Sporting Life

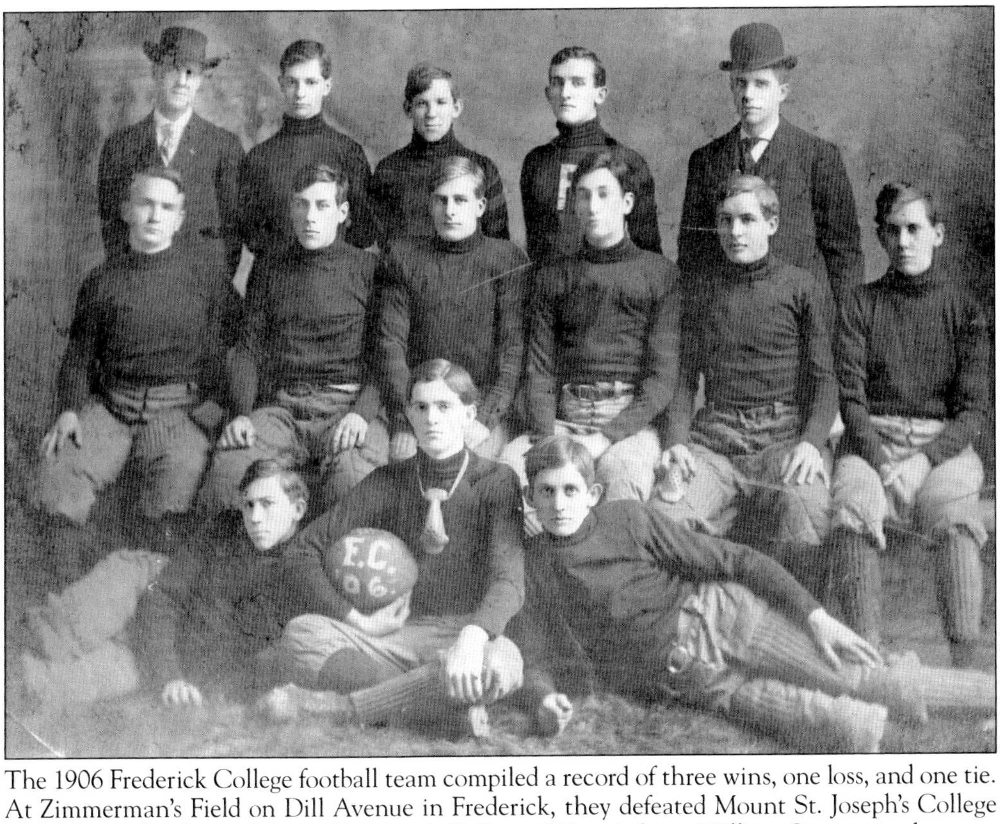

The 1906 Frederick College football team compiled a record of three wins, one loss, and one tie. At Zimmerman's Field on Dill Avenue in Frederick, they defeated Mount St. Joseph's College of Baltimore but lost to Mount St. Mary's College of Emmitsburg. William Storm was the team captain, Albert Gill the manager, and D. John Markey the coach. Note the rubber nose guard worn by the player holding the ball.

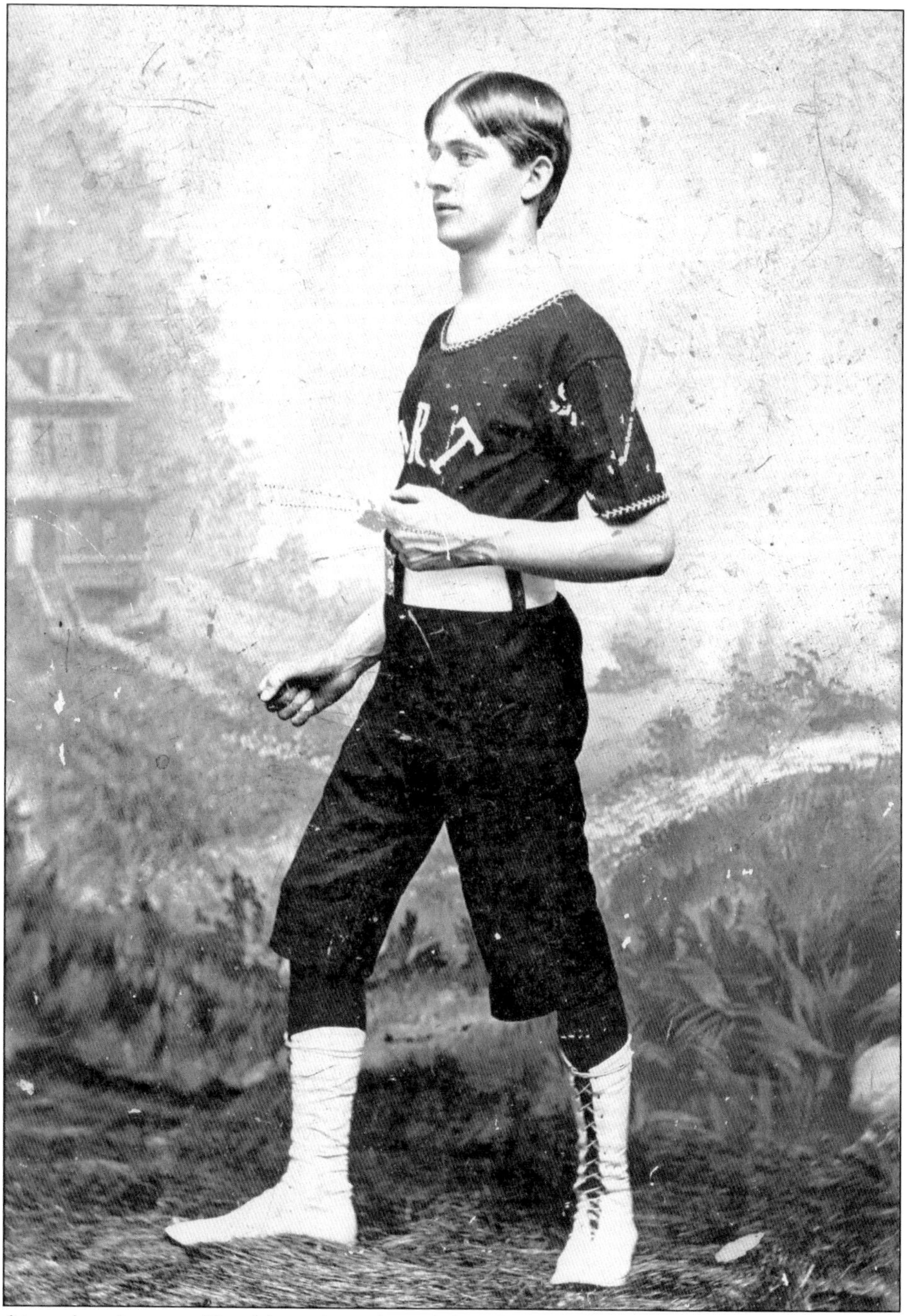

Looking the picture of health and vitality, Adam Lewis Abrecht poses in his "reel runner" costume *c.* 1896. Born in 1875, Abrecht was a member of Frederick's Independent Hose Company. In 1894, and again in 1900, the Independent's Hose Reel Team won first place by running 200 yards with a reel, laying out 50 yards of hose, and attaching one end to a hydrant and the other to a nozzle in less than 41 seconds. Just two years after their win, Abrecht died of complications from a workplace injury incurred at the Palmetto Fibre Works, forerunner of the Ox Fibre Brush Company. He died in 1902 at age 26, leaving behind his wife of four years, Edith Entler.

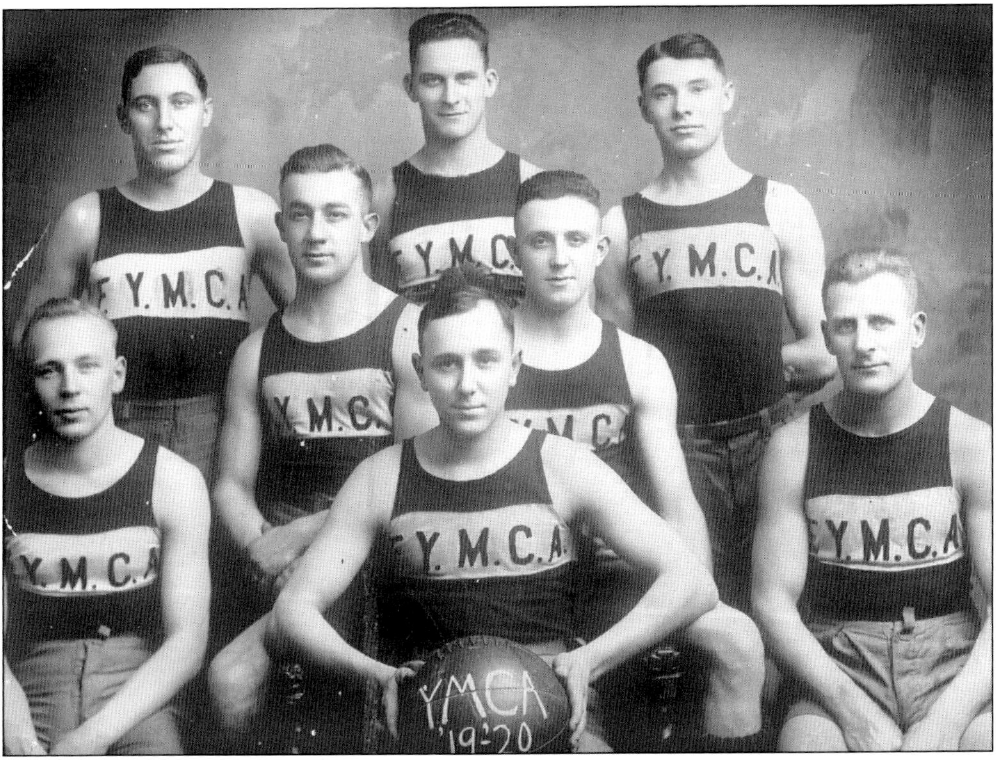

The Frederick Young Men's Christian Association (YMCA) was organized in the late 1860s "to endeavor to impress our young men with proper appreciation . . . of the Bible, and promote the moral tone of the community." By 1906, the "Y" had built a facility at West Church and Court Streets. Early on, it provided arithmetic and grammar classes, as well as sports. Boys—and after 1901, girls—could participate in activities including basketball, bowling, and swimming.

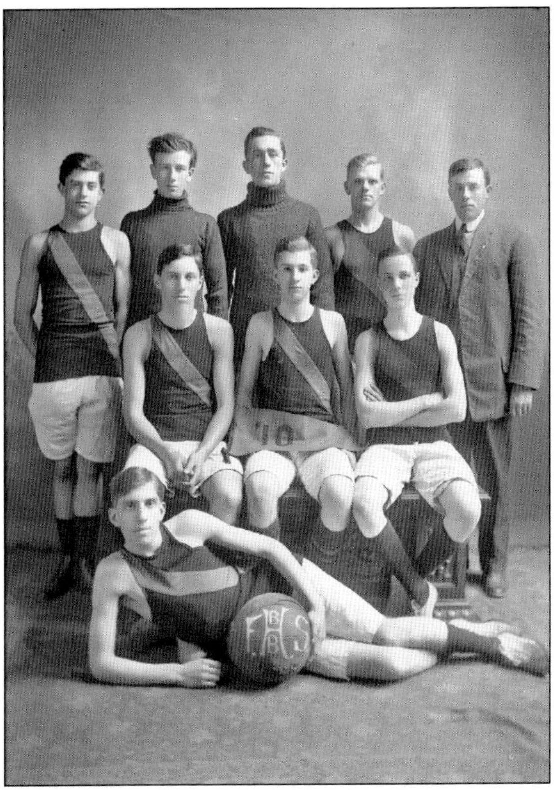

High school athletics, introduced at the Frederick Male High School during the 1905–1906 school year, included three intramural basketball teams. When the 1910 school team posed for their group photograph, they were part of a five-team city league that included squads from Frederick College, the Maryland State School for the Deaf, and two other teams named the Beavers and the Barkers. The YMCA gymnasium hosted the games.

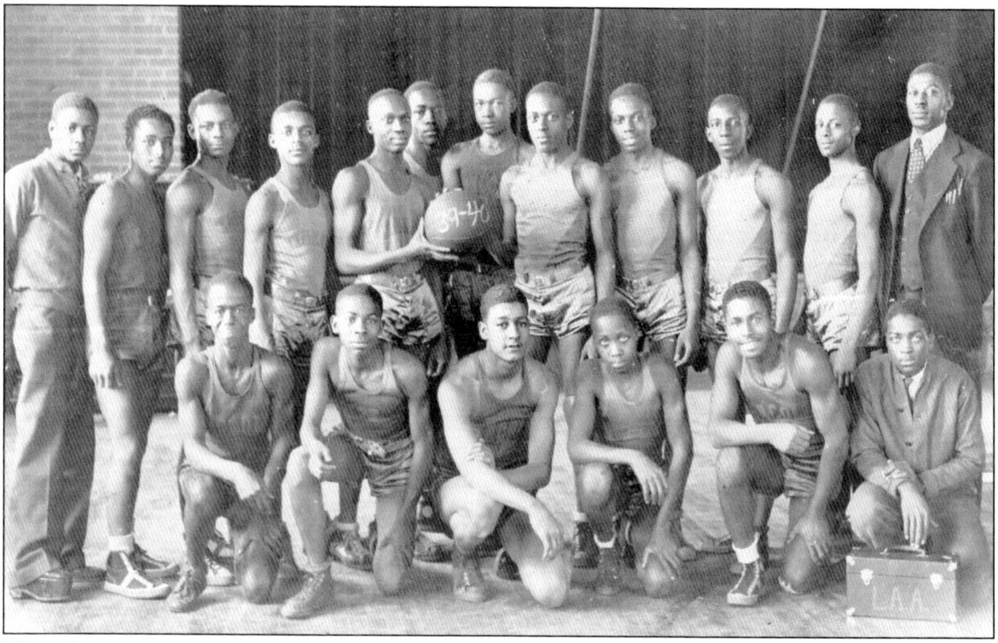

The players, coaches, and managers of the 1930–1940 Lincoln High School basketball team gathered for this photograph in the gymnasium at Lincoln. At this time, Lincoln played other black high schools in the area, including teams from Hagerstown, Cumberland, and Leesburg. The school later joined the Tri-State League, which pitted them against schools from Rockville, Westminster, Martinsburg, and Charlestown.

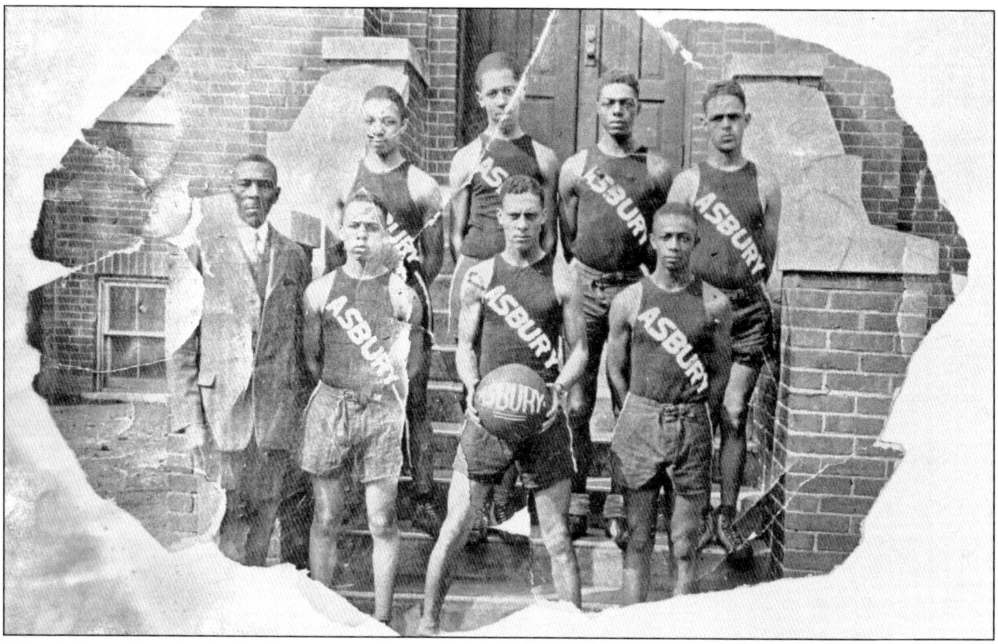

The Asbury Five basketball team was formed in 1927 and played their home games in the basement of the Asbury Methodist Church in Frederick. The team was sponsored by Ulysses G. Bourne, a local doctor, and played other teams from the area, including Lincoln High School. The Asbury Five continued to compete until they disbanded in 1941.

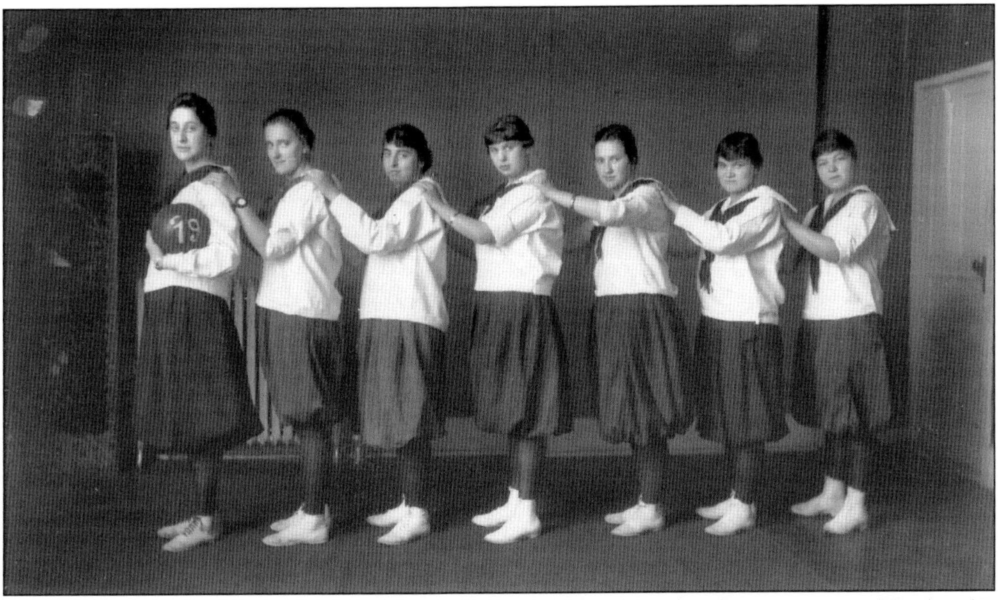

Men and boys were not the only ones who played a good game. The "biggest event of Frederick's winter sporting world" took place on March 1, 1919, according to the *Frederick Post*, when Swarthmore College in Pennsylvania sent a basketball club to the Armory in Frederick. There they played against the Hood College basketball club, which was under the direction of coach Woener, physical director at the college.

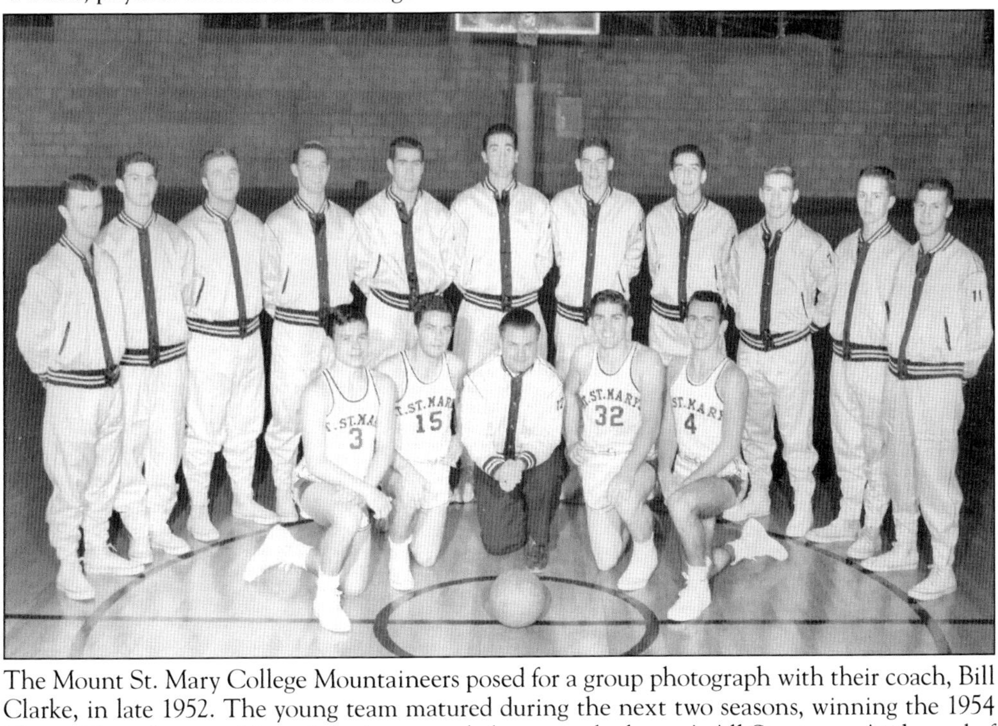

The Mount St. Mary College Mountaineers posed for a group photograph with their coach, Bill Clarke, in late 1952. The young team matured during the next two seasons, winning the 1954 Mason-Dixon League title and placing several players on the league's All-Star team. At the end of the 1953–1954 season, Clarke moved on to a coaching position in Rhode Island. He was followed by the Mount's legendary Jim Phelan.

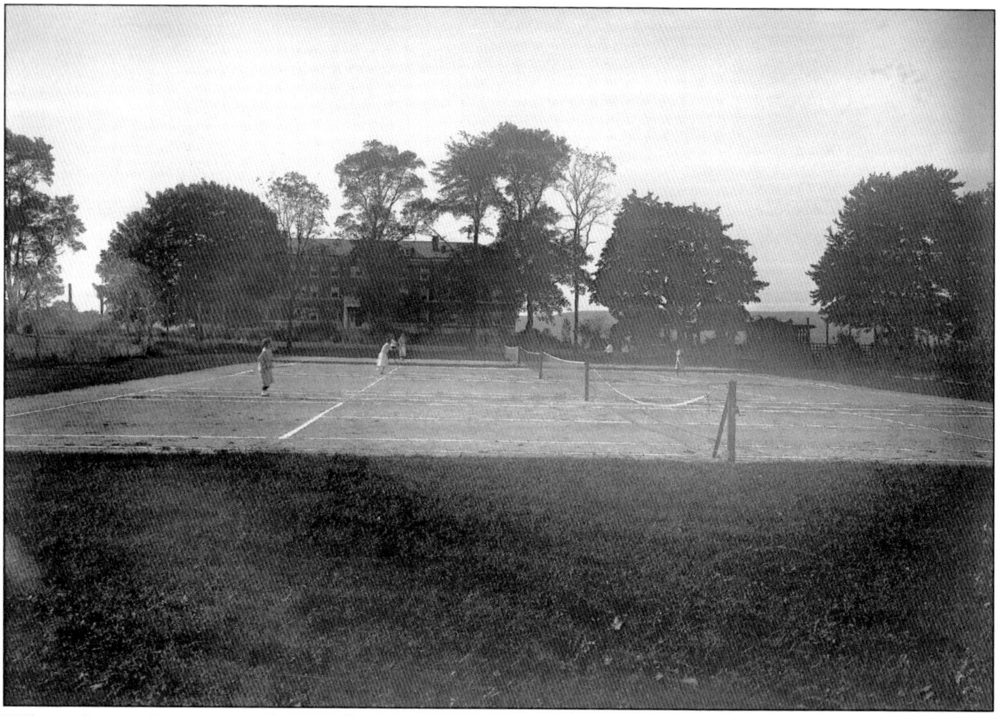

When the students arrived at Frederick's Hood College campus in September 1916, they not only were greeted by new classrooms and dormitories but also by four tennis courts and a hockey field (above). Though they didn't have a gymnasium until later, the women of Hood still could enjoy basketball at the Armory and swimming at the YMCA, as well as tennis, field hockey, croquet, and archery in the rear of the campus. Field hockey was a particular favorite of Dr. Joseph Apple, president of Hood for 41 years, who is credited with introducing it to women's colleges in the United States. In 1927, concrete tennis courts were installed, assuredly welcomed by white-skirted players such as these.

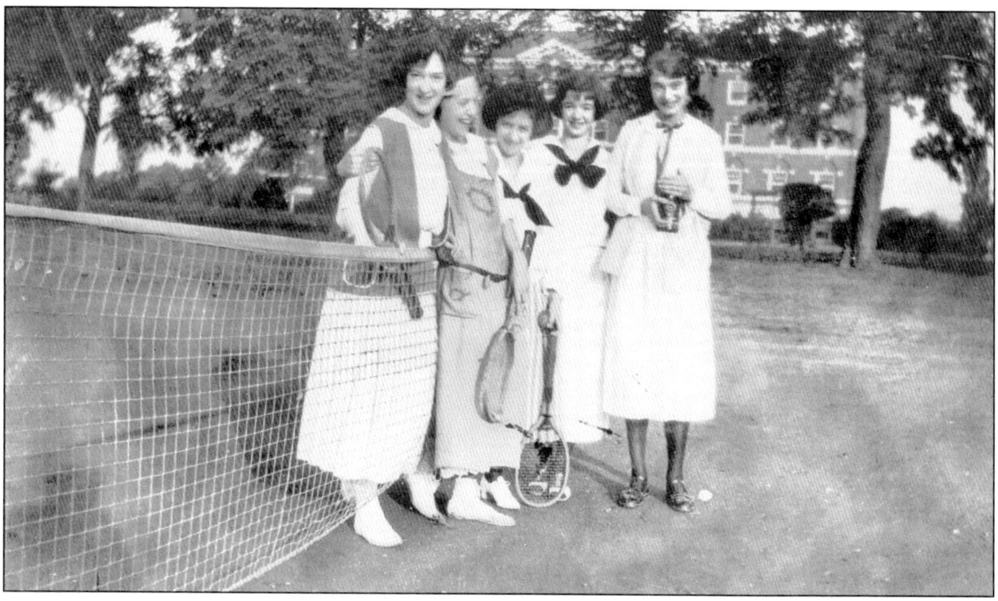

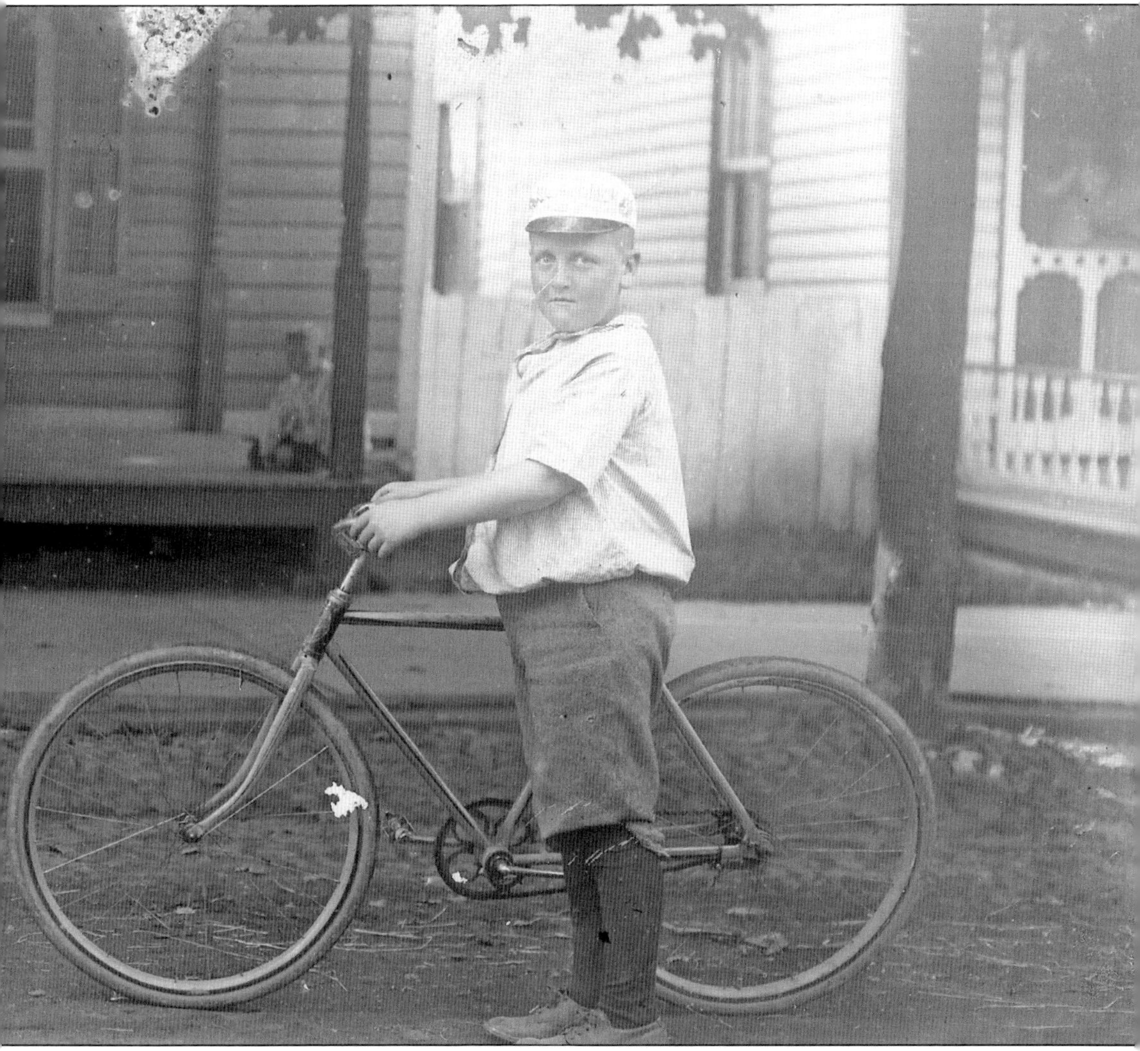

Looking like he could find trouble around every corner, this young fellow from Emmitsburg wears a cap emblazoned with "Cracker Jack," which helps date this photograph to sometime after 1896. His bicycle, a *c.* 1900 model, was made when bicycling was new and all the rage. In 1897, the Frederick Bicycle Club, a chapter in the Maryland Division of the League of American Wheelmen, hosted a bicycle meet attracting cyclists from across the region and from as far away as Philadelphia and Chicago. Local entries came from the Frederick club as well as from chapters in Hagerstown, Westminster, and the Crescent Bicycle Club in Baltimore.

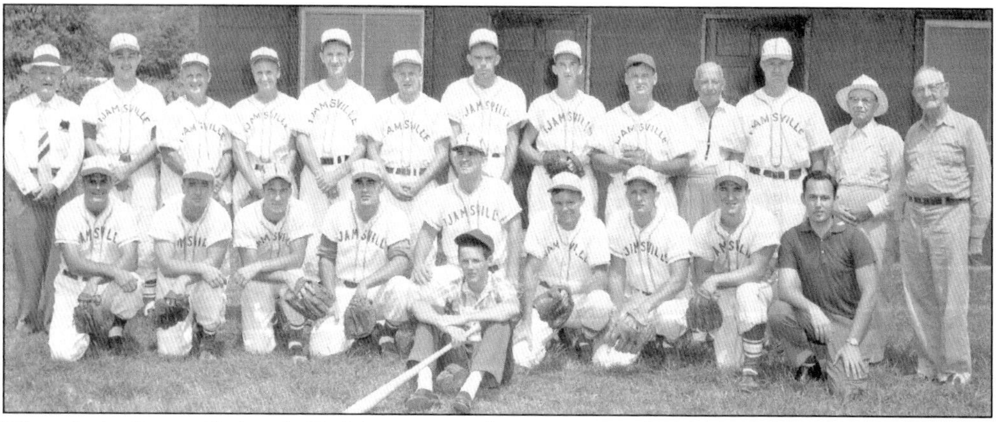

Though the Ijamsville baseball club consistently won statewide semipro titles, it folded in 1964 after nearly 60 years. The 1958 players and team officials pictured are, from left to right, as follows: (kneeling) Bill Crone, "Buzz" Wagner, Donnie Neel, John Harper, Frank Martz, Bob Shores, Ronnie Tyeryar, Rick Zimmerman, and Charles E. Moylan Jr.; (standing) Charles E. Moylan, Howard Smith, "Dottie" Staley, Charley Holland, John Trout, Fred Young, John Carpenter, Dick Sweadner, "Chiz" Staley, Edgar R. Smith, Robert Marendt, Harvey Hargett, and Charles Morhiser.

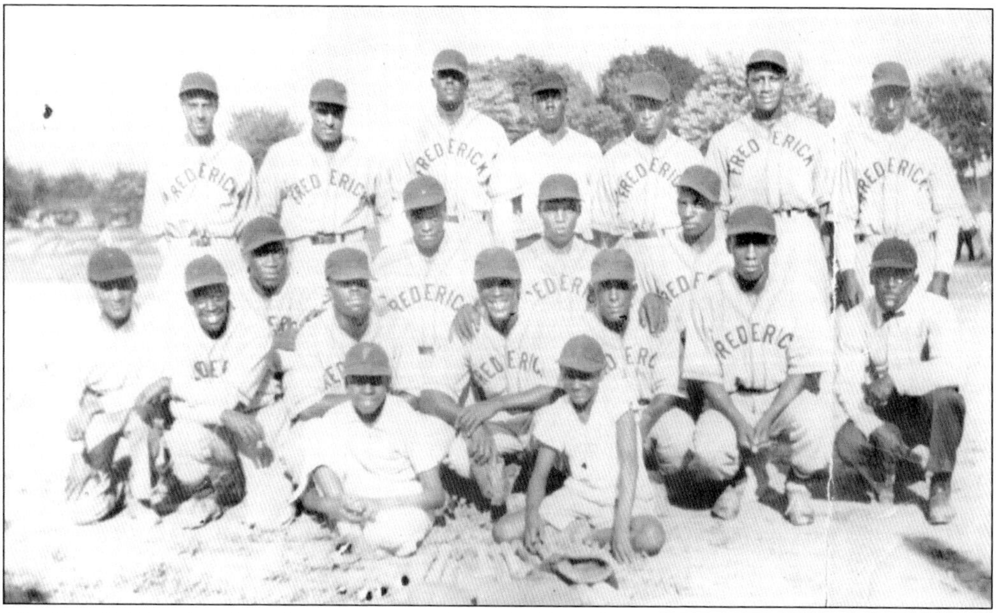

The Richfield Eagles played home games at Lincoln High School and competed against all-black teams from Leesburg, Hagerstown, Baltimore, and other communities. Players in this 1939 image are, from left to right, as follows: (seated in front) mascots G. Jenkins and E. Lyles; (first row kneeling) M. Tighman, E. Mason, J. Keys, F. Grey, G. Moore, J. Smith, and C. Shern; (second row) M. Addison, G. Fredericks, M. Smith, and R. Foreman; (third row) T. Wagner, C. Dickett, E. Lee, A. Rollins, C. Summers, C. Cooper, and manager Cliff Hoy.

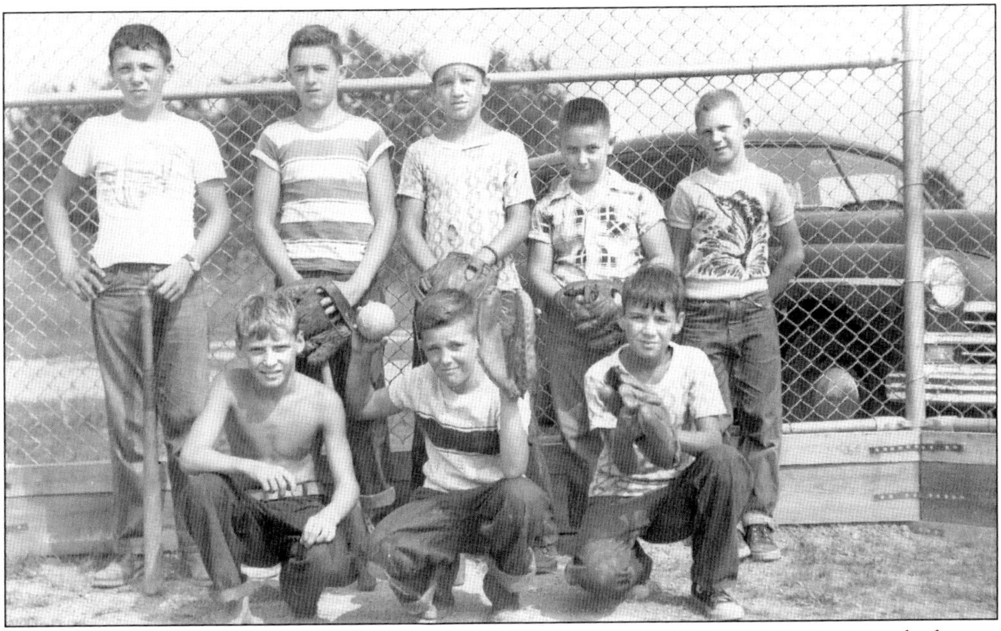

The Frederick Midget Softball League champs, the North Market Street team, posed after its 10-0 triumph over the Harmon Field team in a playoff game at Baker Park on August 28, 1951. The league was sponsored by the Frederick City Recreation Commission. Pictured from left to right are the following: (first row) John Hane, Dehaven Toms, and Wayne Jones; (second row) Edward Garrett, Robert Heffner, Tommy Jones, Ronnie Engle, and Tinker Michael.

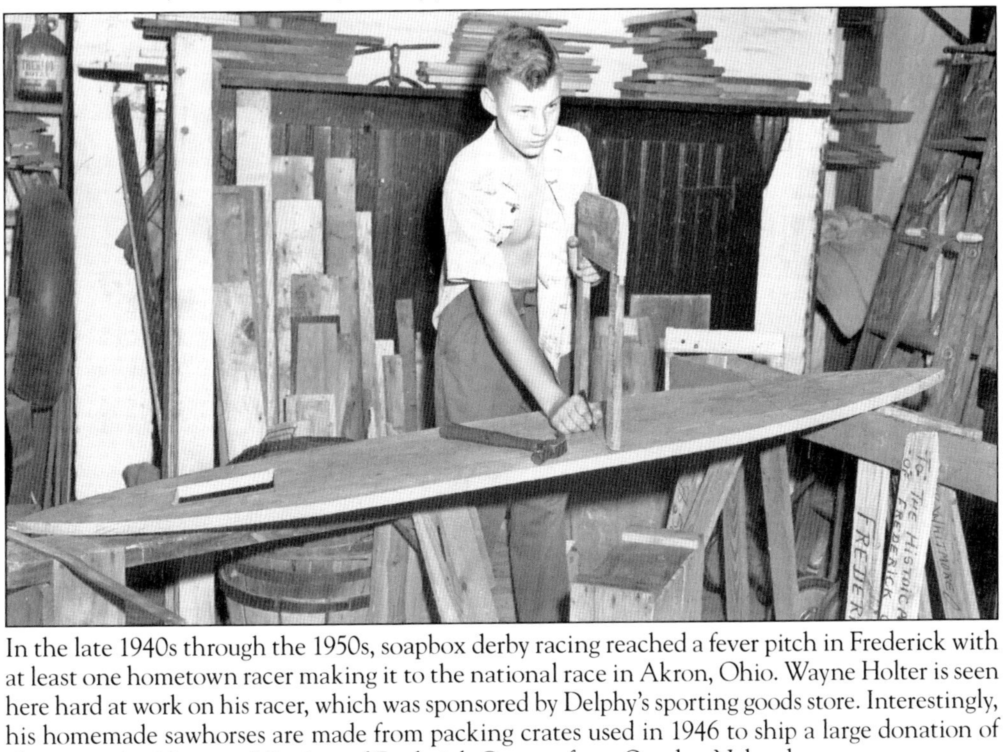

In the late 1940s through the 1950s, soapbox derby racing reached a fever pitch in Frederick with at least one hometown racer making it to the national race in Akron, Ohio. Wayne Holter is seen here hard at work on his racer, which was sponsored by Delphy's sporting goods store. Interestingly, his homemade sawhorses are made from packing crates used in 1946 to ship a large donation of objects to the Historical Society of Frederick County from Omaha, Nebraska.

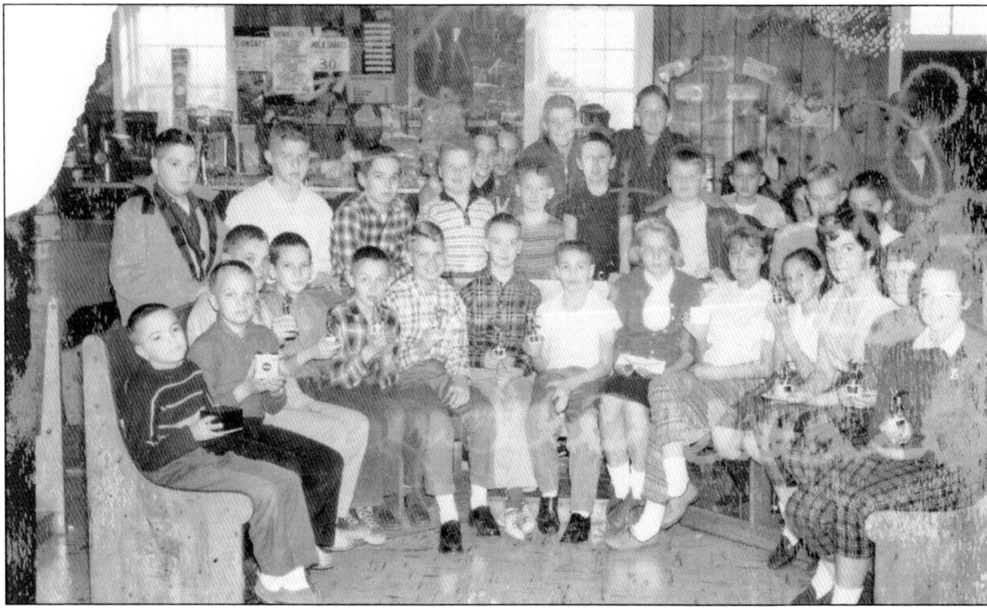

On December 12, 1960, boys and girls gathered for a Junior Bowling Tournament party sponsored by the Jaycees at Arcade Alleys on North Market Street in Frederick. Bowling has been popular throughout the county since the mid-19th century, and bowling alleys were present in a number of communities by the early 20th century. Arcade Alleys (later Arcade Bowling Lanes) catered to a number of youth and church leagues.

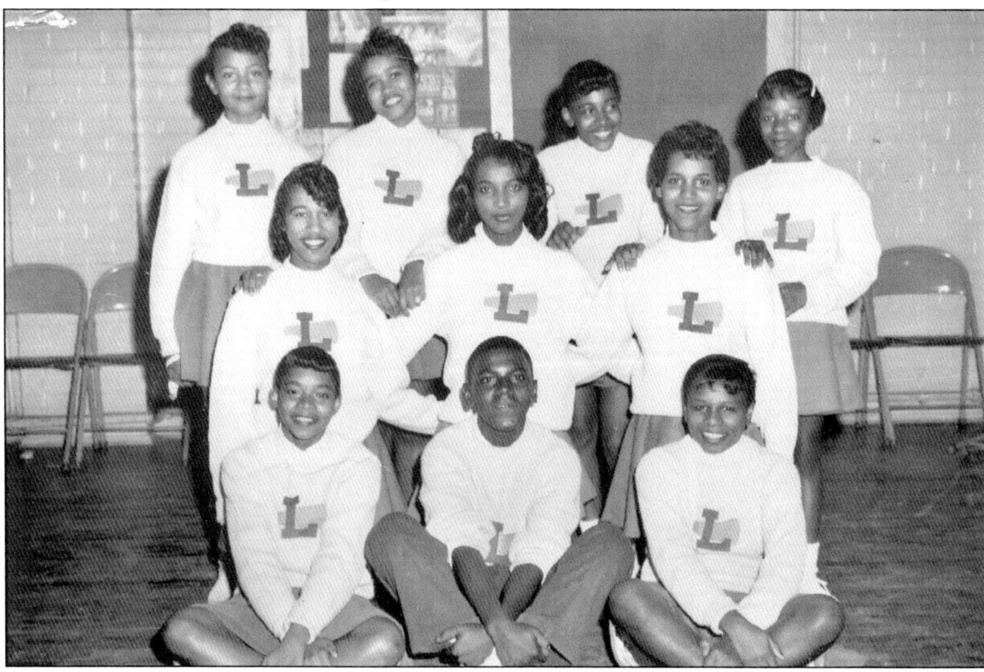

As far as school athletics programs go, cheerleading is one that supports all others. Cheering on the other athletes of Lincoln High School in 1961 are, from left to right, the following: (first row) Elizabeth Marie Thomas, Charles Shern, and Savannah Virginia Rivera; (second row) JoAnn Harris, Shirley Lee, and Betty Proctor; (third row) Rose Dorsey, Carol White, Jane Onley, and Patricia Lee.

Three

Old-Time Religion

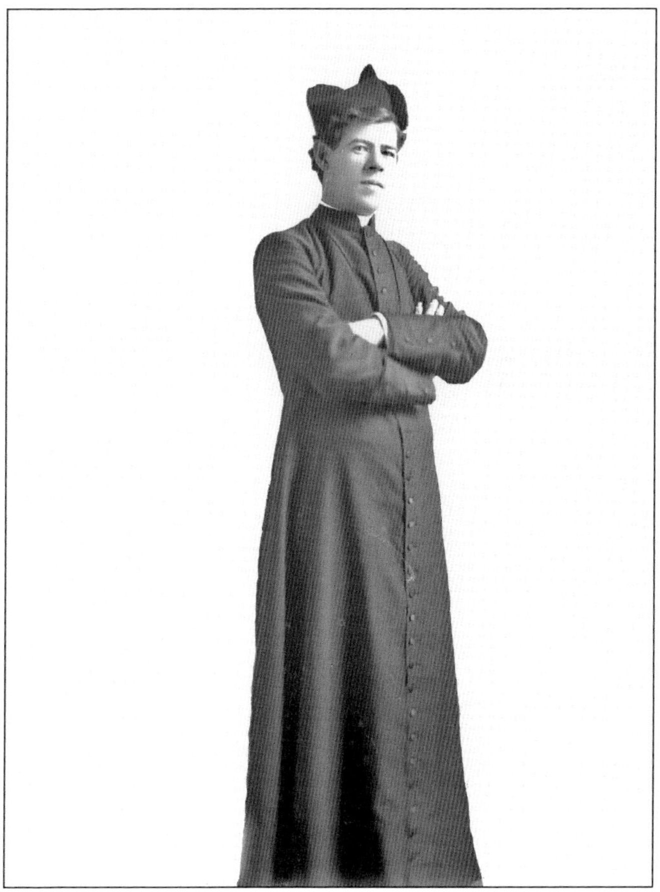

For nearly 200 years, young Catholics have received training at Mount St. Mary's College (now University) and Seminary in Emmitsburg. For about 70 years of the 19th century, many began their religious life in the Jesuit Novitiate in Frederick. The novitiate left the city in 1902. This young man, attired in biretta and cassock and likely a part of one of these institutions, was photographed *c.* 1900 at the Byerlys' Frederick studio.

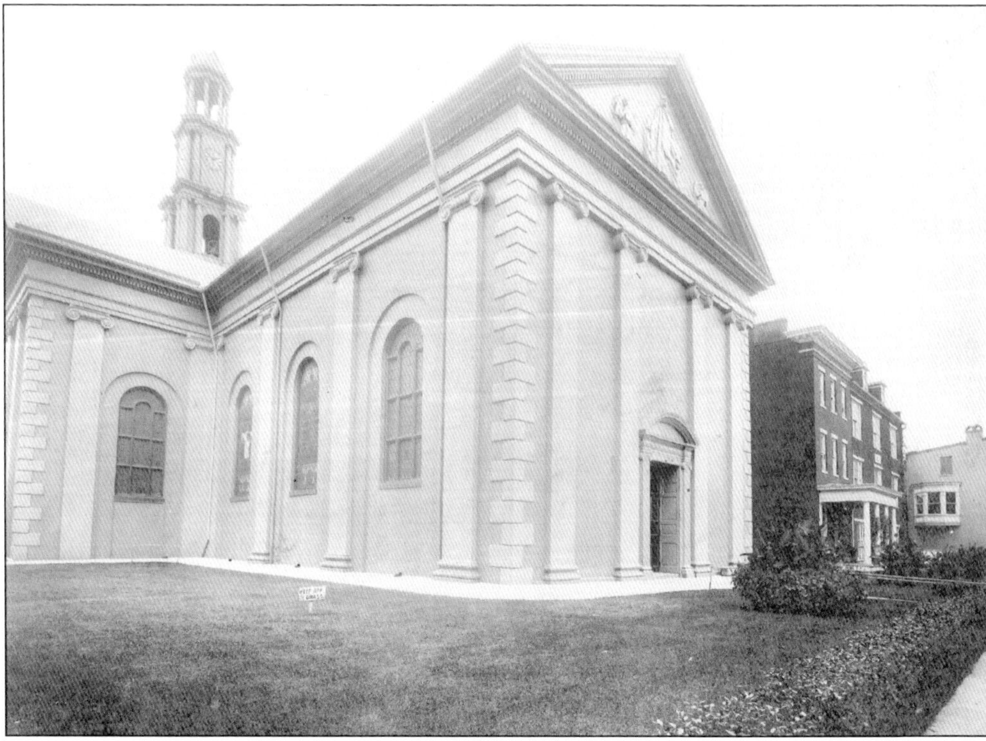

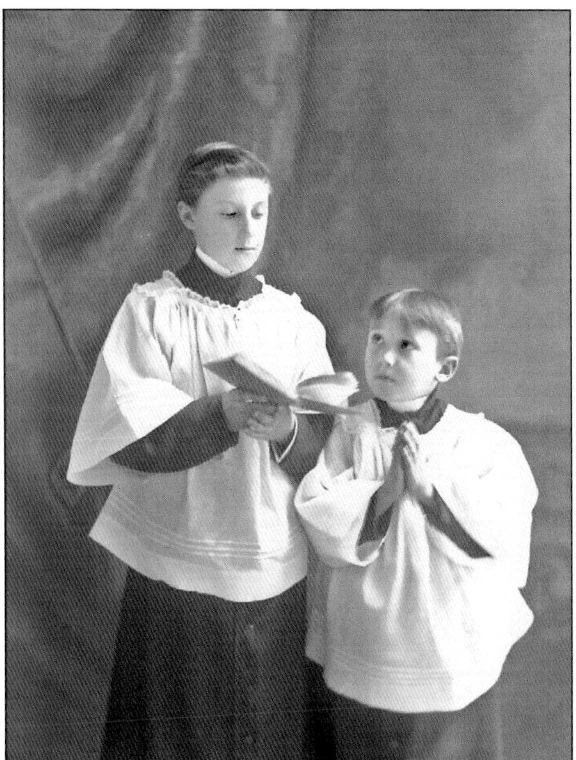

Judging by the small sign in the photograph above, St. John the Evangelist Roman Catholic Church in Frederick may have had problems with people trampling its well-manicured lawn. The church had removed an iron fence, replacing it with a hedge, in 1902. Of course, such trespasses never crossed the minds of the angelic altar boys photographed by Charles Byerly about that time. St. John's was designed in the shape of a Latin cross by local architect John Tehan and completed in 1837 on East Second Street at a cost of nearly $37,000. It replaced modest churches that had been built in 1763 and 1800. St. John's was the largest parish church in the United States at that time. The church's gilded tower was finally finished in 1854. The altar boys likely were part of the congregation.

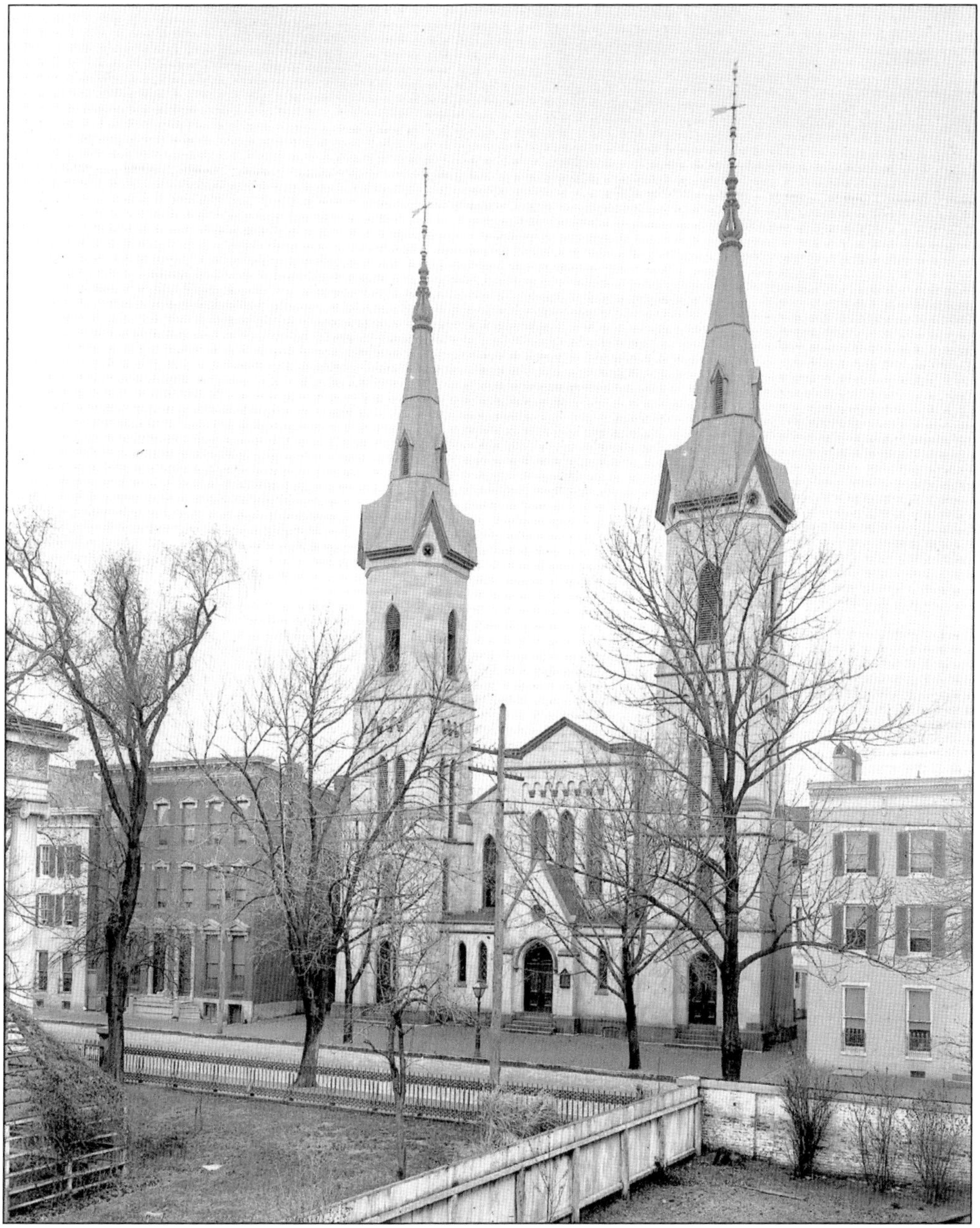

The cornerstone for the Evangelical Lutheran Church building on Church Street in Frederick was placed on August 24, 1854. The stucco brick building with its twin towers was built to replace an earlier, smaller church that had been dedicated in 1762. The front portion of the older building was removed to accommodate construction of the new one. The remaining portion constitutes one of the oldest stone structures in the county. During late 1862, the church was used as a hospital for some of the more than 4,000 soldiers wounded in the Battles of Antietam and South Mountain during the Civil War. The church property extends to Second Street and includes the Schaeffer Center, which houses Sunday school classrooms and a preschool, and several other buildings. This photograph was taken from a vantage point at the rear of the Loats orphanage next door to Winchester Hall. The lawns between the two buildings are now a parking lot.

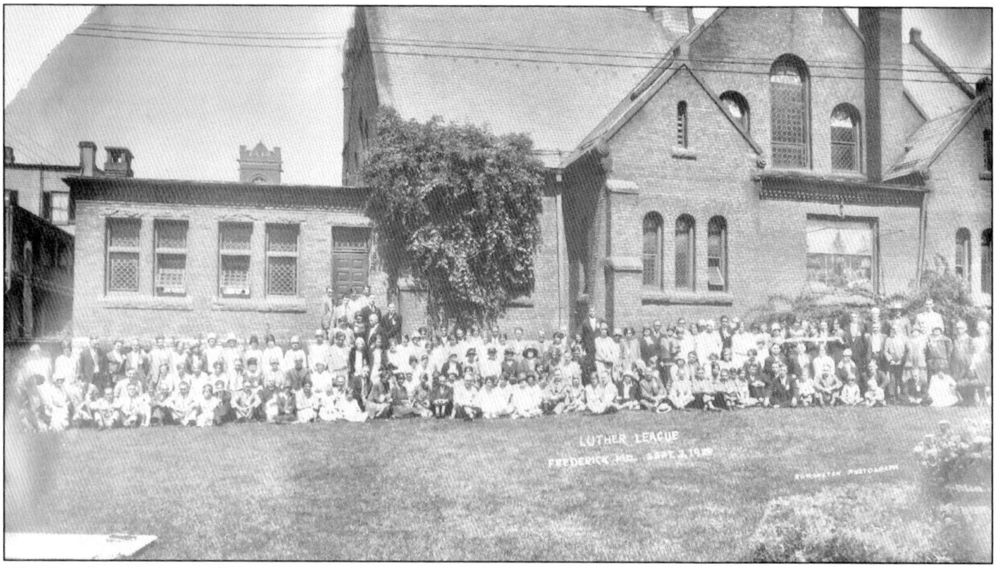

The Luther League of the Evangelical Lutheran Synod of Maryland convened its seventh annual convention in the Sunday school building of the Evangelical Lutheran Church on Church Street in Frederick on September 2, 1928. The league was formed in 1888 as a religious association for young people. Pictured here are the delegates, many from throughout the county, who attended. The gathering concluded with a banquet at the Hotel Braddock.

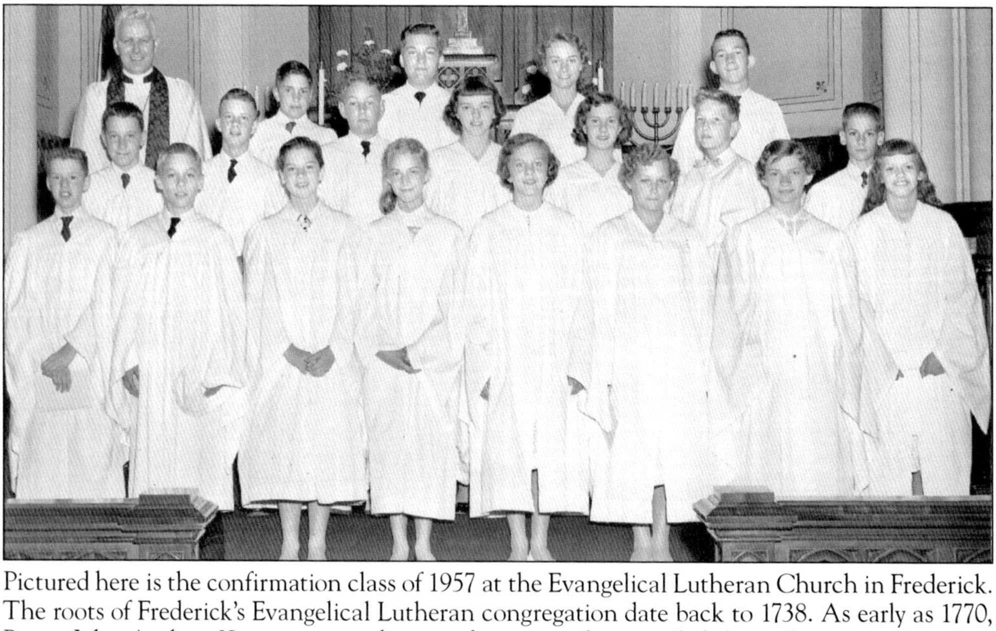

Pictured here is the confirmation class of 1957 at the Evangelical Lutheran Church in Frederick. The roots of Frederick's Evangelical Lutheran congregation date back to 1738. As early as 1770, Pastor John Andrew Krug was recording confirmations; he recorded the male names in English script and the female names in German, presumably to easily distinguish between the two while looking at the ledger.

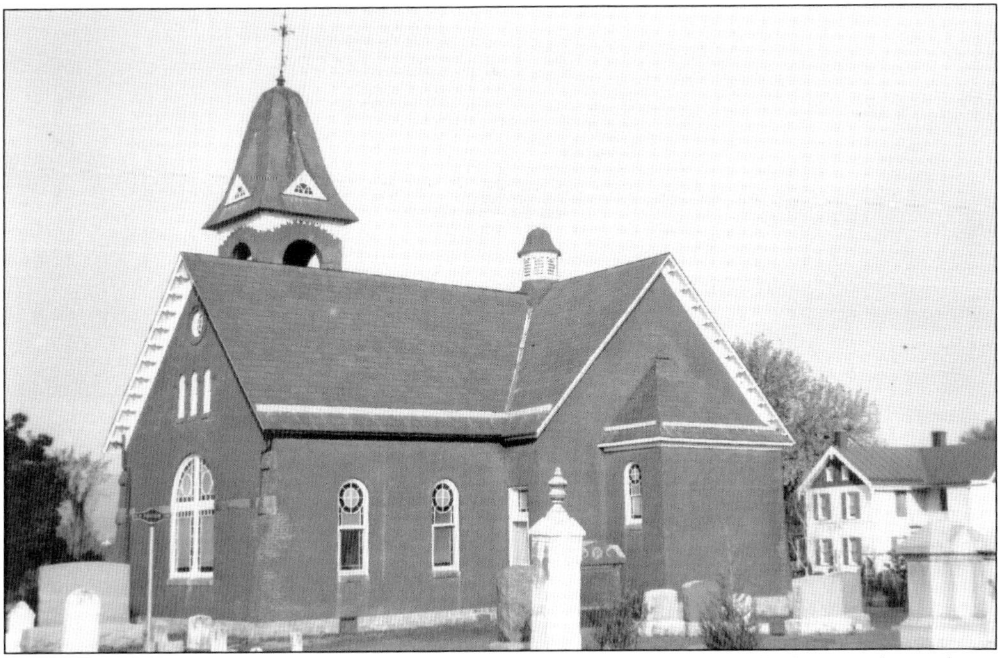

The congregation of St. Paul's Evangelical Lutheran Church in Utica Mills first worshipped in a log meeting house built about 1769 and shared with several other denominations. About 1800, the church constructed a stone addition to the log structure, in which the Lutheran and Reformed congregations continued to worship until 1889, when they constructed this building. Since 1964, the church has been used solely by the Lutheran congregation.

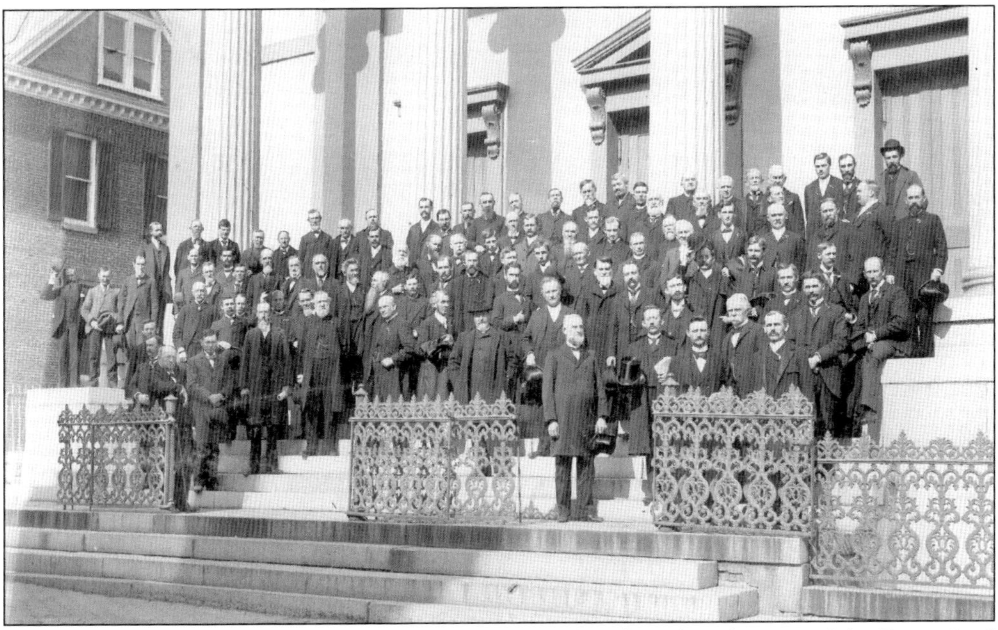

Ministers of the Potomac Synod of the Reformed Church gathered on the steps of the Evangelical Reformed Church on Church Street in Frederick for this commemorative photograph. Frederick diarist Jacob L. Engelbrecht reported that the synod was in session locally the week of October 24, 1895. The synod was organized in 1873.

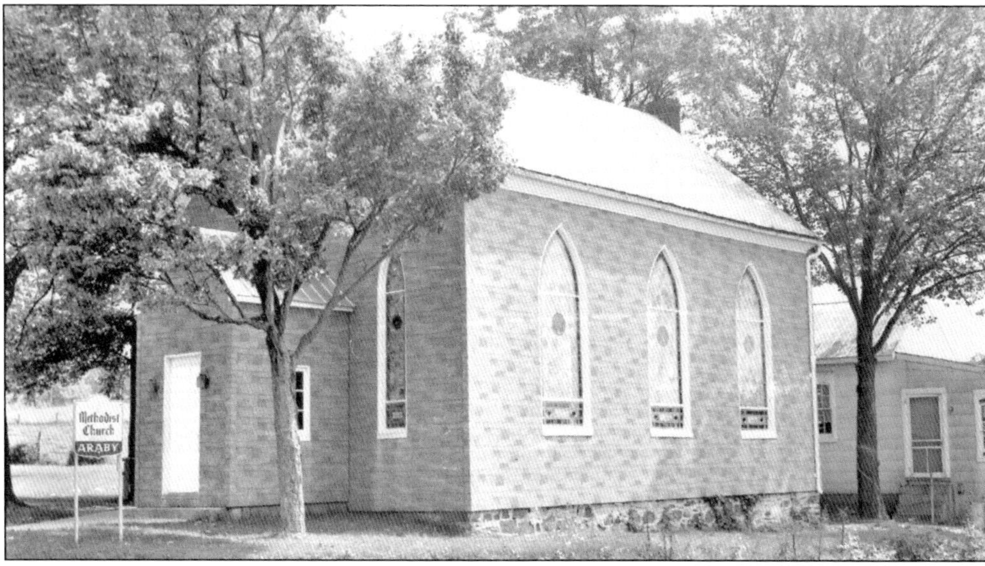

This small church was constructed in 1887 at the intersection of Araby and Baker's Valley Roads. Throughout its history, the church served Lutheran, Reformed, Dunkard, and Methodist congregations. The latter congregation formed as a part of the Buckeystown Methodist circuit in 1896. This c. 1959 photograph shows the shingled exterior before the congregation faced it with brick in 1970.

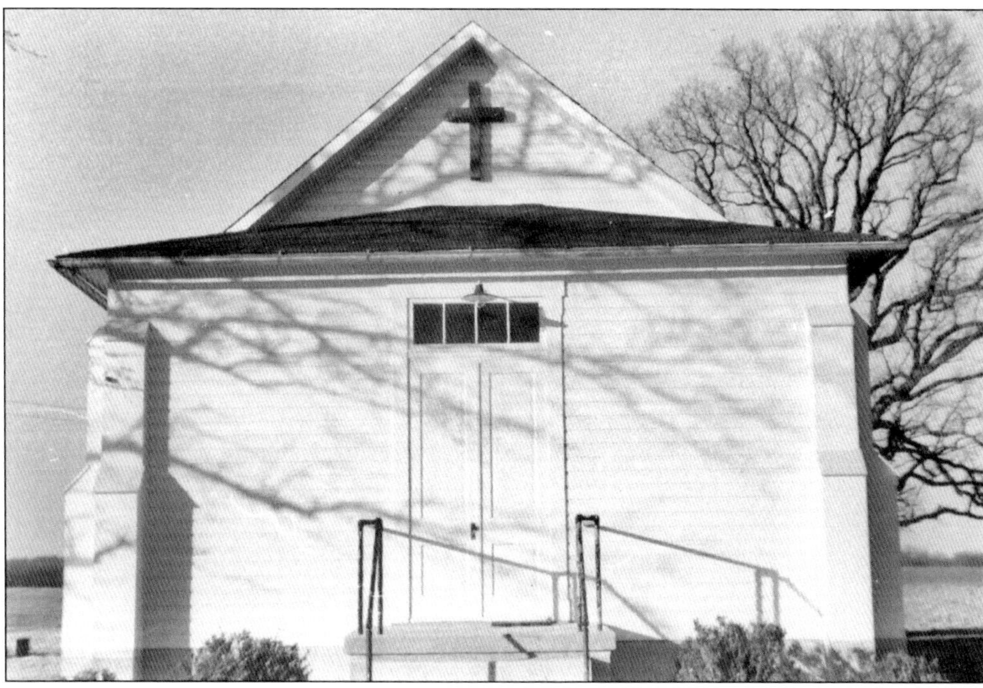

What is now the Forest Grove United Methodist Chapel congregation first met about 1871 in a log cabin across the road from its later church building. That structure, shown here in 1957, incorporates sections of an Episcopal chapel that was dismantled in Washington, D.C. The pieces were transported up the C&O Canal by barge and moved to the church site just inside the Frederick County line on Route 28.

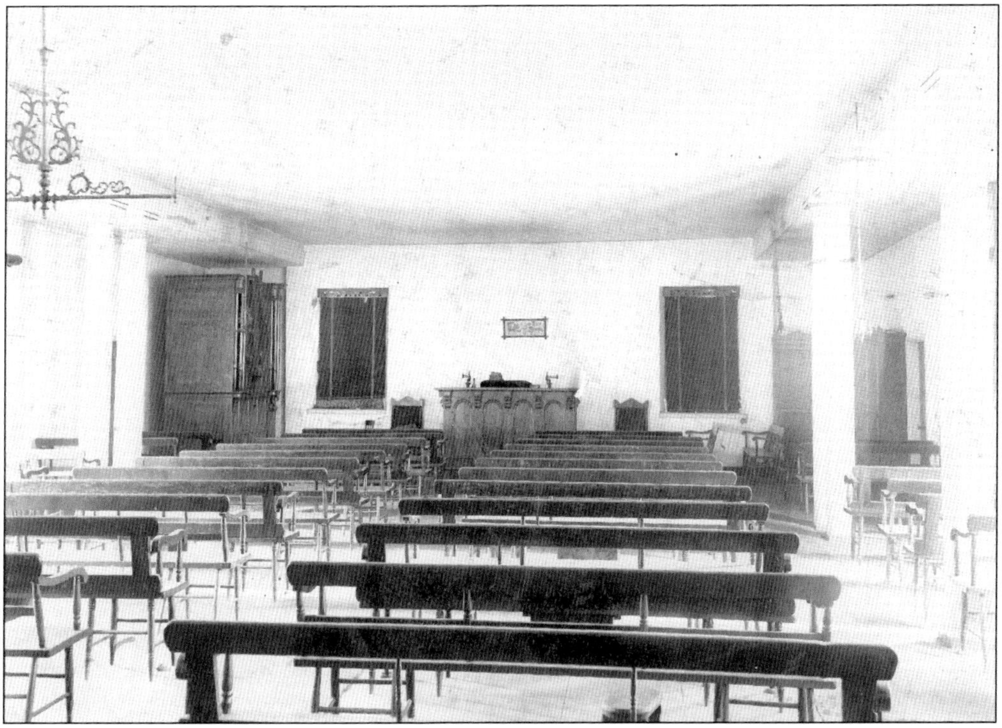

This *c.* 1879 view of the interior of Frederick's All Saints' Episcopal parish chapel provides clues to its appearance when constructed on North Court Street in 1813. Its simplicity reflected the "low church" form of worship then favored by the congregation. The pillars support the original galleries that provided seating for servants of church members. At the left front is the organ purchased by the congregation in 1826.

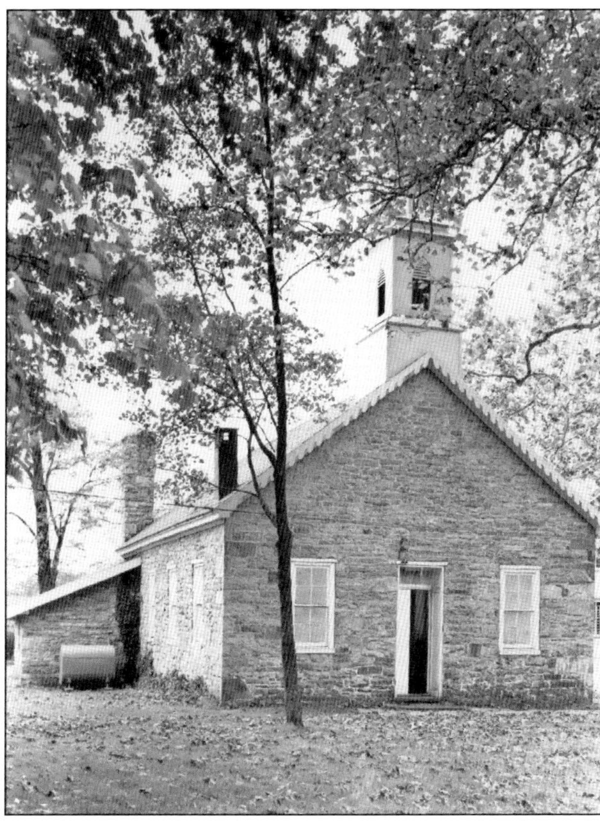

Harriet McPherson Brien found the 24-mile round-trip from her home near the Catoctin Furnace to Frederick for services at All Saints' Episcopal Church difficult. In 1827, the year of her death, her husband began construction of the Harriet Chapel, which was consecrated in October 1833. The chapel remained a part of All Saints' Parish until the Catoctin Parish was formed in 1844.

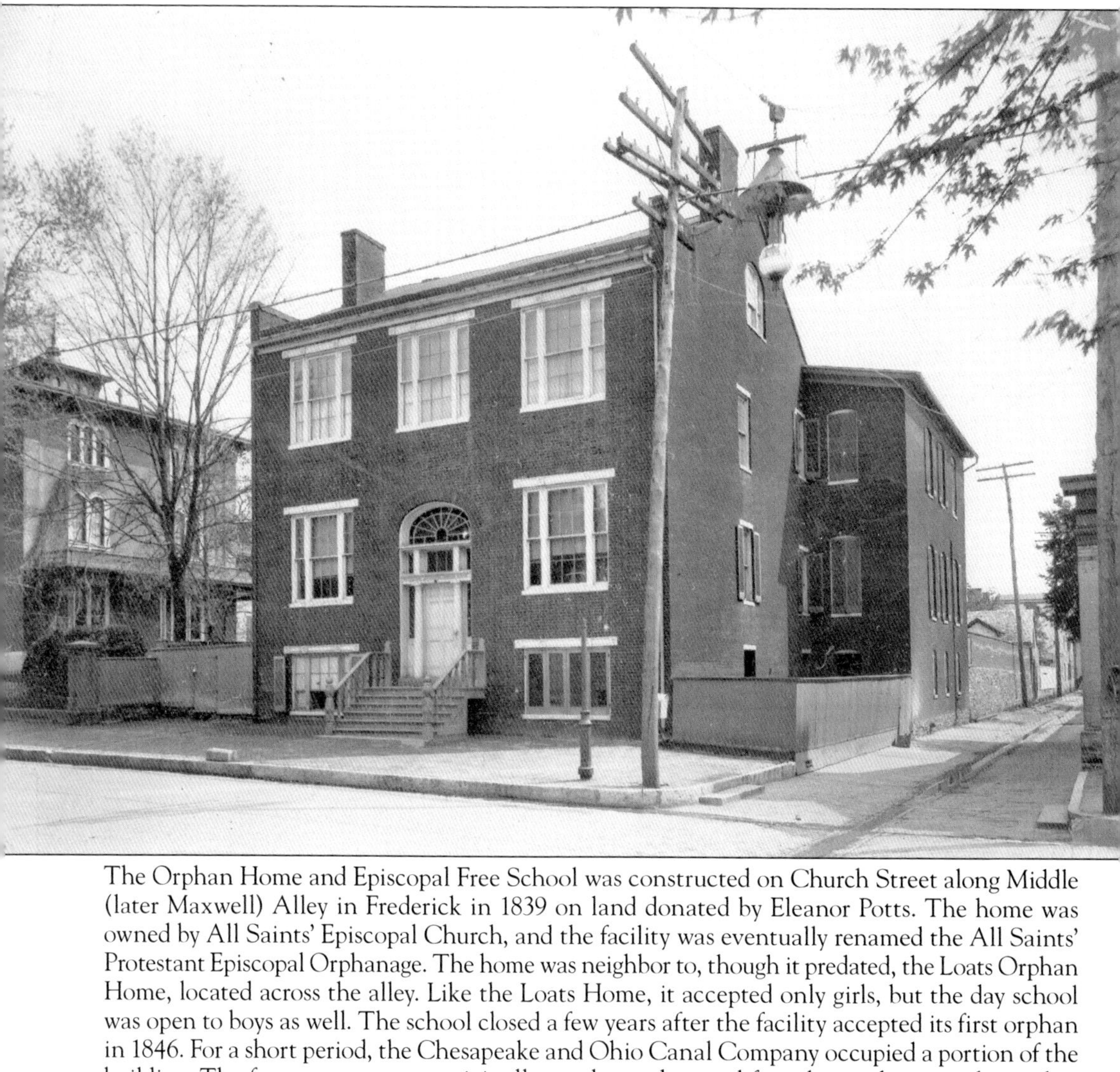

The Orphan Home and Episcopal Free School was constructed on Church Street along Middle (later Maxwell) Alley in Frederick in 1839 on land donated by Eleanor Potts. The home was owned by All Saints' Episcopal Church, and the facility was eventually renamed the All Saints' Protestant Episcopal Orphanage. The home was neighbor to, though it predated, the Loats Orphan Home, located across the alley. Like the Loats Home, it accepted only girls, but the day school was open to boys as well. The school closed a few years after the facility accepted its first orphan in 1846. For a short period, the Chesapeake and Ohio Canal Company occupied a portion of the building. The front entranceway originally was located several feet above where it is located in this c. 1920 photograph. It was done away with entirely after the orphanage closed in 1947, and the building was converted to apartments. Located next door in this image is the Trail Mansion, now the Keeney-Basford Funeral Home.

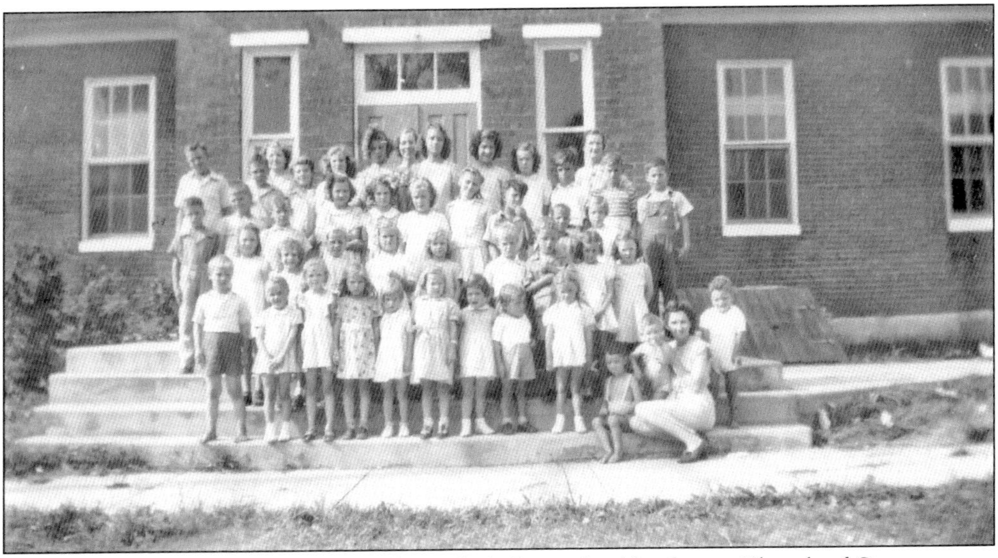

In the late 1920s, the congregation of St. John's Evangelical Lutheran Church of Creagerstown purchased the old school building across the road from the church for use as a parish hall. The children of the Sunday school posed on the front steps of the building, still serving an educational function, sometime in the late 1940s.

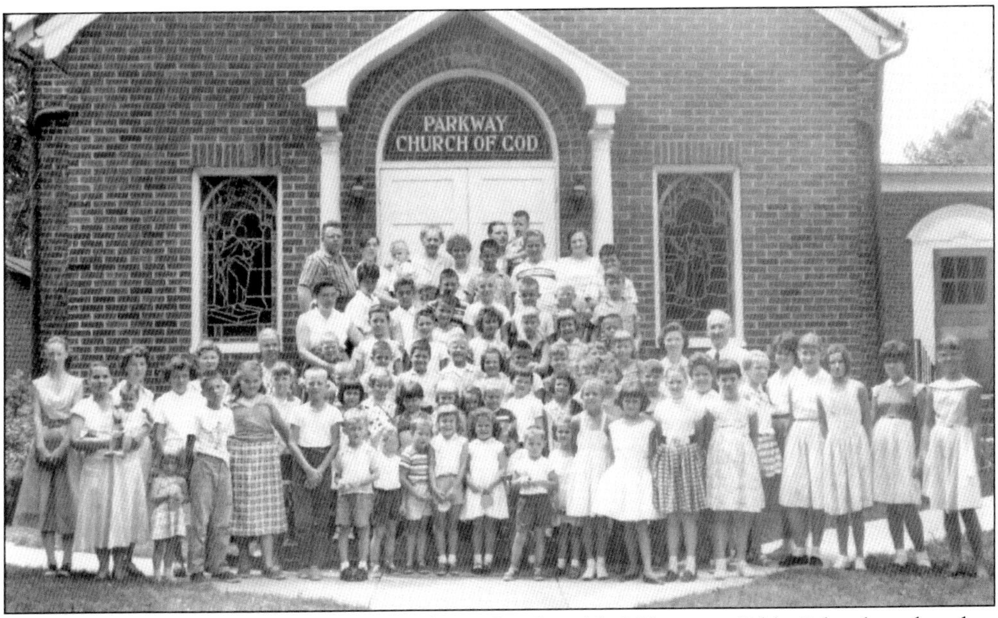

For over a century, the end of the school year has heralded Vacation Bible School at churches throughout the county. The children and teachers at Parkway Church of God posed in front of their church building one mid-20th-century summer day during Vacation Bible School. The congregation worshipped in this building on Carroll Parkway in Frederick for nearly 50 years before moving to a new location in 1986.

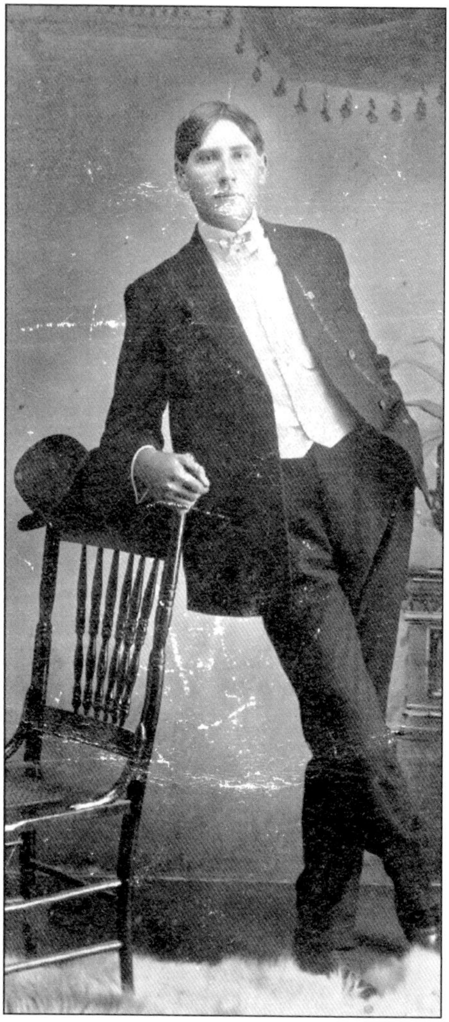

Born in North Carolina about 1885, Rev. William Carson Royal served the First Baptist Church of Frederick from 1916 until his retirement from the ministry in 1957. Those who knew him described him as a warm man with a genial personality. His ministerial philosophy was to be a "friend to man," a philosophy he put into practice in his involvement with his church and the wider Frederick community.

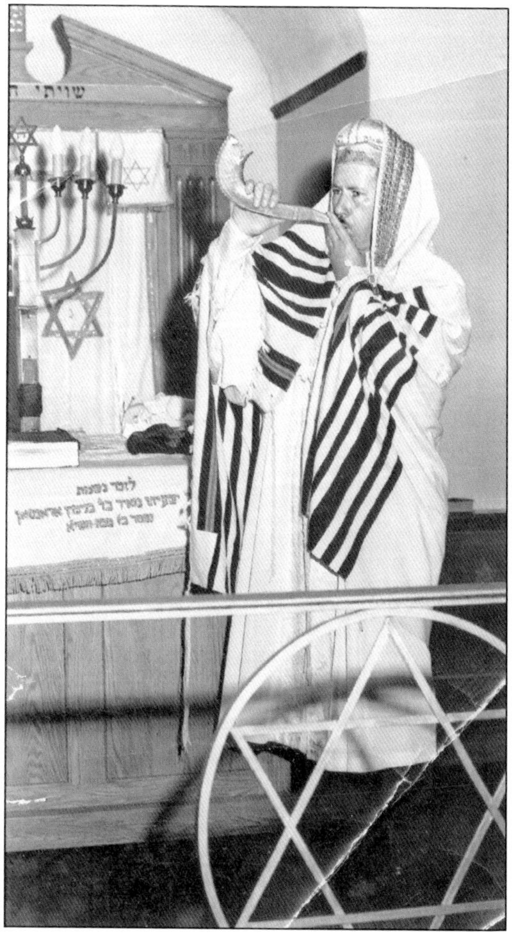

Rabbi Yehudah E. Perkin was the spiritual leader of Frederick's Beth Shalom Synagogue in 1959. In this photograph, he blows the shofar, or ram's horn, for Yom Kippur, the Day of Atonement and the most solemn day on the Jewish religious calendar. In 1858, Sussman Goebricker became Frederick's first rabbi—in fact, the first rabbi anywhere in Maryland outside Baltimore—to serve the city's small but active Jewish population.

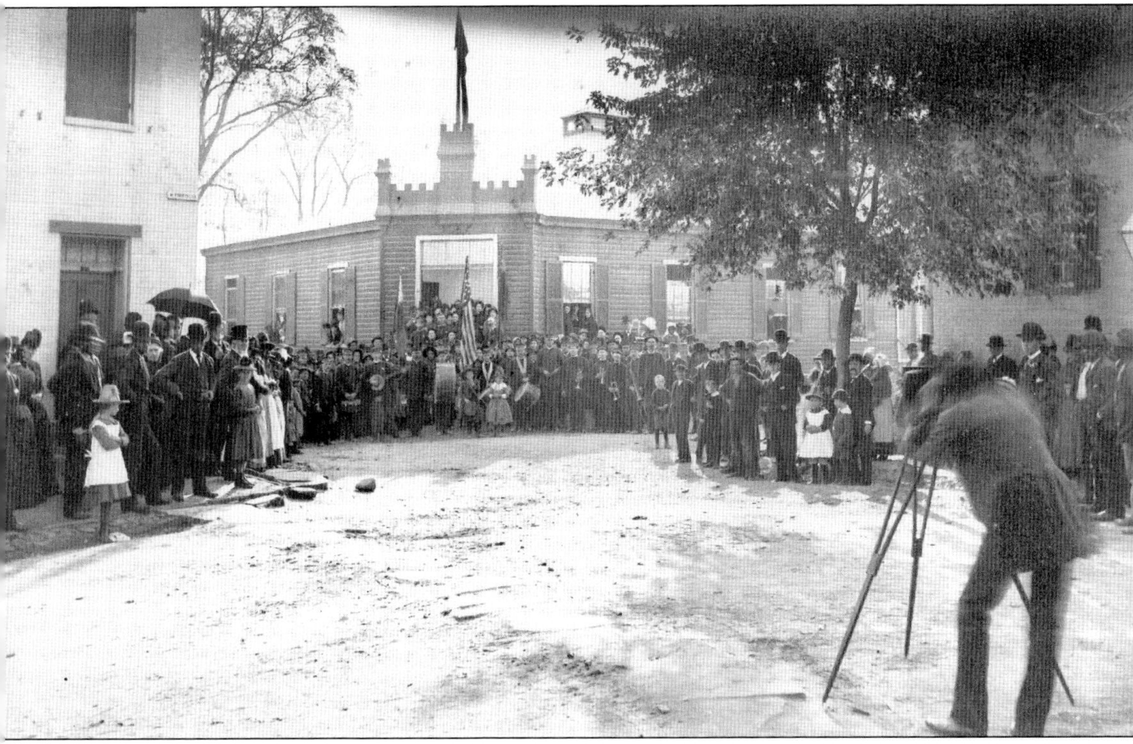

The Salvation Army Corps No. 1 dedicated its new barracks on Fourth and Bentz Streets in Frederick on October 15, 1887. The Salvation Army was established at Frederick in 1885 with the aim to "reach a class not susceptible to the ordinary influences of missionary effort; to excite a spirit of religious fervor in persons who rarely, if ever, enter a regular place of worship." By recorded accounts, the "Salvationists" were wildly successful. Hundreds and sometimes thousands came out for the group's downtown open-air meetings, lectures, services, ice cream and cake festivals, and camp meetings held throughout the county. Until the completion of the new building, the organization used the Roller Rink Building on Patrick Street. It also held meetings at Koontz Hall on North Market Street. In 1886, the No. 2 Colored Corps was formed and subsequently established a barracks on West Fourth Street. Both groups are credited with many benevolent activities. This photograph likely depicts the dedication of the Fourth Street Barracks in 1887. The photograph is credited to the Byerly Studio, and the second photographer in the foreground also may be a Byerly.

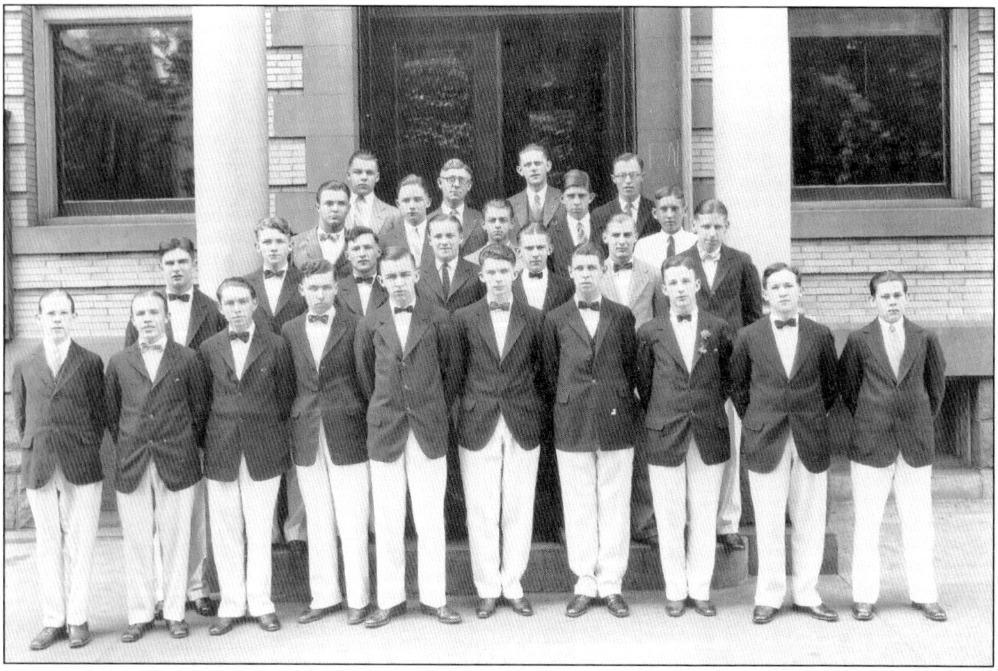

The Frederick YMCA traces its beginning to 1868 when the Frederick *Examiner* ran an advertisement announcing a meeting to start a group. While athletics may have been a major part of the program, the organization first emphasized Bible and moral teachings. The Hi-Y Club was the name for the YMCA teen and youth clubs. Shown here is the group in 1925.

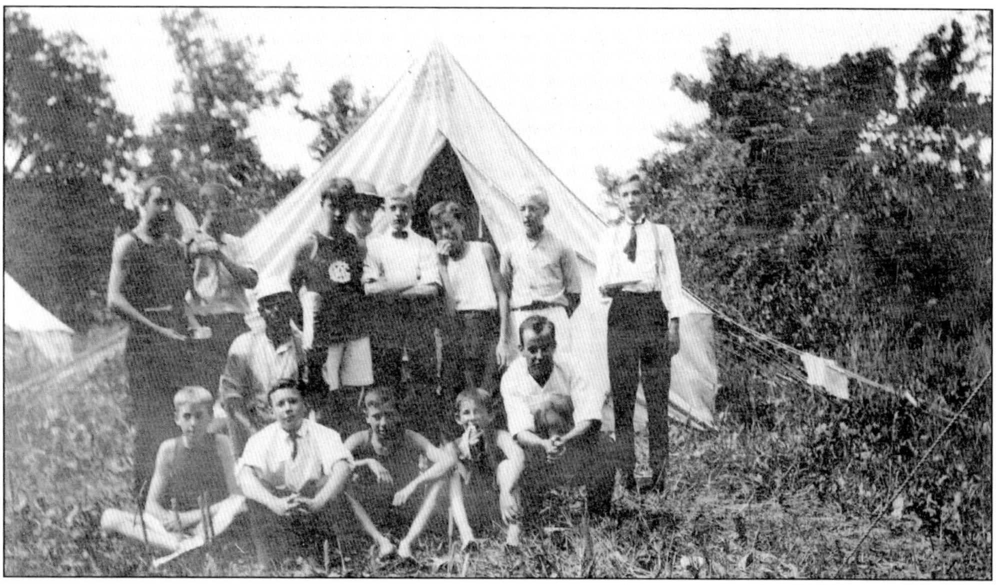

Many young county men attended the YMCA camp at Hanging Rocks, Maryland. On June 23, 1908, the Frederick *News* reported that the following boys were attending the camp: George D. Stull, Stephen Eader, William Bennett, Marvin Shirley, Harry Zeigler, Earl Zeigler, Harry Burkhart, S. Sponseller, Frank Castle, C. Fisher, Austin Mantz, Charles Hagan, John Ebert, Arthur Brown, Paul Brown, Lewis Knock, Dean Hendrickson, Edward Delaplaine, Charles Doll, and Charles Chew.

Four

THAT'S ENTERTAINMENT

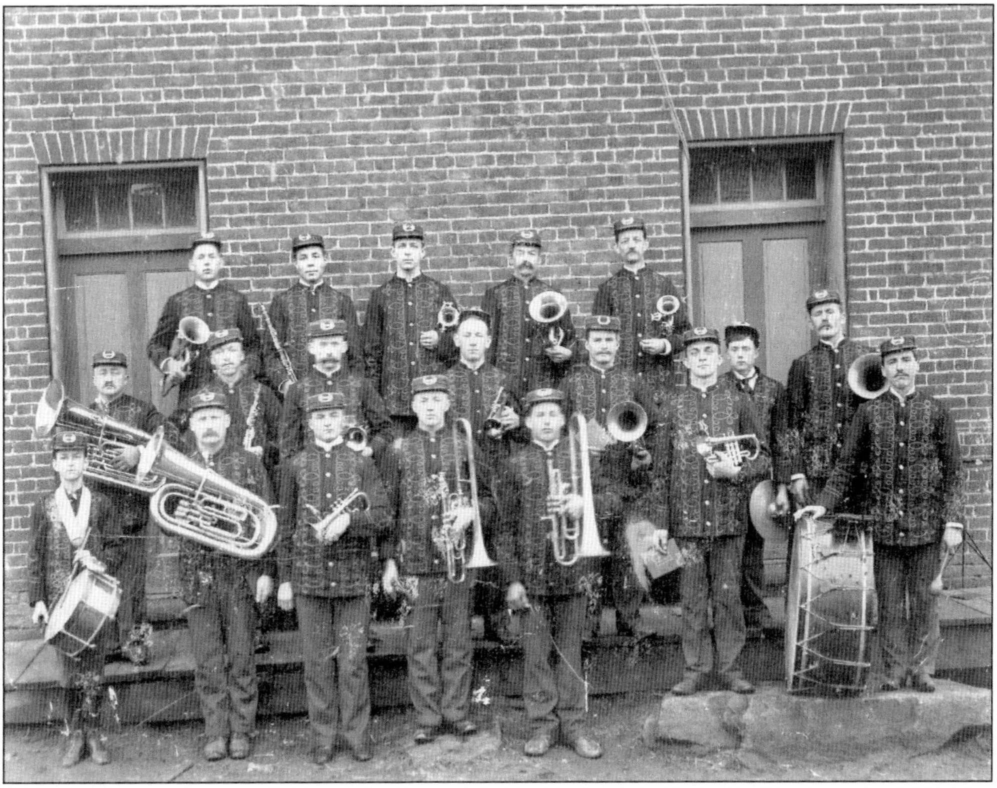

In the late 19th and early 20th centuries, many communities in Frederick County had their own bands to perform at concerts, parades, picnics, and socials. The American Band of Middletown, pictured here c. 1900, in 1901 boasted of having the finest bandwagon in the state, it having been refurbished and elaborately painted by Hagan Brothers of Frederick. F. C. Remsberg was leader of the band.

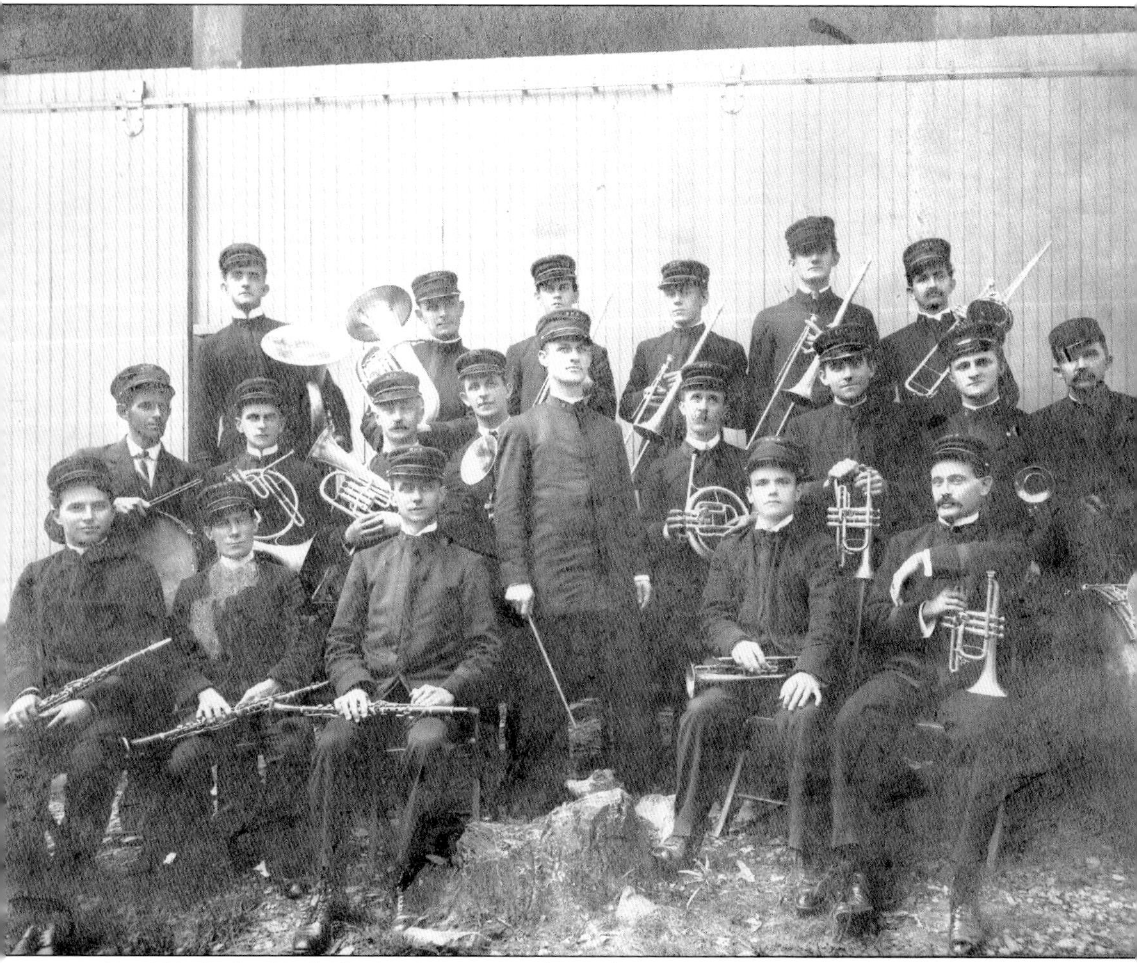

By 1908, the Braddock Heights Concert Band was "famous"—at least according to the advertisements for their concerts in the Frederick *News*. "Professor" Irving S. Biser (standing) led the band from its early days in the late 19th century until about 1915. When this photograph was taken in 1909, the band was a fixture at the Braddock Heights Auditorium. Many of its members also moonlighted at the Hotel Braddock. According to one, under the Professor's leadership, the band did not play popular music but instead was limited to "the operas, descriptive and romantic fantasia, heavy overtures and light selections." Members pictured from left to right are as follows: (first row) Homer D. Kepler, William Wastler, William L. O. Fisher, Professor Biser, Emile Raspellaire, and Albert R. Wallis; (second row) Charles Weaver, Frank Derr, Mantz Rhoades, Frank Brunner, Charles R. Holter, E. R. Stockman, Roger Harp, and Charles Willhide; (third row) Albert A. Schroeder, William Aumen, Wilber Hahn, Joseph B. Price, Harry O. Schroeder, and Foster Remsburg.

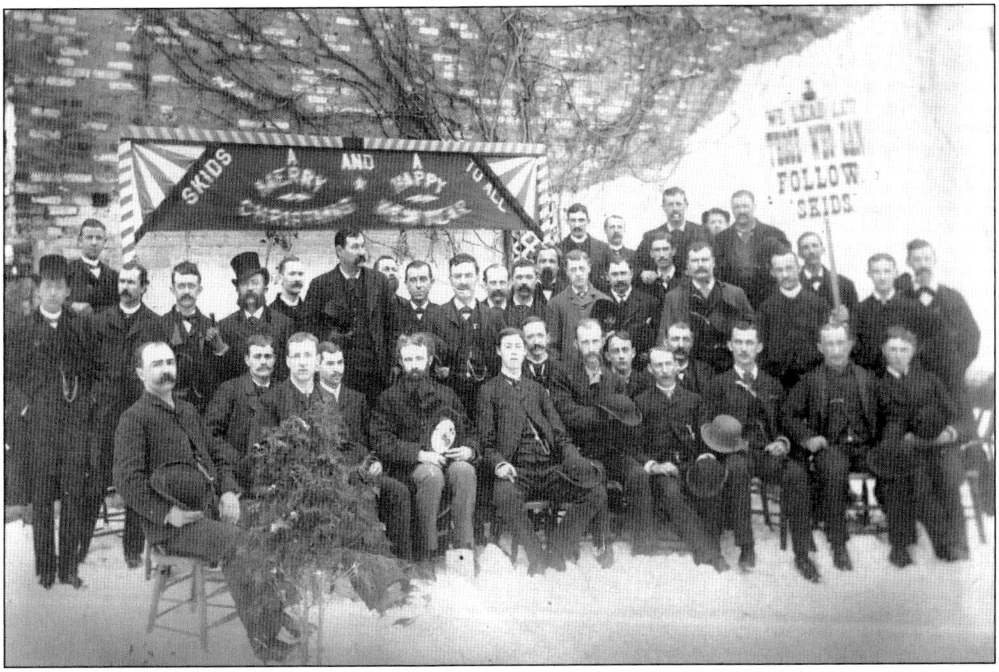

The 1880s were a particularly prolific time for the creation of men's social clubs. The Skids was a Frederick men's club initially formed in 1879 and reorganized in 1883 that took its name from a popular song, "Skids are Out Tonight," and whose motto was, "Friendship, Love and Fun." Along with staging elaborate banquets and entertainments, the group had a brass band that would roam around downtown Frederick serenading people.

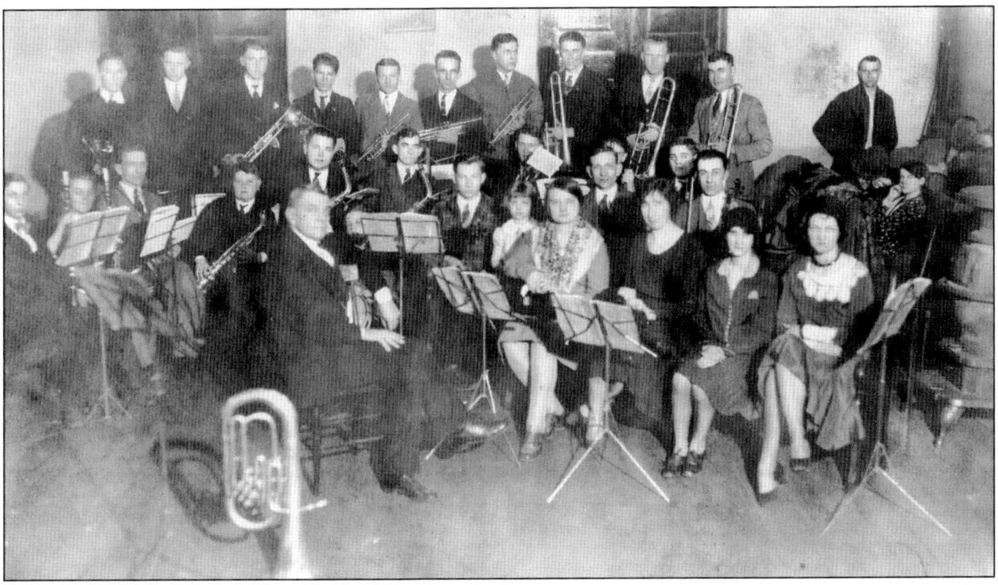

Aside from community bands, musicians often joined together to express their music. Assembled here are members of the Cassell Concert Society at their monthly gathering in February 1935. They are joined in this photograph with members of the Frederick Concert Society for a concert directed by John Francis Fisher, given after the Cassell club's business meeting. Following the meeting, the club spent time practicing choral pieces for the spring recital.

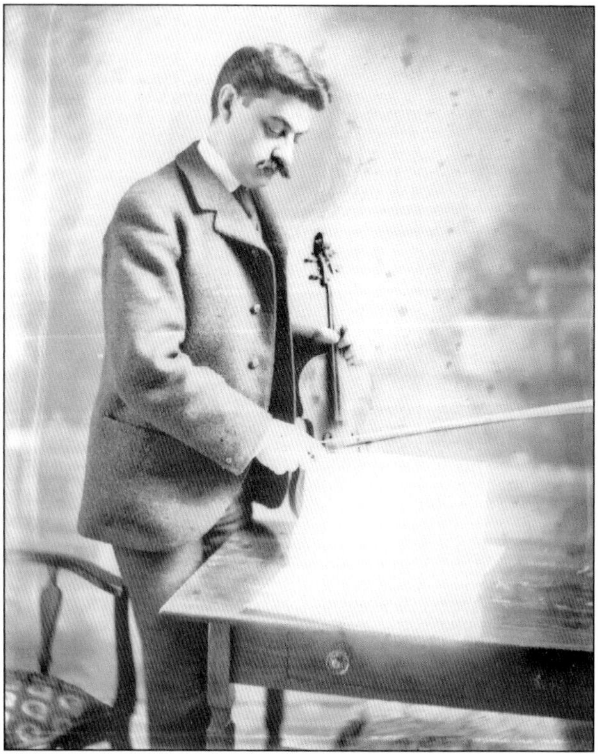

Bion Firestone had a remarkable career as a musician in Frederick County during the late 1800s and early 1900s. During his career, he would earn a living as a professor of music, as a conductor in the Frederick Philharmonic Orchestra, and as an accomplished violinist, organist, and pianist. Some of his many involvements were working for the Signor Hazazer School of Dance and the Lutheran Sunday School Orchestra.

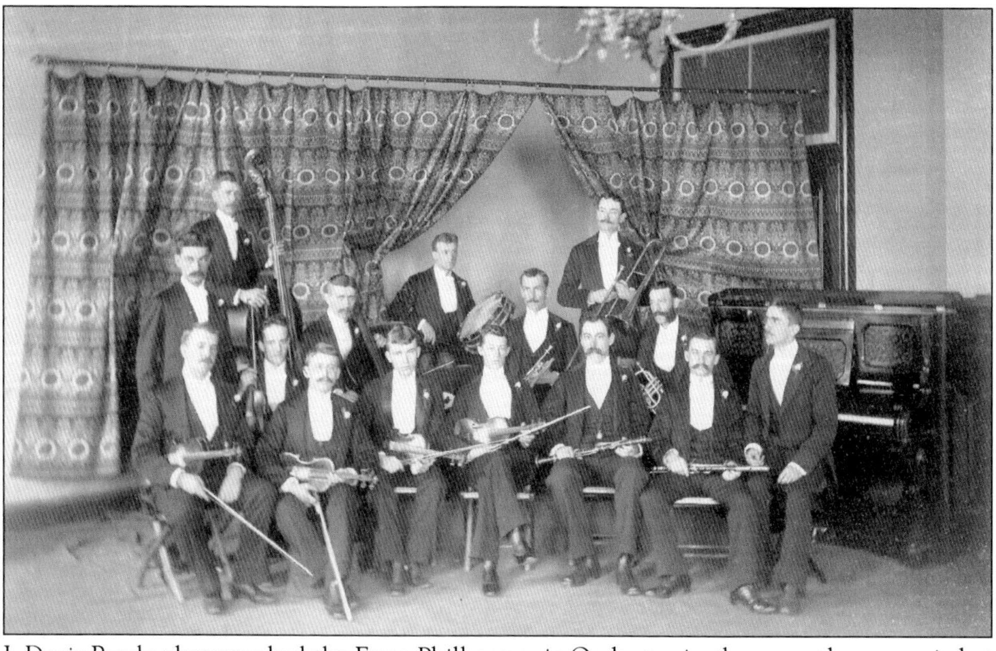

J. Davis Byerly photographed the Estey Philharmonic Orchestra in the room they occupied at Frederick's city hall building in 1890. The orchestra performed around town under the direction of Bion Firestone (standing second row far left). Other members of the group included Dr. Albert L. Pearre (second from left, holding up his violin) and Charles W. Wertheimer (first row, third from right).

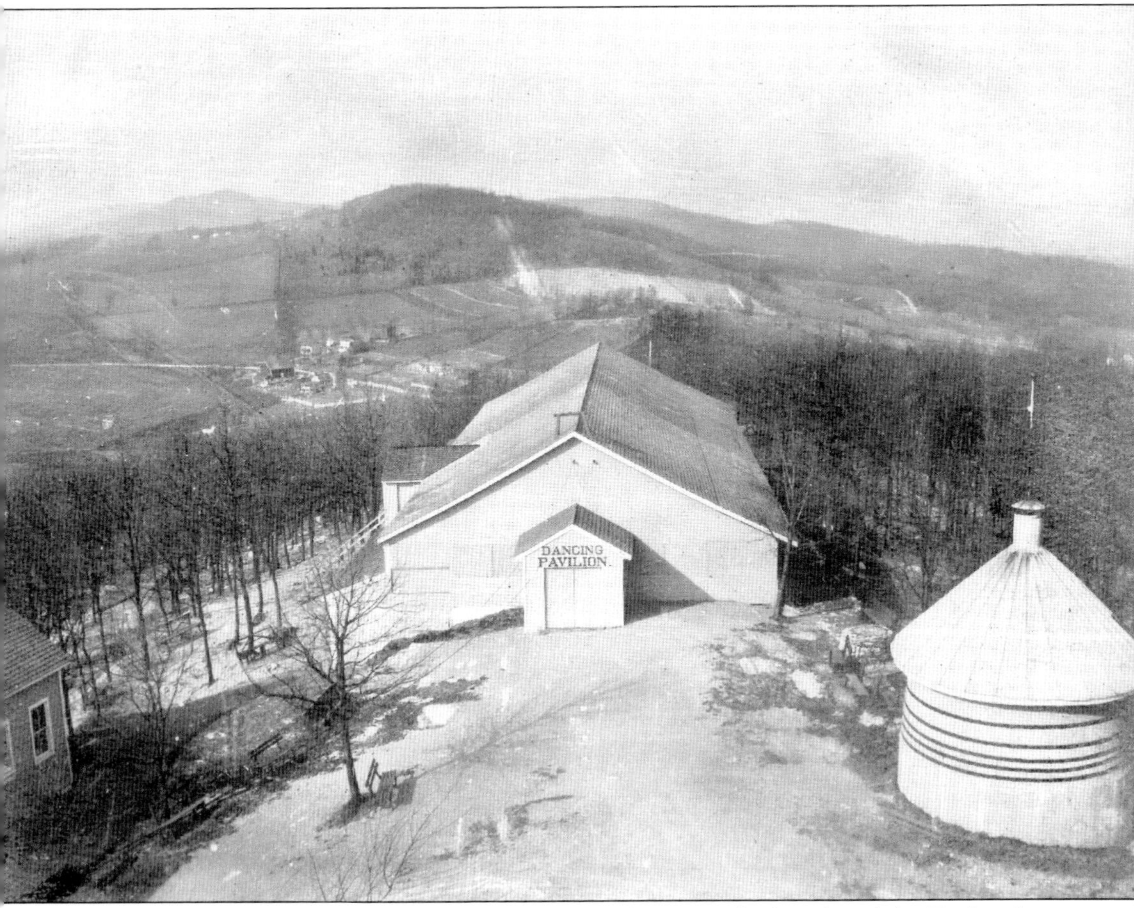

Braddock Heights Park was established by George William Smith, founder of the Frederick Railroad Company and the Braddock Heights Improvement Company, in 1896. What was originally a quiet picnic area would expand to include an amusement arcade, skating rink, and dance pavilion by 1908. The pavilion, pictured here, was the second structure built in the park; the first was an observation tower, which was torn down and rebuilt in 1931 and 1971. Because of its popularity, the dance pavilion was renovated in 1924 to expand the dance floor to 6,000 square feet. In 1933, people were allowed to participate in "fancy dancing," which included such dances as the tango and the turkey trot. Weekday evening dances were held there from 8:00 p.m. to 11:00 p.m. The park was closed in 1964 but was reopened for a time in the 1970s. The dancing pavilion was destroyed by a fire in 1987.

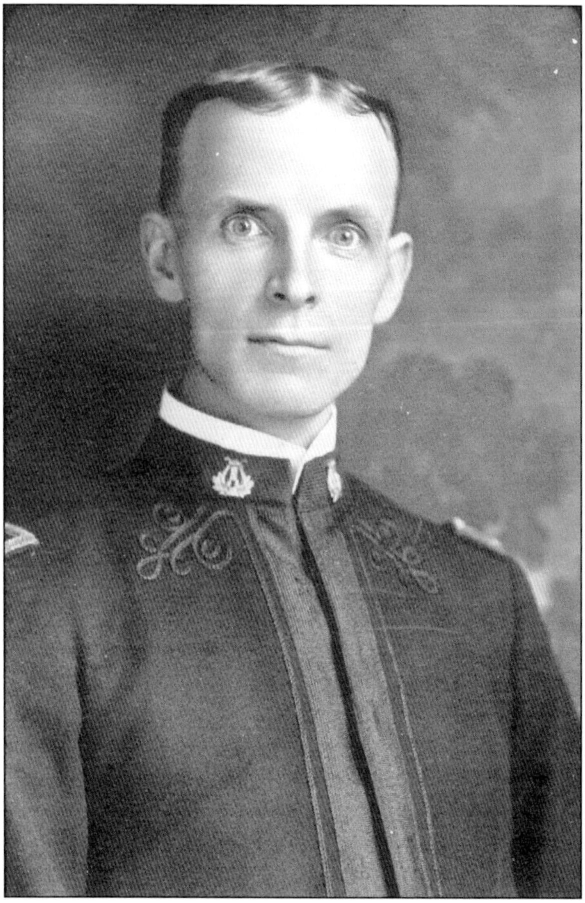

Fenton Harris is pictured here in his Boys' High School Band uniform, a fitting ensemble given that he started the school band—the first in the county—in 1913. Unlike most bandleaders, Harris did not teach music but was head of the Commercial Department. He taught at Boys' High School and Frederick High School for 35 years, retiring in 1943. He later was elected to the state legislature.

In April 1960, a group of Frederick High School band members, directed by W. Gray Buckley III, provided background music for student demonstrations following the nominations of each of six candidates at a mock Democratic National Convention at Hood College, which involved 600 delegates from 18 colleges. Buckley, a senior at Frederick High School, received the Frederick County Senatorial Scholarship to the Peabody Conservatory in Baltimore.

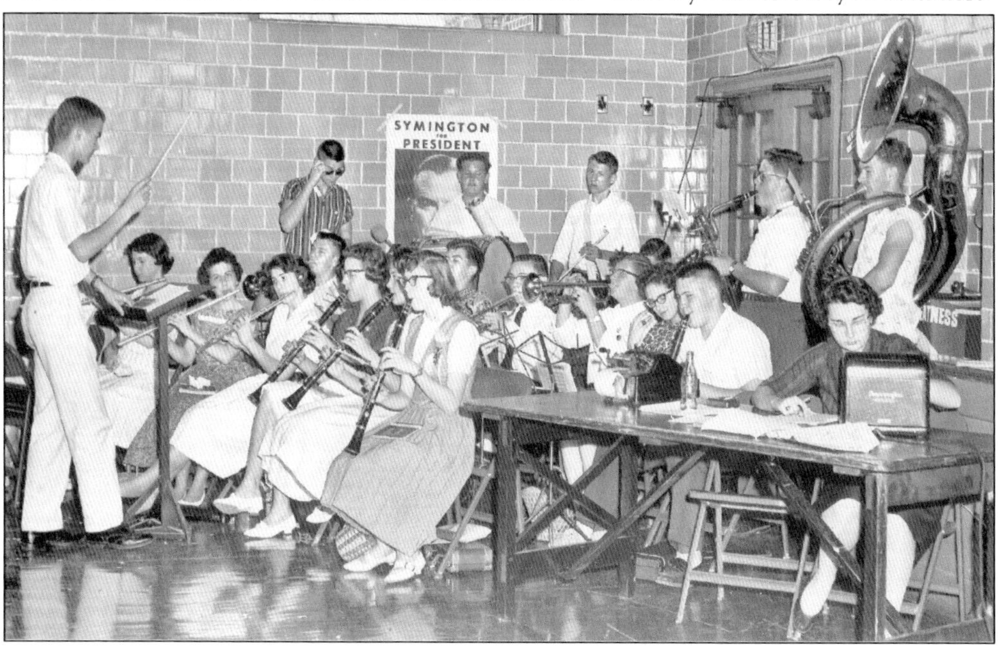

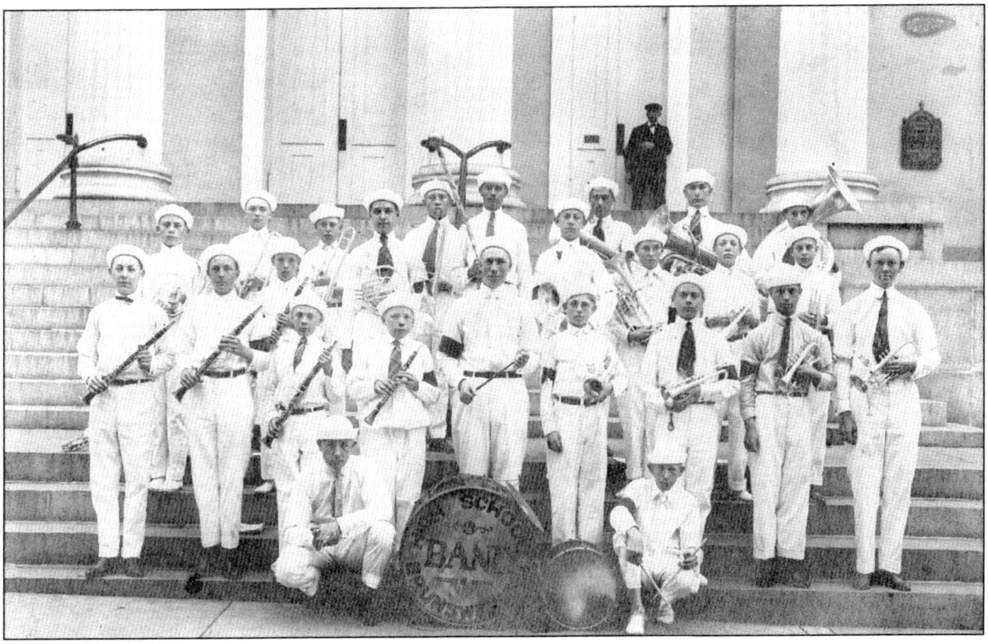

The Brunswick High School band, established in 1917 by Charles T. Stull, was one of Frederick County's earliest high school bands. The exact date on which the band posed on Frederick's Evangelical Reformed Church steps is unknown. A May 1922 newspaper article about a Brunswick parade mentioned the "natty suits of white" worn by the band members.

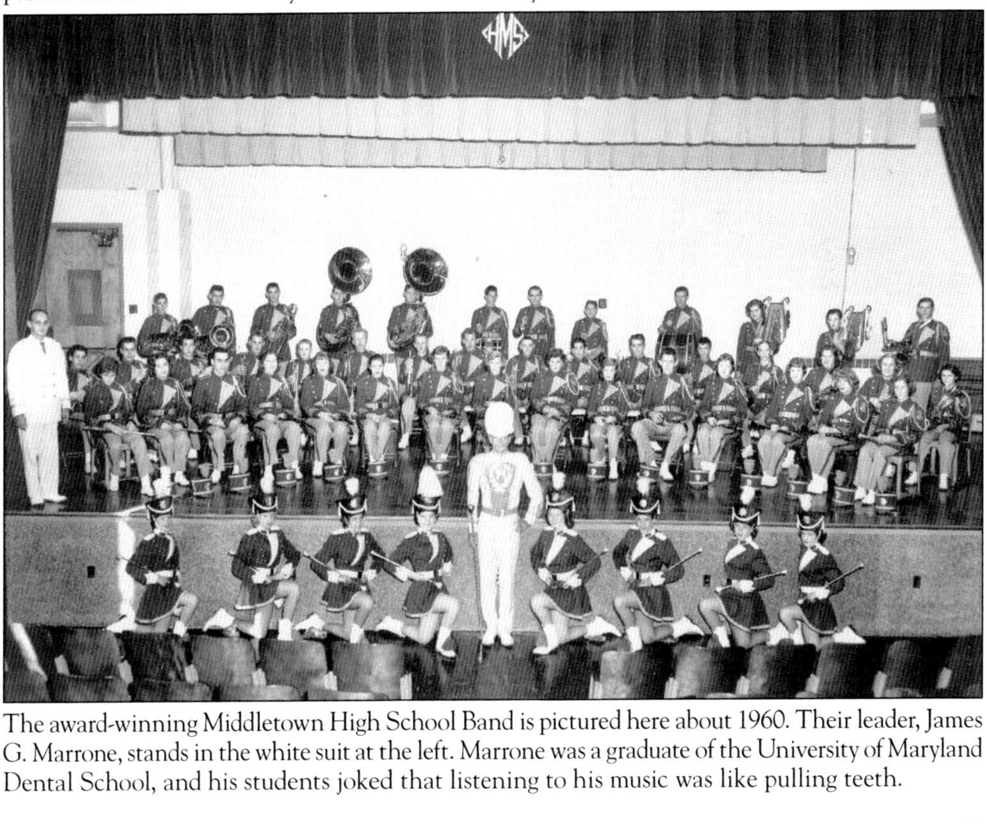

The award-winning Middletown High School Band is pictured here about 1960. Their leader, James G. Marrone, stands in the white suit at the left. Marrone was a graduate of the University of Maryland Dental School, and his students joked that listening to his music was like pulling teeth.

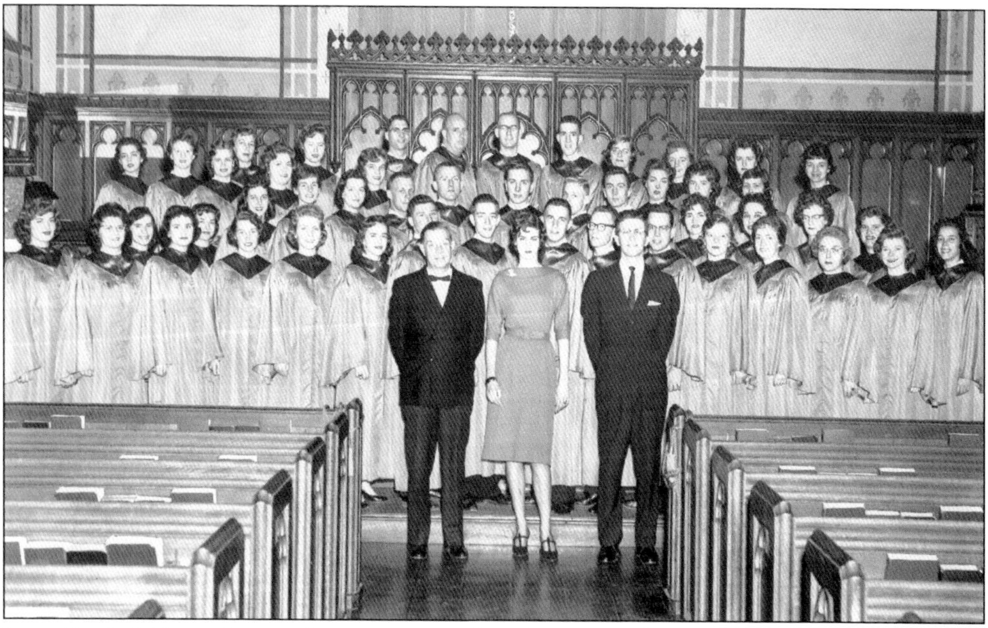

From Frederick's earliest settlement, music played an integral part in religious worship. John Thomas Schley, the Reformed Church's first schoolmaster, was also a musician and composer whose beautifully illuminated songbooks still survive in the collection of the Historical Society of Frederick County. The choir of Frederick's Evangelical Reformed Church, pictured here sometime in the mid-20th century, carried on the musical tradition of Schley and the church.

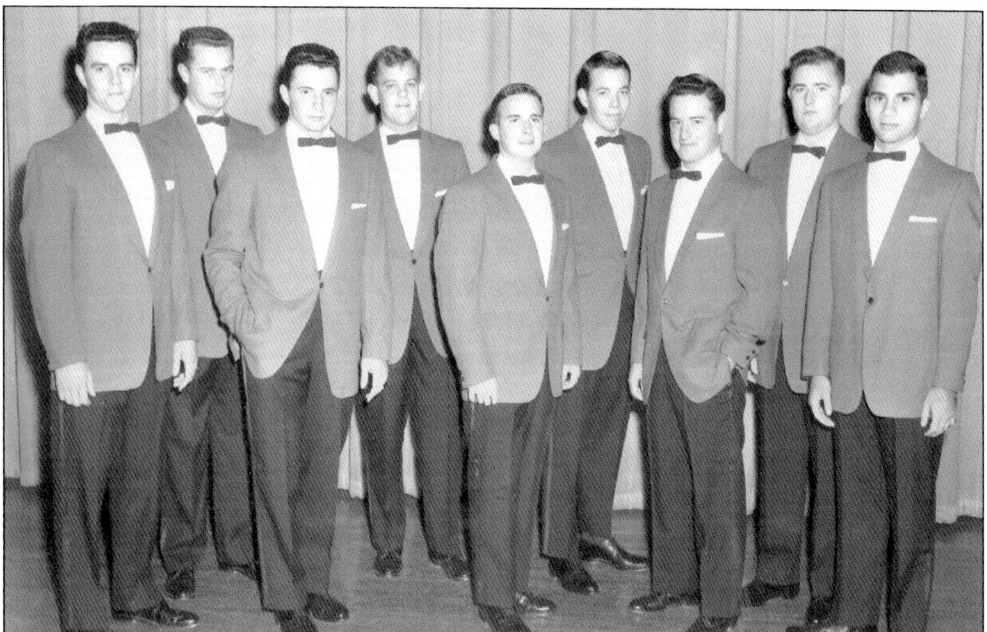

Mount St. Mary's College was founded in 1808 by Fr. John Dubois. The Emmitsburg school has always provided a number of activities in which students may participate. These students were members of the glee club, which performed an annual Christmas concert as well as community events. The college changed its name to Mount St. Mary's University in 2005.

"Happy Johnny" Zufall (left), pictured c. 1936 with "Handsome Bob" Bouch, was a popular radio personality and entertainer. Born in Pennsylvania in 1909, John Zufall, his fiddle, and guitar traveled with various performers. Known for his country twang and corny jokes, Zufall gained a national following working as a Baltimore disc jockey. He was a morning disc jockey at WFMD in Frederick from 1953 to 1973 and became a favorite at events throughout the county. He passed away in 1990.

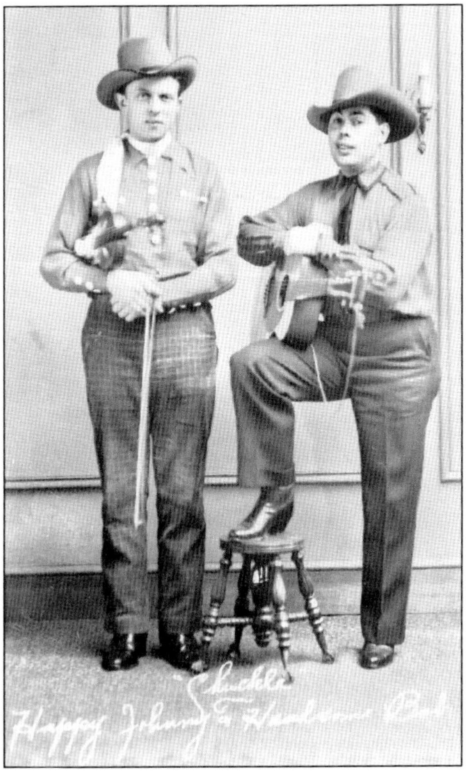

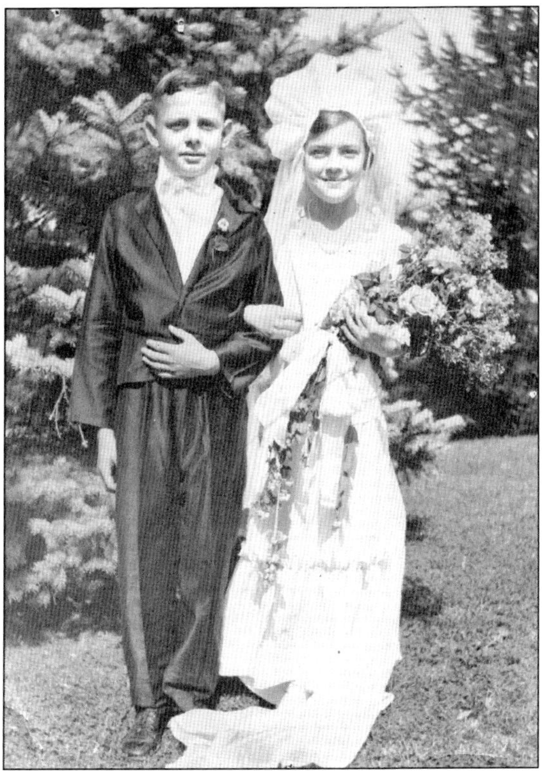

Arthur Fouche and Joyce Yingling portrayed the bride and groom in the *Tom Thumb Wedding* held at the Adamstown Odd Fellows' Hall in September 1935. The cast of characters were personalities of the day, including Pres. Franklin Roosevelt, Charles Lindbergh, Shirley Temple, and Jean Harlow. Performances were followed by a "Pageant of Brides" featuring local wedding gowns from 1873 to 1935. The program was presented by the Rainbow Class of Adamstown church.

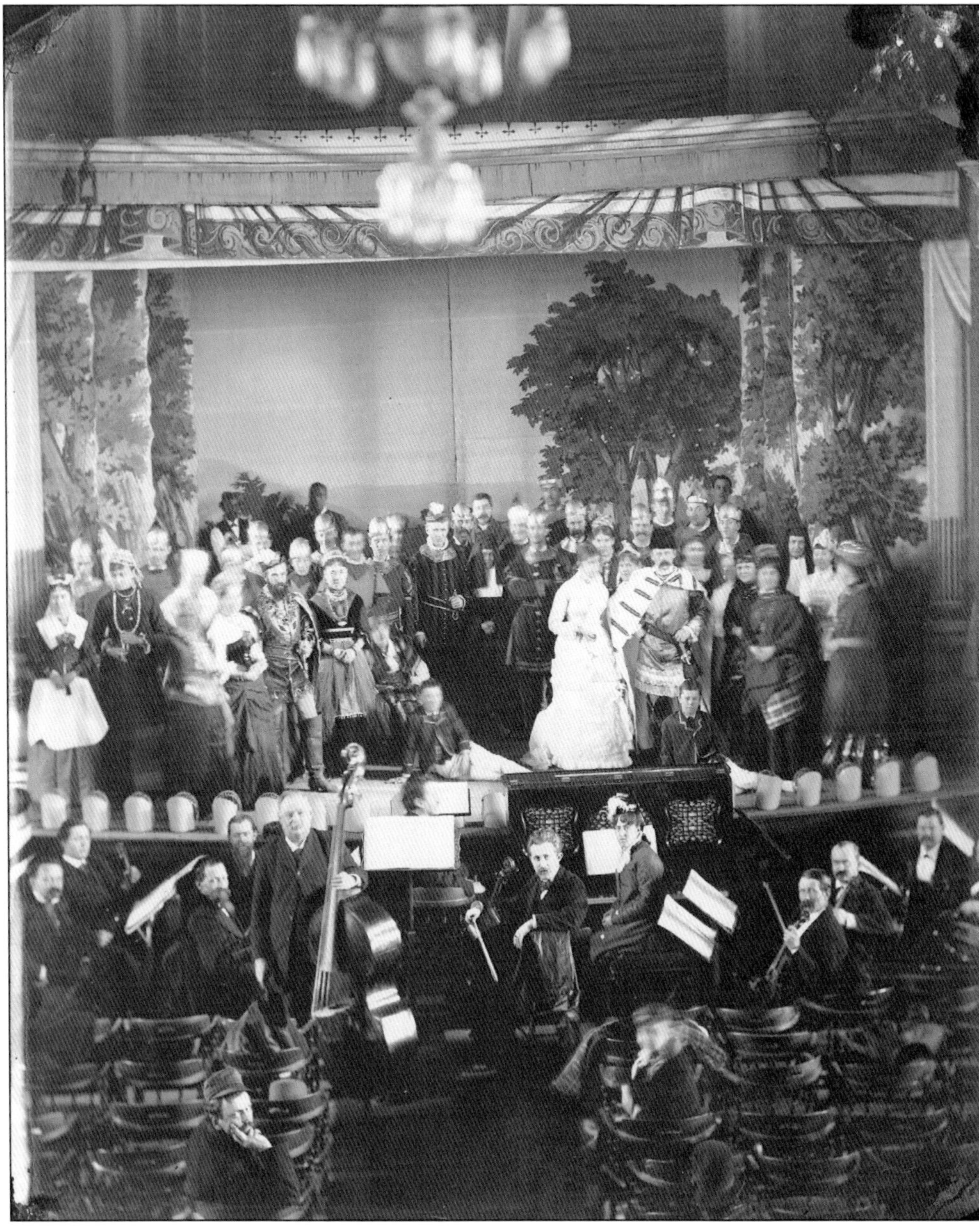

In 1950, the newly renovated City Opera House reopened to patrons who could enjoy Ebert's ice cream while they watched *Mister 880*, starring Burt Lancaster. The opera house originally was built in 1873. It housed the City Market House and town hall on its first floor and a 1,100-seat auditorium on the second. In 1900, the building was renovated to include an auditorium on its first floor with balconies. For many years until its conversion to a movie theater, its stage presented shows by touring companies and local theater troupes, symphonies and dances, and lectures and special services. On September 19, 1901, it was the location of memorial services for the recently deceased Pres. William McKinley. Although the production for which this cast and orchestra are assembled is unknown, the costuming and scenery are reflective of the extravagant spectacles that could be experienced at the opera house. Today the building has been renovated as a restaurant but still contains many of its historical architectural features.

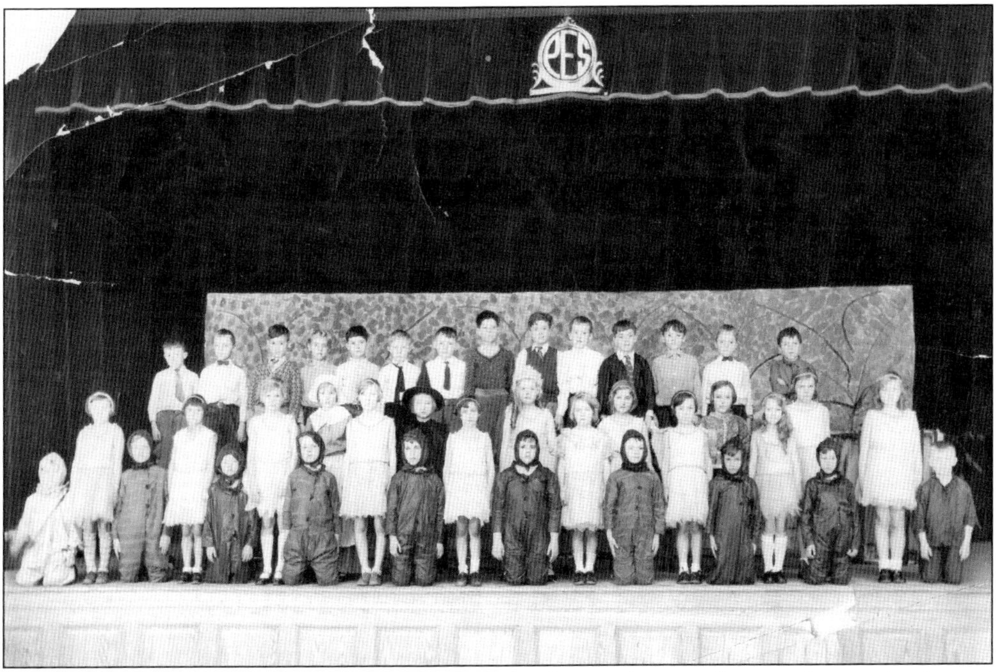

To the delight of their parents, children have long been reluctant flowers, farm animals, and storybook characters in school plays. This photograph, dated 1932, of the players in *Hansel and Gretel* shows the cast of third graders from Parkway Elementary School in Frederick. The school had just opened the previous school year.

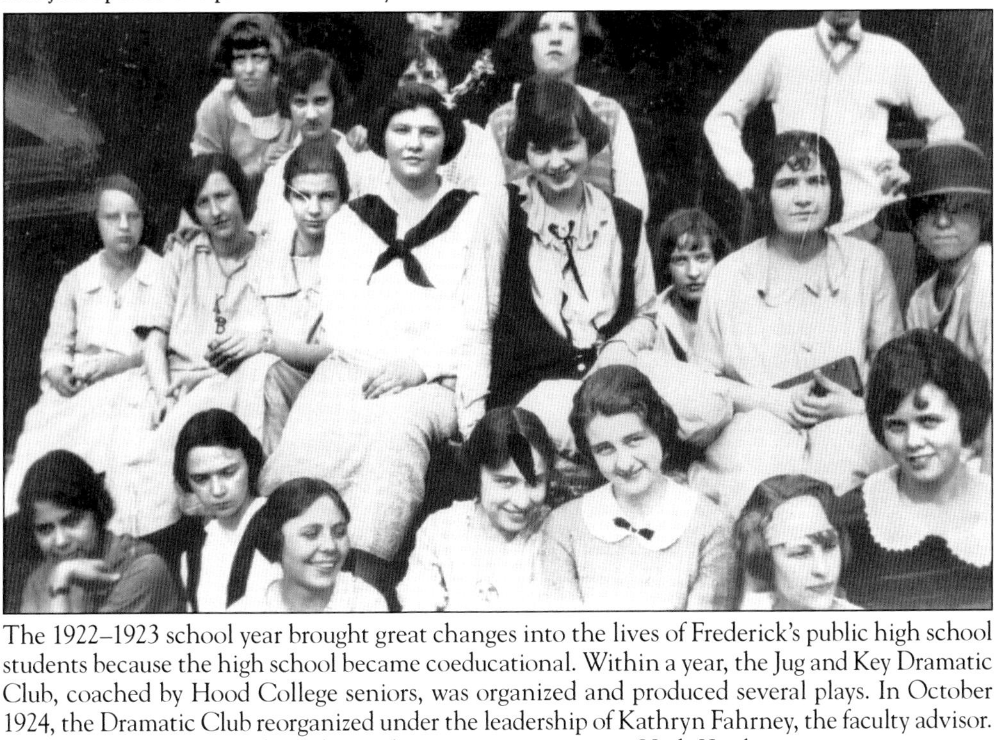

The 1922–1923 school year brought great changes into the lives of Frederick's public high school students because the high school became coeducational. Within a year, the Jug and Key Dramatic Club, coached by Hood College seniors, was organized and produced several plays. In October 1924, the Dramatic Club reorganized under the leadership of Kathryn Fahrney, the faculty advisor. In this c. 1925 photograph, club members enjoy an outing to High Knob.

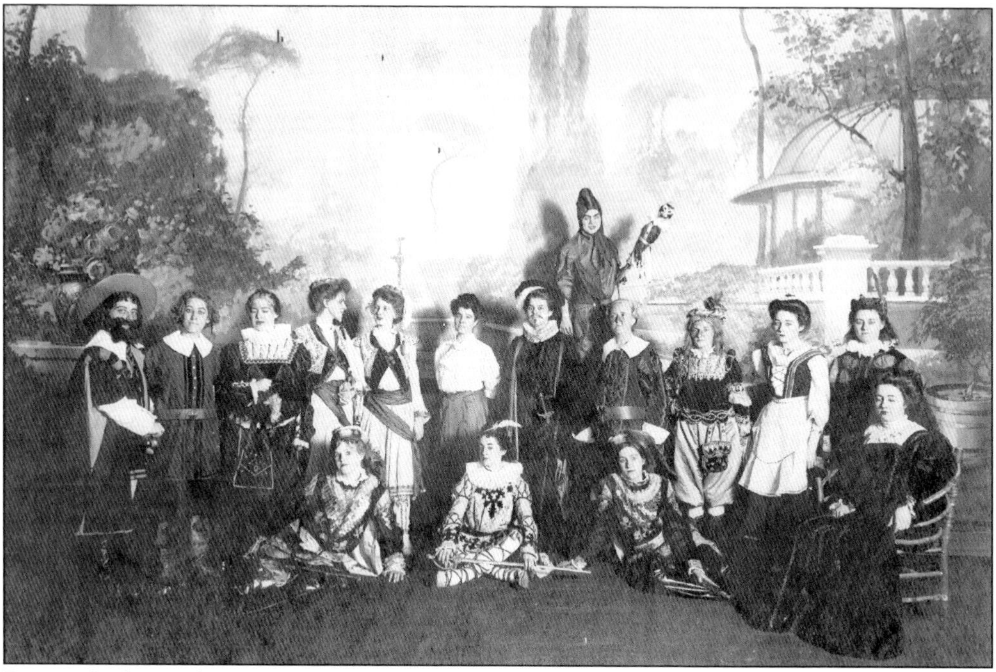

During the late 19th century, the students of Frederick Female Seminary produced annual spring programs of music, recitations, and drama. The alumnae also presented dramas, sometimes including local male talent in the show. This photograph includes the cast of one of these dramas, probably produced by the seminary students.

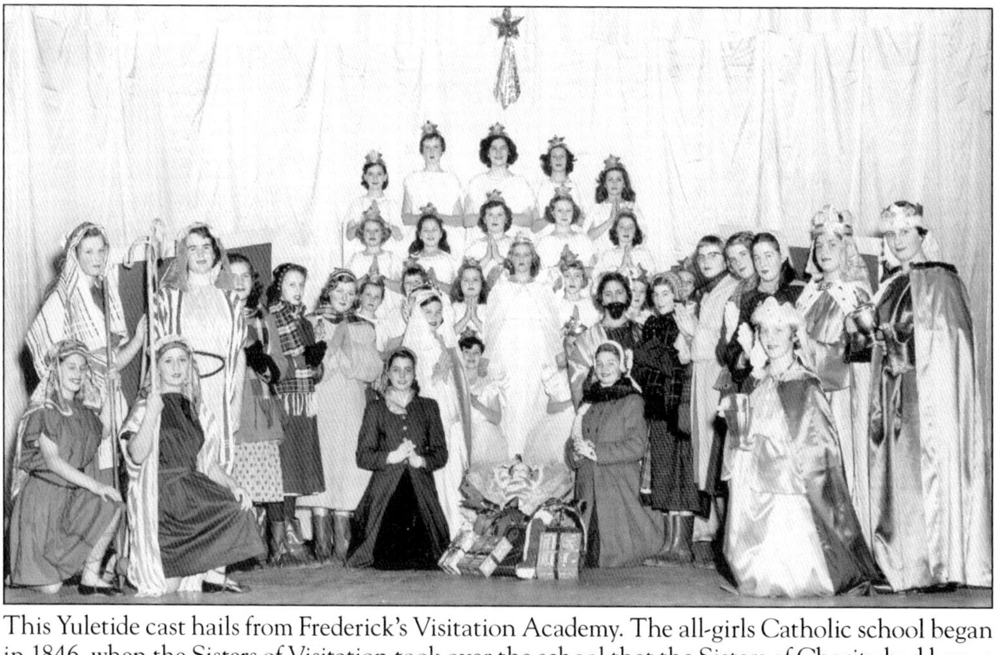

This Yuletide cast hails from Frederick's Visitation Academy. The all-girls Catholic school began in 1846, when the Sisters of Visitation took over the school that the Sisters of Charity had begun in 1824. In the past, many of the girls were boarders and came from many different states and even from other countries. Today it is a day school but continues many of the traditions begun in its early years.

Five

FROM FARM TO MARKET

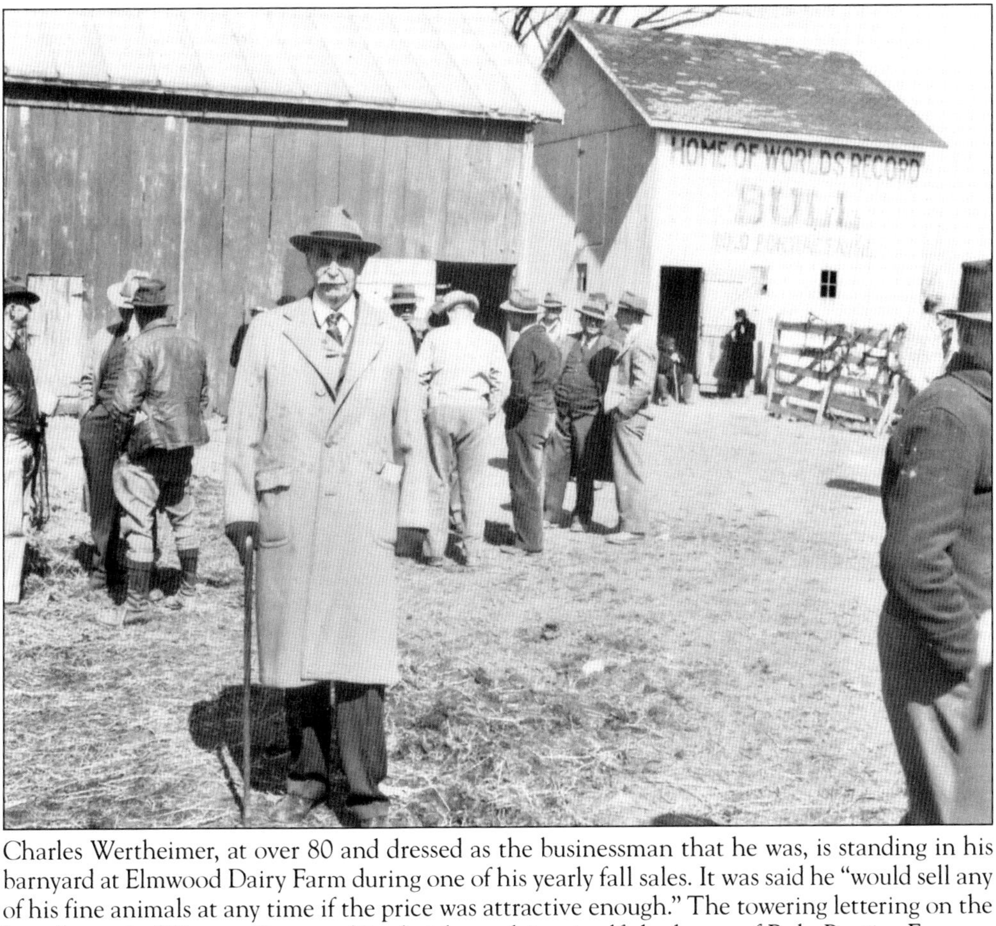

Charles Wertheimer, at over 80 and dressed as the businessman that he was, is standing in his barnyard at Elmwood Dairy Farm during one of his yearly fall sales. It was said he "would sell any of his fine animals at any time if the price was attractive enough." The towering lettering on the barn located off Route 40 west of Frederick proclaims itself the home of Rolo Pontiac Fayne, a bull Wertheimer bought in 1923 for $2,500, which sired a bevy of record-breaking dairy cows.

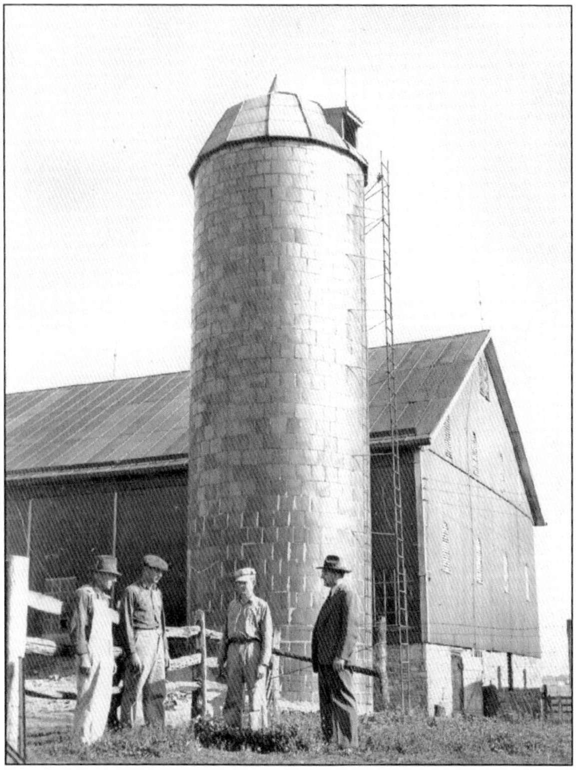

These men stand on the Thomas farm in Adamstown, where international cooperation was embraced in 1950. That year, Ashok Choksi, a U.S. graduate student and Indian citizen, spent months gaining practical knowledge of American agriculture working as a hired hand for manager William Fouche on the 185-acre dairy farm. He was particularly impressed by the county's 4-H program for youth, mechanization, and efficient farm practices.

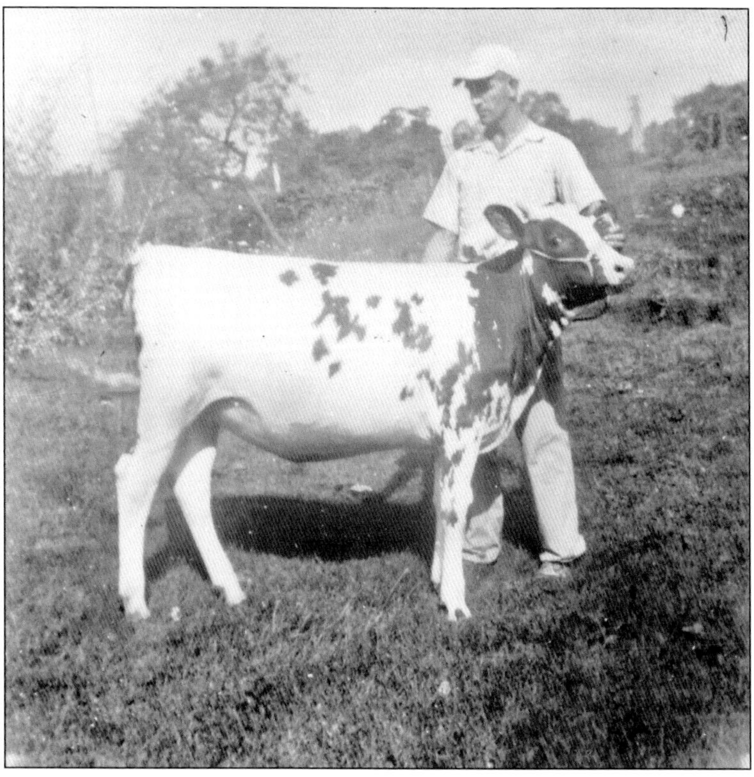

Webster G. MacCartee and his children raised champion cattle on his Frederick County farm. Numerous articles in the local newspapers mention his Ayrshires' fine showing at the Great Frederick Fair, 4-H, and Western Maryland Ayrshire Field Day competitions. This mid-20th-century photograph features his young cow, Minamae Helen, junior champion winner in a competition.

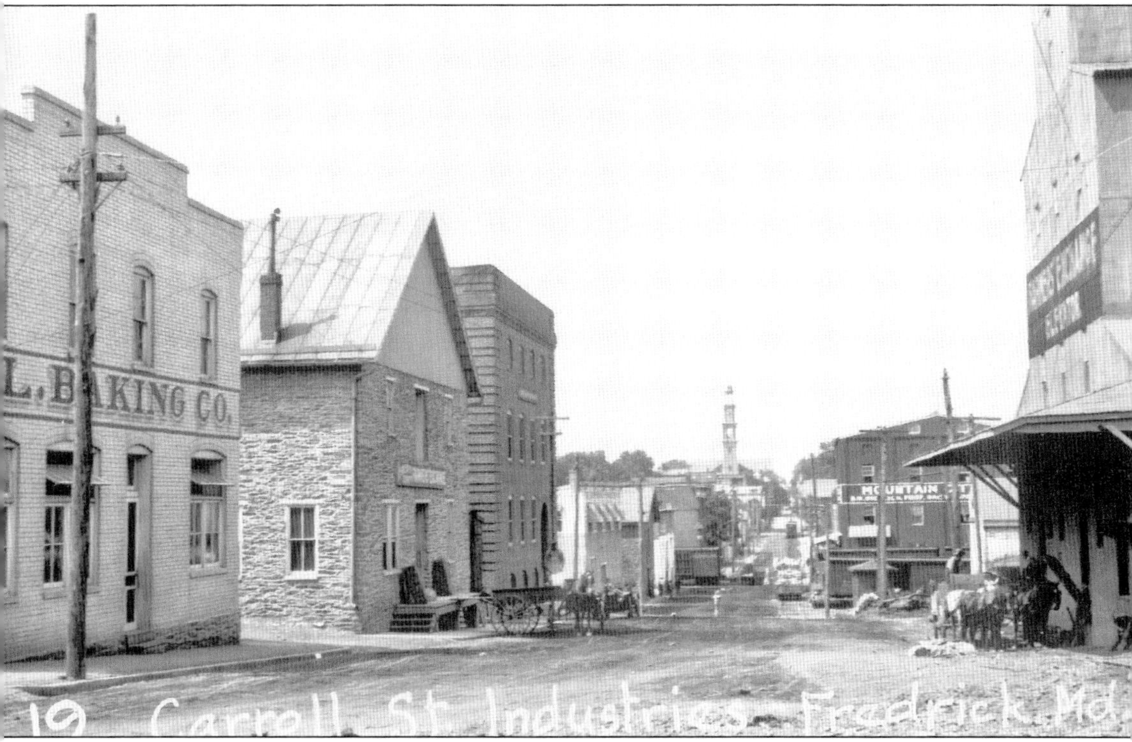

This early-20th-century photograph, looking north along Carroll Street in Frederick, captures some of the businesses associated with Frederick County's largest industry—agriculture. On the right is the Farmers' Exchange Elevator, and visible just beyond it is the Mountain City Mill building constructed in 1893 by James H. Gambrill. One of the mill's popular products was Challenge Flour. Across from the mill were various businesses to help farmers produce more: Ramsburg Fertilizer Company, Tyson's Phosphate, and A. J. Delashmutt Fertilizer, as well as Dietrich and Gambrill's Feedmill. James Gambrill, not satisfied to simply grind flour, started the G. L. Baking Company with Rush Lewis, which produced bread, crackers, and cookies for over eight decades.

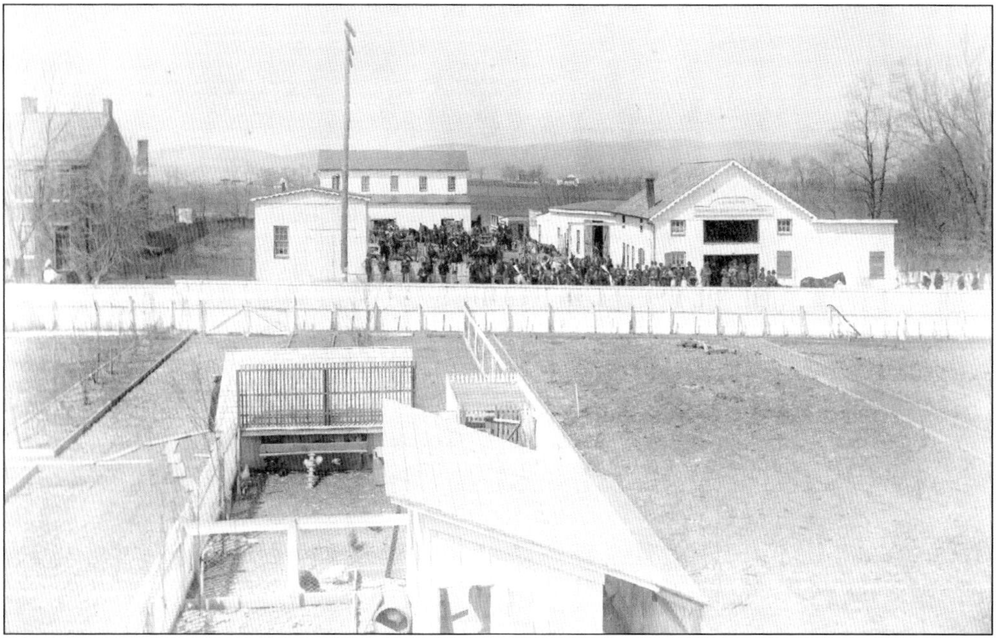

Local farmers gathered at W. R. Steiner's to purchase fertilizer and agricultural implements in this image from about 1890. Steiner's was located on the west side of North Market Street immediately north of Seventh Street in Frederick. The building toward the front right housed agricultural implements such as reapers and mowers; the building in the rear was a fertilizer factory.

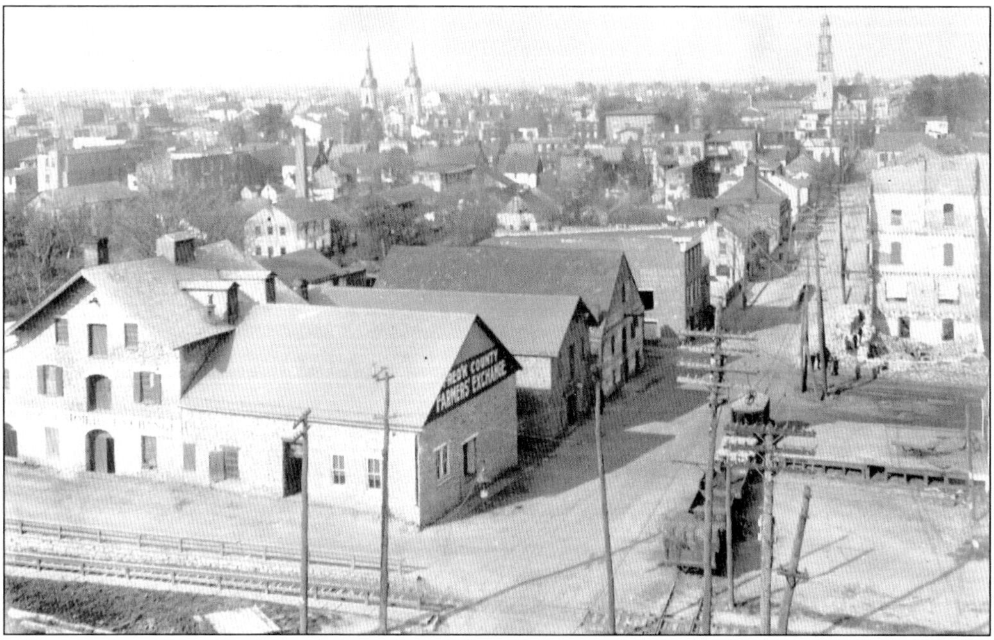

The spires of the Evangelical Lutheran Church and St. John's Roman Catholic Church can be seen along the skyline of this 1906 image by Charles Byerly. In the foreground is the Frederick County Farmers' Exchange, which supplied agricultural implements, hay, grain, flour, and seed to area farmers. Across the street are the ruins of the Mountain City Flour Mill, which had recently been destroyed by fire.

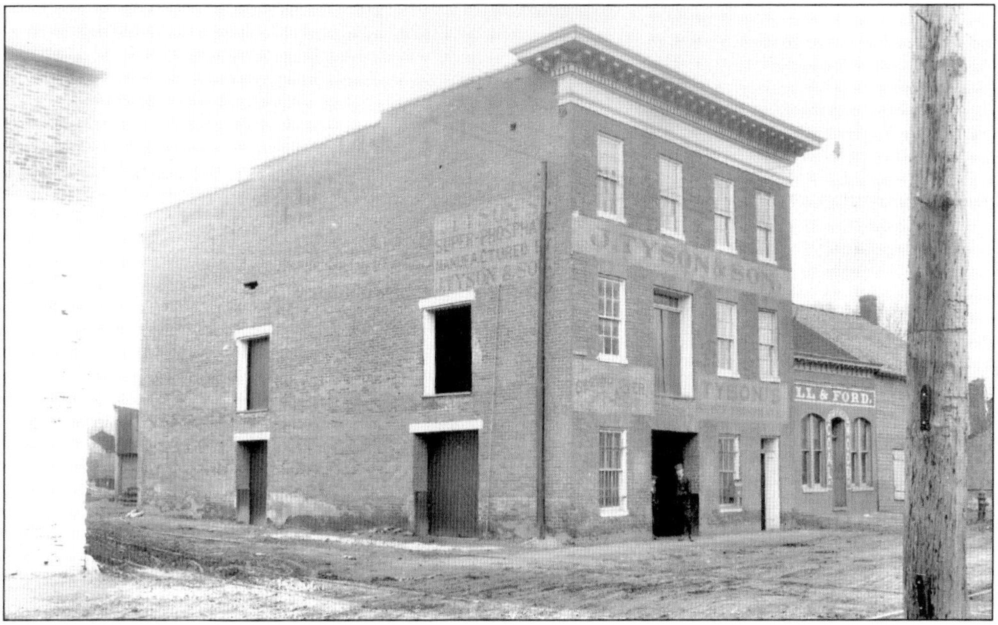

J. Tyson and Son was an agricultural fertilizer manufacturing firm in downtown Frederick, strategically located near the Freight Depot on South Carroll Street. Established about 1864 by Jonathan Tyson and his son, Jacob, who managed it for many years, the firm was one of the pioneer fertilizer manufacturers in Western Maryland. Jacob Tyson retired and sold the business to the Central Chemical Company of Hagerstown in 1920.

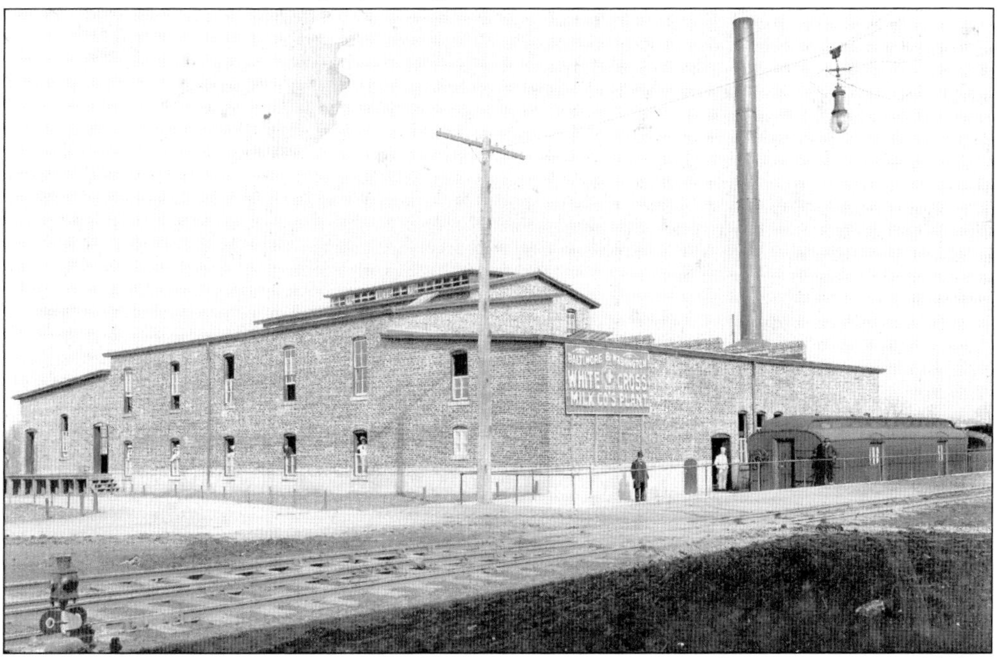

The Frederick branch of the Baltimore and Washington White Cross Milk Company was established in December 1909. The building had a creamery and a laboratory and produced 2,500 gallons of product daily that was taken to market by refrigerated train cars. In 1910, the company also advertised that it would deliver its pasteurized milk to anywhere in Frederick for 7¢ a quart.

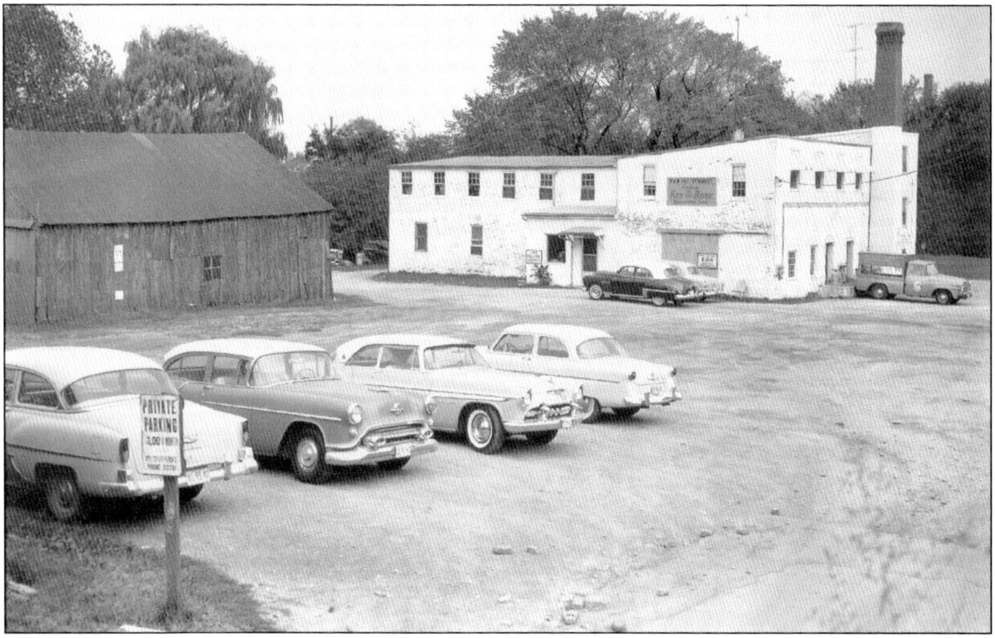

W and W Poultry moved from South Street to this location along Carroll Creek on East Patrick Street in Frederick in 1955. Owned by Alton T. Williar and F. S. Warner, it specialized in live and dressed poultry, eggs, and poultry feed. The building and the adjoining lot were on the site of the former Birely Tannery. In April 1960, an automobile was stolen from this lot and was involved in a fatal crash with a bus in Baltimore while being pursued by police.

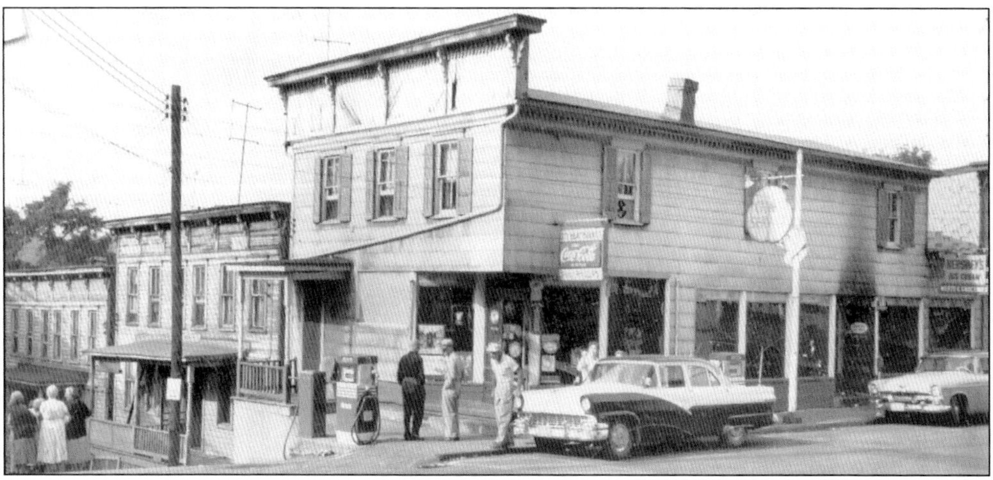

Pictured is the City Meat Market operated by Teddy Phillips. It was located in Brunswick in various locations along West Potomac Street but remained at 200 West Potomac from 1940 until September 1959, when the building, located at the corner of West Potomac Street and Virginia Avenues, burned down. In its place now stands the Brunswick Volunteer Ambulance Company.

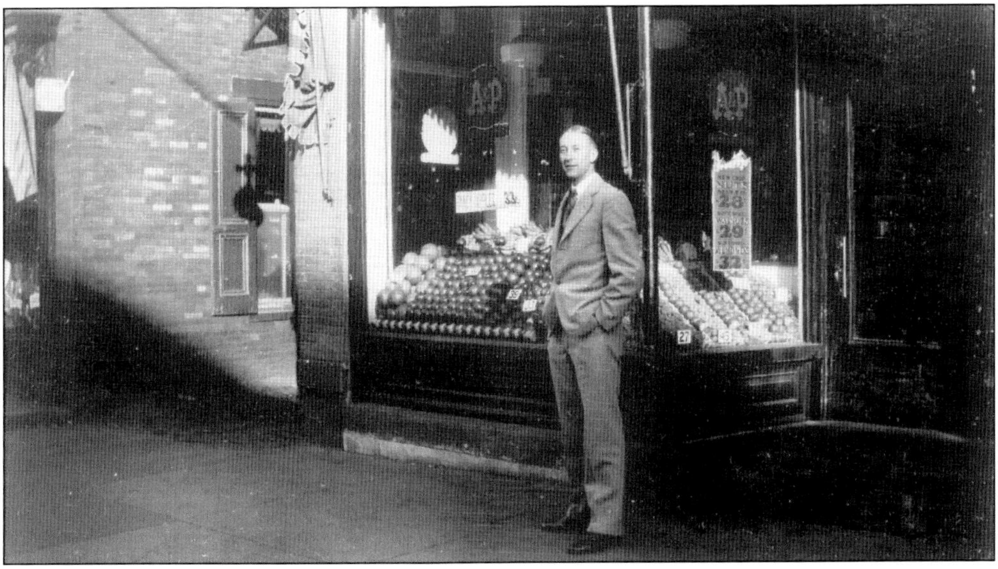

Before the advent of the supermarket, one could find a small grocery store on nearly every Frederick city block and one or more in every town of any size. They sold locally grown food and more exotic items. In 1935, the Frederick *City Directory* listed four Great A&P Tea Company stores—the precursor to today's Super-Fresh grocery chain—three on Market Street and one on Patrick Street.

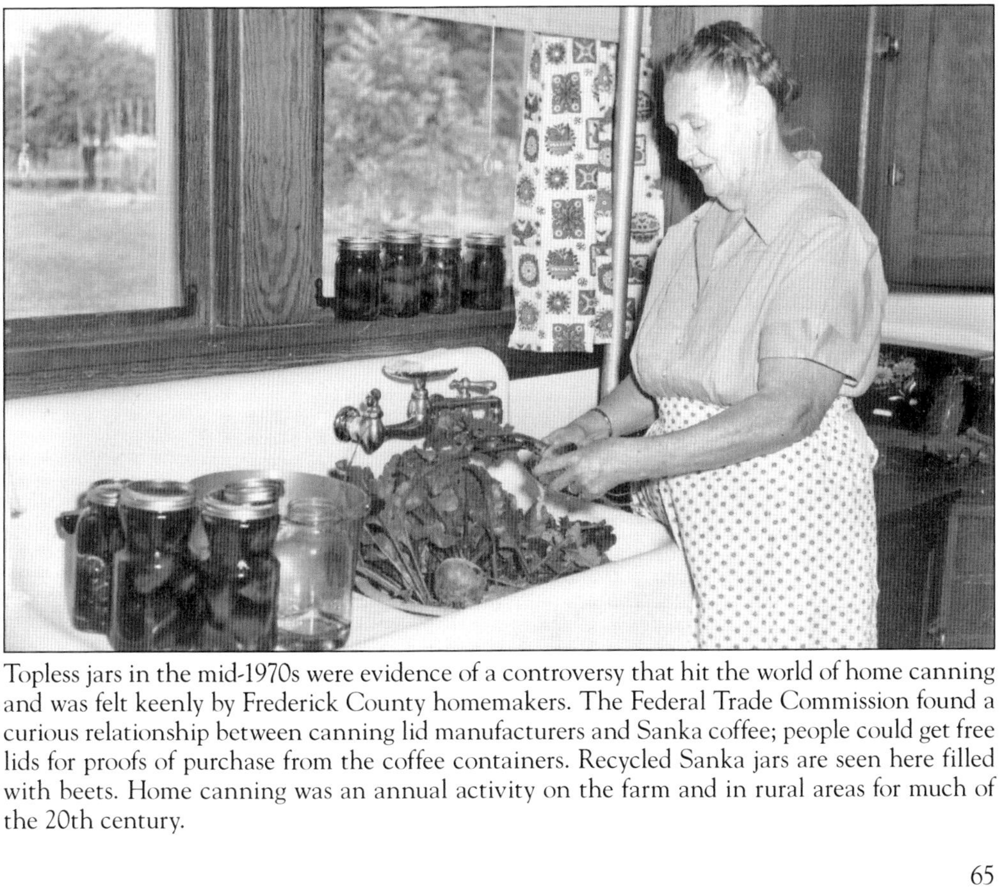

Topless jars in the mid-1970s were evidence of a controversy that hit the world of home canning and was felt keenly by Frederick County homemakers. The Federal Trade Commission found a curious relationship between canning lid manufacturers and Sanka coffee; people could get free lids for proofs of purchase from the coffee containers. Recycled Sanka jars are seen here filled with beets. Home canning was an annual activity on the farm and in rural areas for much of the 20th century.

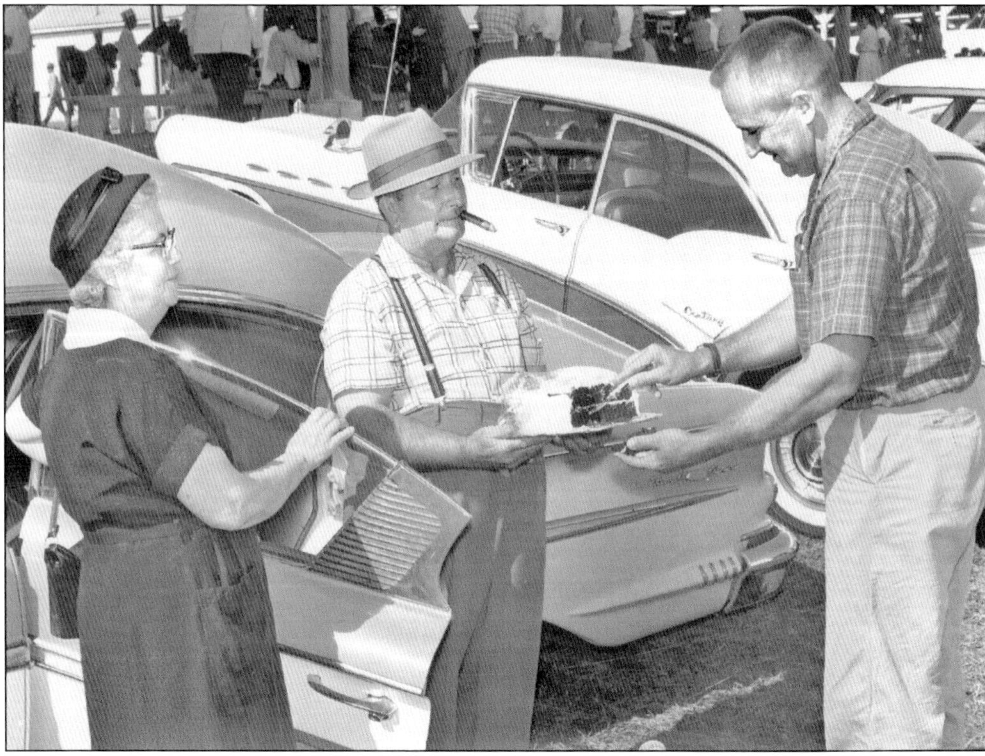

Mr. and Mrs. Roger Hildebrand of Woodsboro shared a piece of cake with Frank Long Jr. for photographer Frank Keefer at the Great Frederick Fair in September 1961. The prizewinning cake was bought by the Hildebrands at the Girls 4-H club auction. The agricultural society, the fair's organizer, was created in 1820 and has held a fair celebrating Frederick County's agriculture nearly every year since.

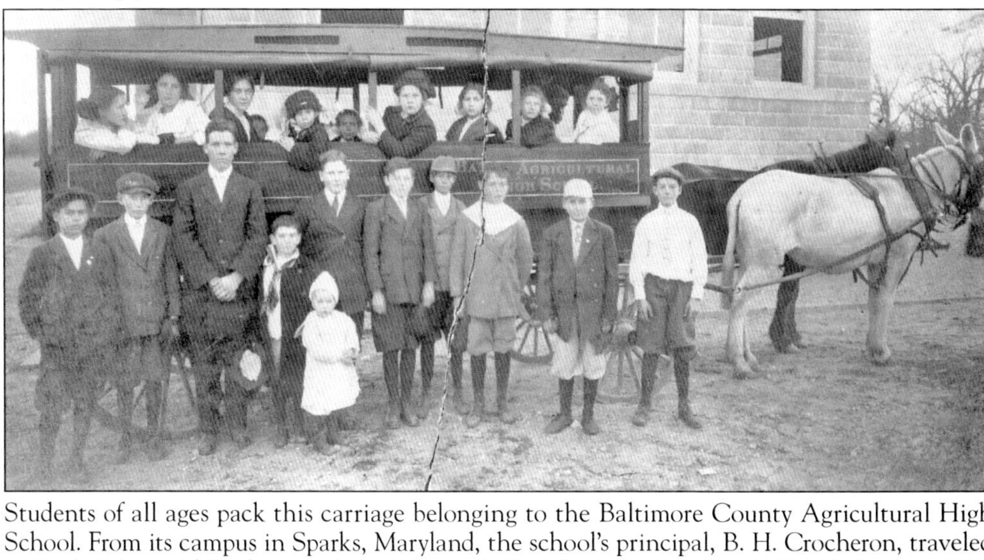

Students of all ages pack this carriage belonging to the Baltimore County Agricultural High School. From its campus in Sparks, Maryland, the school's principal, B. H. Crocheron, traveled to Frederick to aid in the creation of the agricultural program at Boys' High School in 1911. Four years later, the Frederick County Agricultural Society introduced Maryland's first student stock-judging contest.

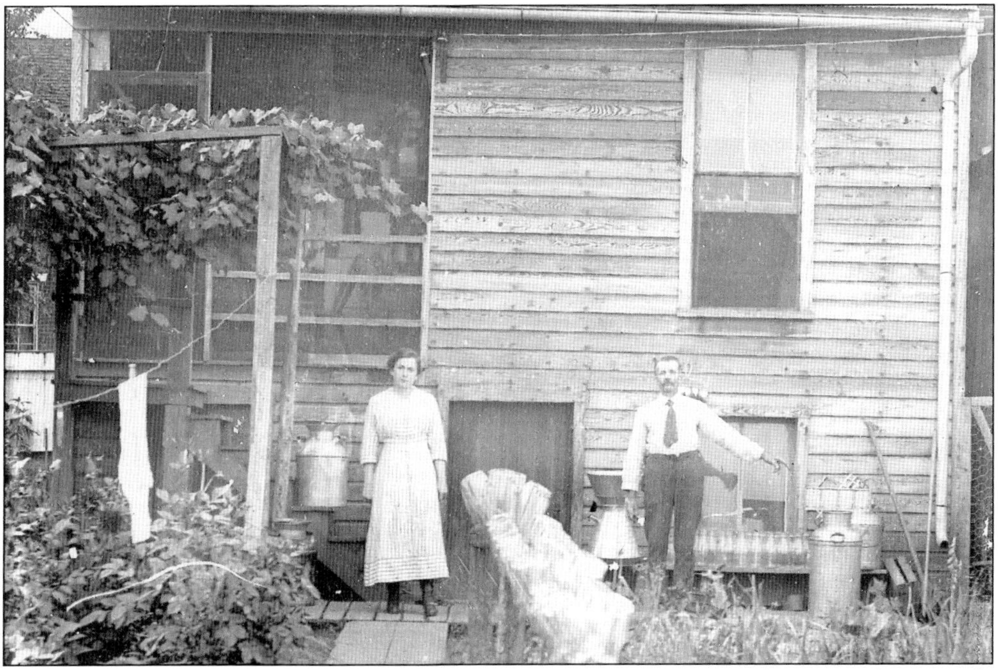

Agricultural pursuits were not restricted to large farms or big businesses. This Emmitsburg couple shows off some of the equipment and materials of their *c.* 1900 dairy operation. Returned quart bottles waiting to be filled again are drying in the foreground.

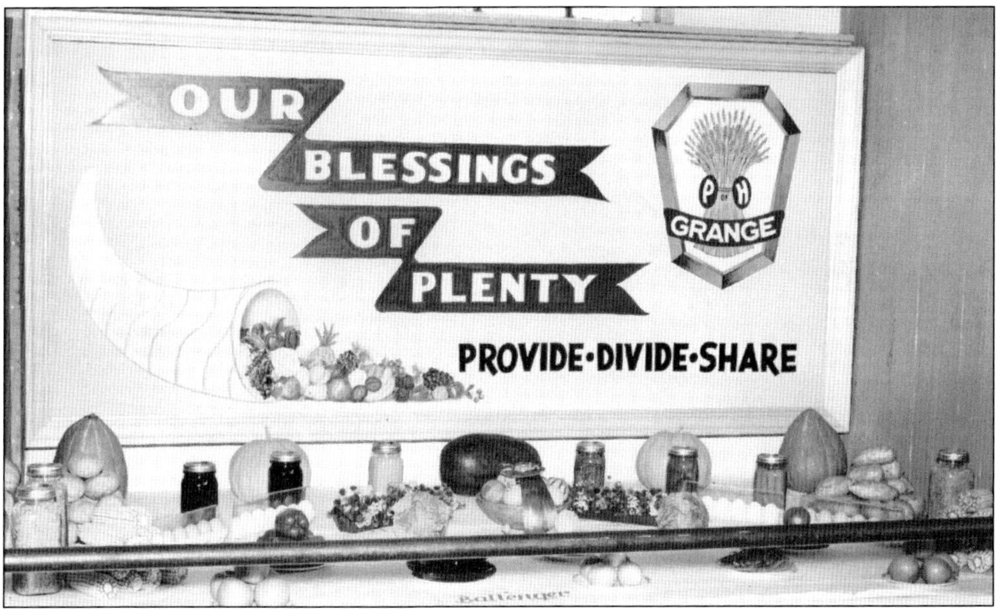

A number of organizations have actively supported the county's agricultural pursuits and heritage over the years. Local chapters of the Grange were established in many locales around the county, including Ballenger, Braddock, Carroll Manor, Creagerstown, Emmitsburg, Glade Valley, Jackson, Lewistown, Linganore, Middletown, Mount Pleasant, New Market, Thurmont, and Tuscarora. Jefferson Grange No. 167, founded in 1876, is among the oldest chapters in Maryland. The Frederick County Pomona Grange was formed in 1930.

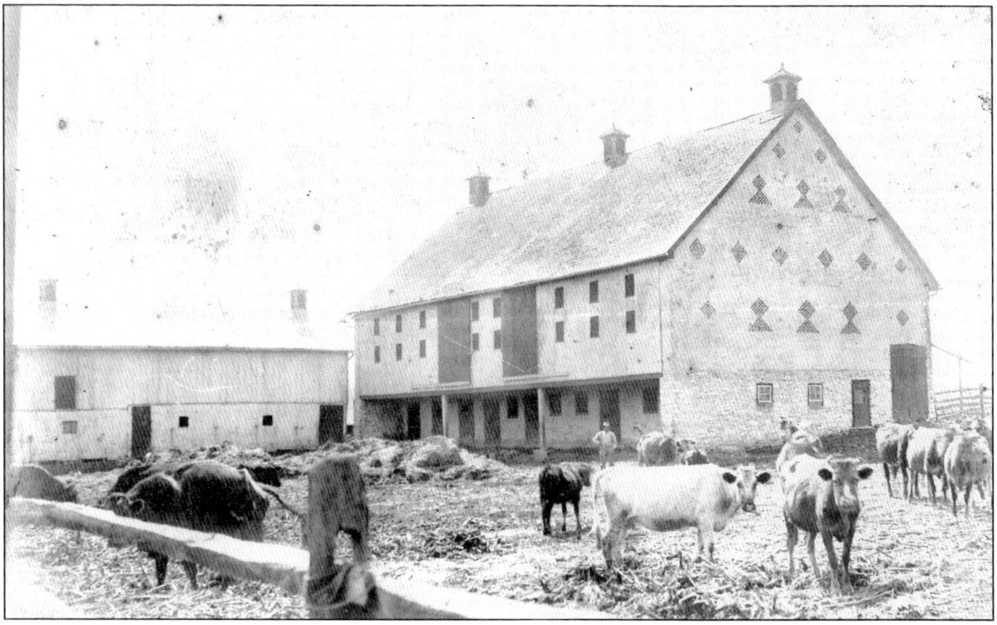

A few curious cows hardly reflect the historical drama that unfolded here. During the Civil War, Araby Farm south of Frederick was near the epicenter of the fighting during the Battle of Monocacy. By the time this photograph was taken in the early 20th century, the farm had returned to a more placid agrarian scene. In 2001, the farm was purchased to eventually become part of the Monocacy National Battlefield.

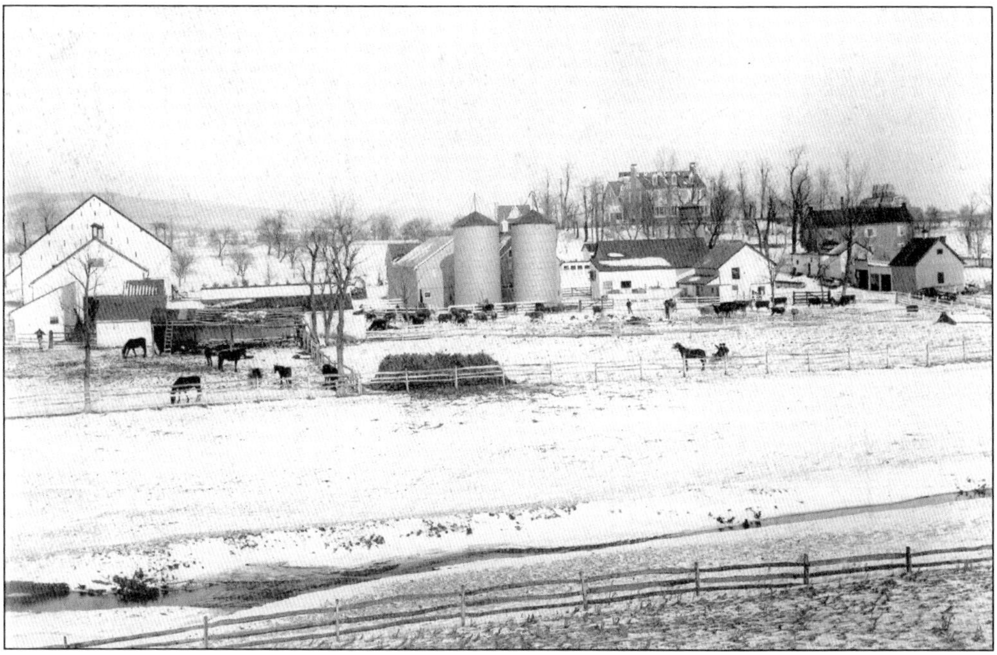

A winter view of the Baughman Farm, located along U.S. Route 40 west, does not foreshadow the explosive growth of the area. A 20-acre portion of the farm was requested to be rezoned in 1971, leading to the current "Golden Mile" shopping corridor. Many other farms also gave way to residential and commercial developments, contributing to Frederick's growth.

Six

Nine to Five

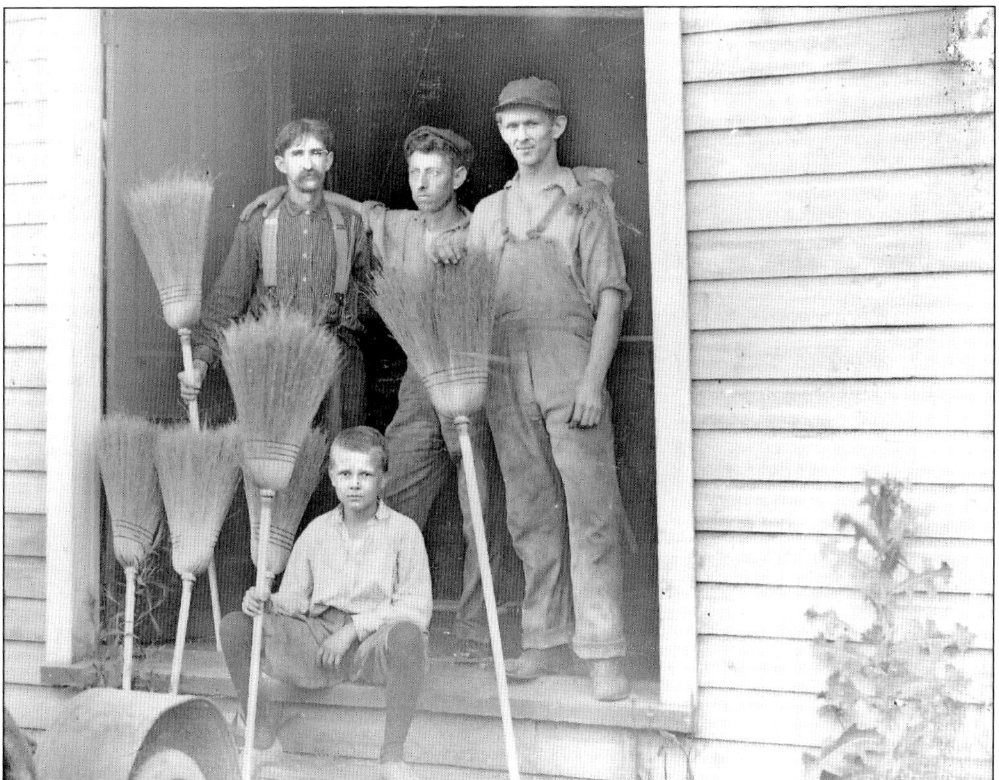

Pictured here are workers from the small Winegardner broom factory, west of Emmitsburg. Broomcorn was brought in by the carload from the west, and the brooms were made up for the local citizens or were sold in various stores in nearby communities.

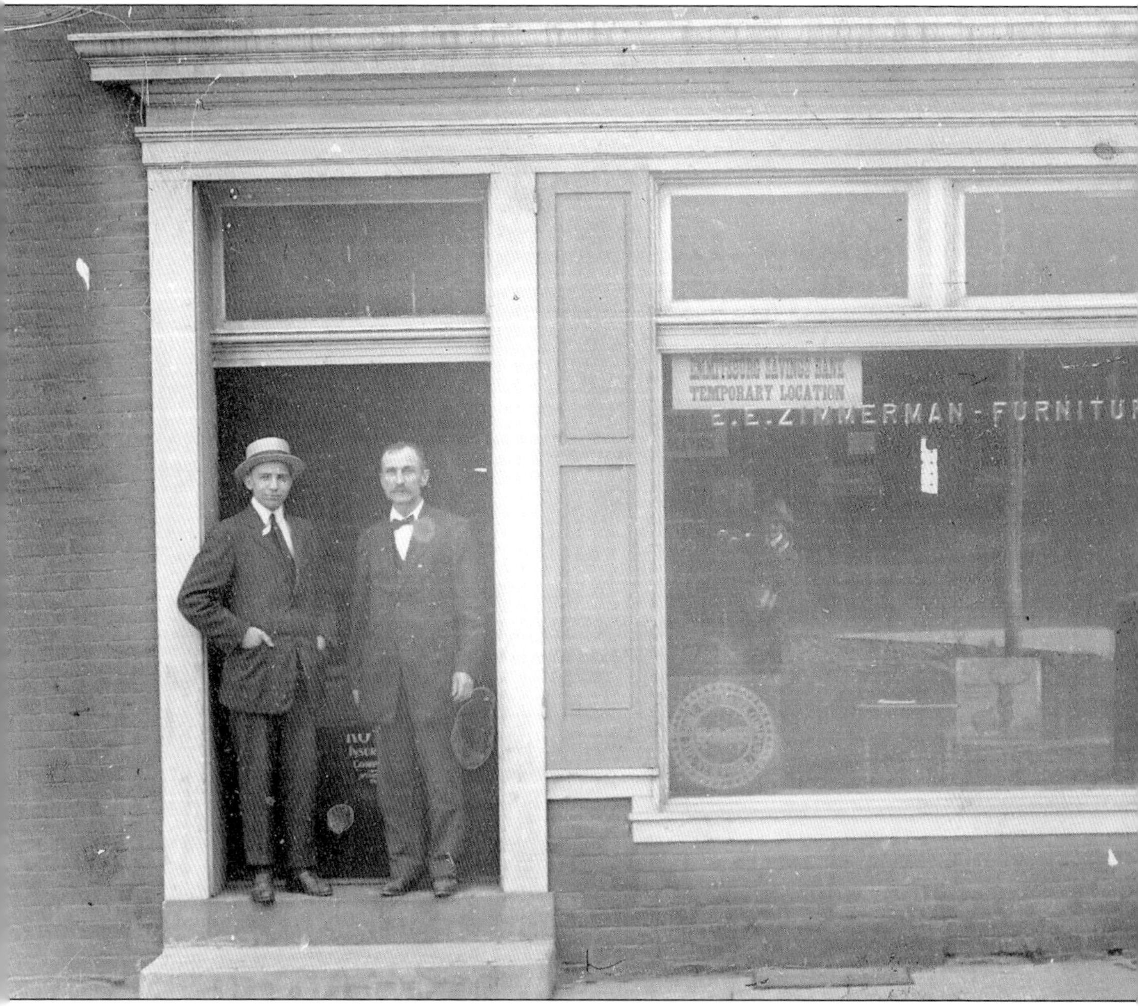

Eugene E. Zimmerman (1866–1927) was a cabinetmaker who owned a furniture business on Main Street in Emmitsburg in the early 1900s. By 1915, he was taking advantage of the tremendous business opportunity brought on by the advent of the automobile and also owned the Emmitsburg Motor Company. At one point, Zimmerman's furniture shop also served as the location of the Emmitsburg Savings Bank, as is evidenced by the sign in the window. Interestingly, a close look at the large window in this photograph also reveals the reflection of the photographer standing with his camera on tripod.

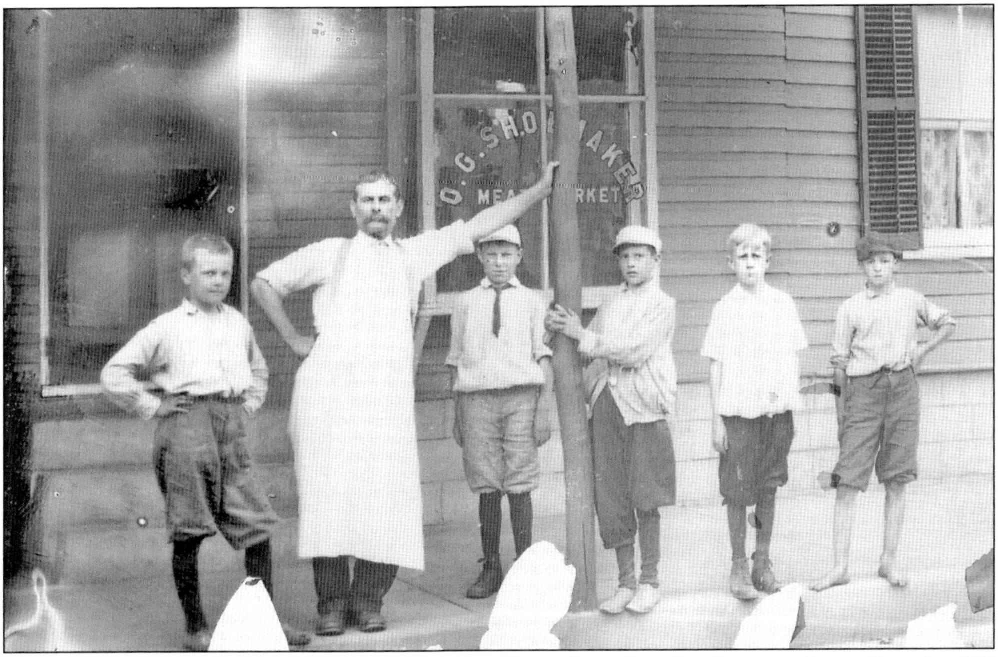

In the early 1900s, Quinsy G. Shoemaker ran a flourishing butcher business located in the 100 block of Main Street in Emmitsburg. He peddled his wares in the Thurmont area as well, treating the boys who followed his truck to raw hot dogs.

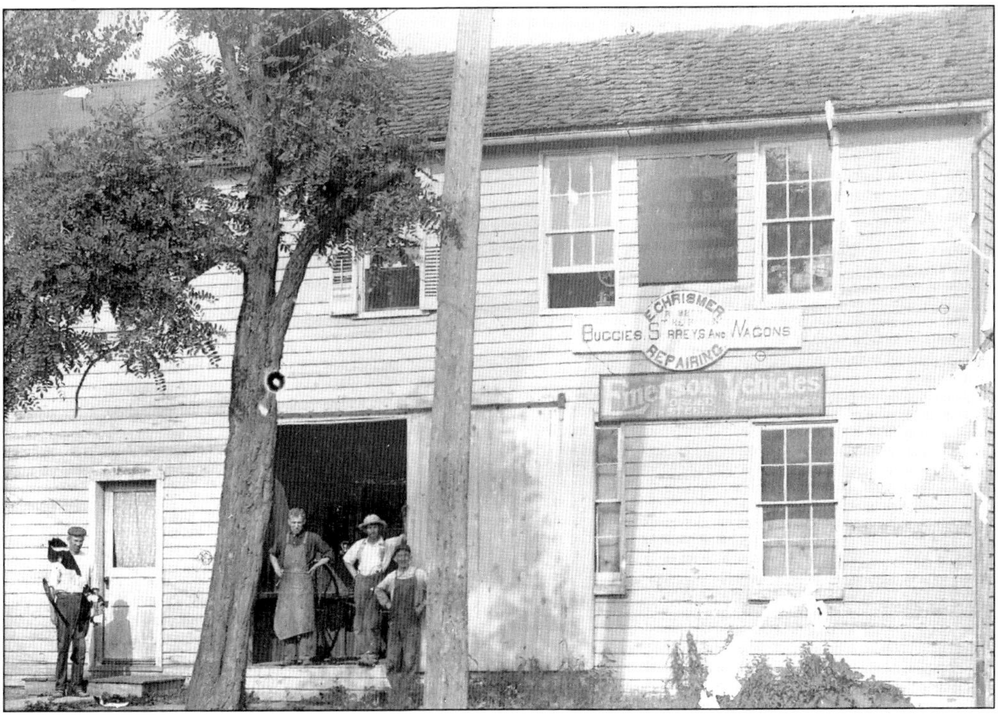

Beginning in the 1840s, Emmitsburg supported a carriage maker. E. Chrismer was one of many through the years who operated a carriage-making and repair business. He advertised for Emerson vehicles on the front of his shop in the early 1900s.

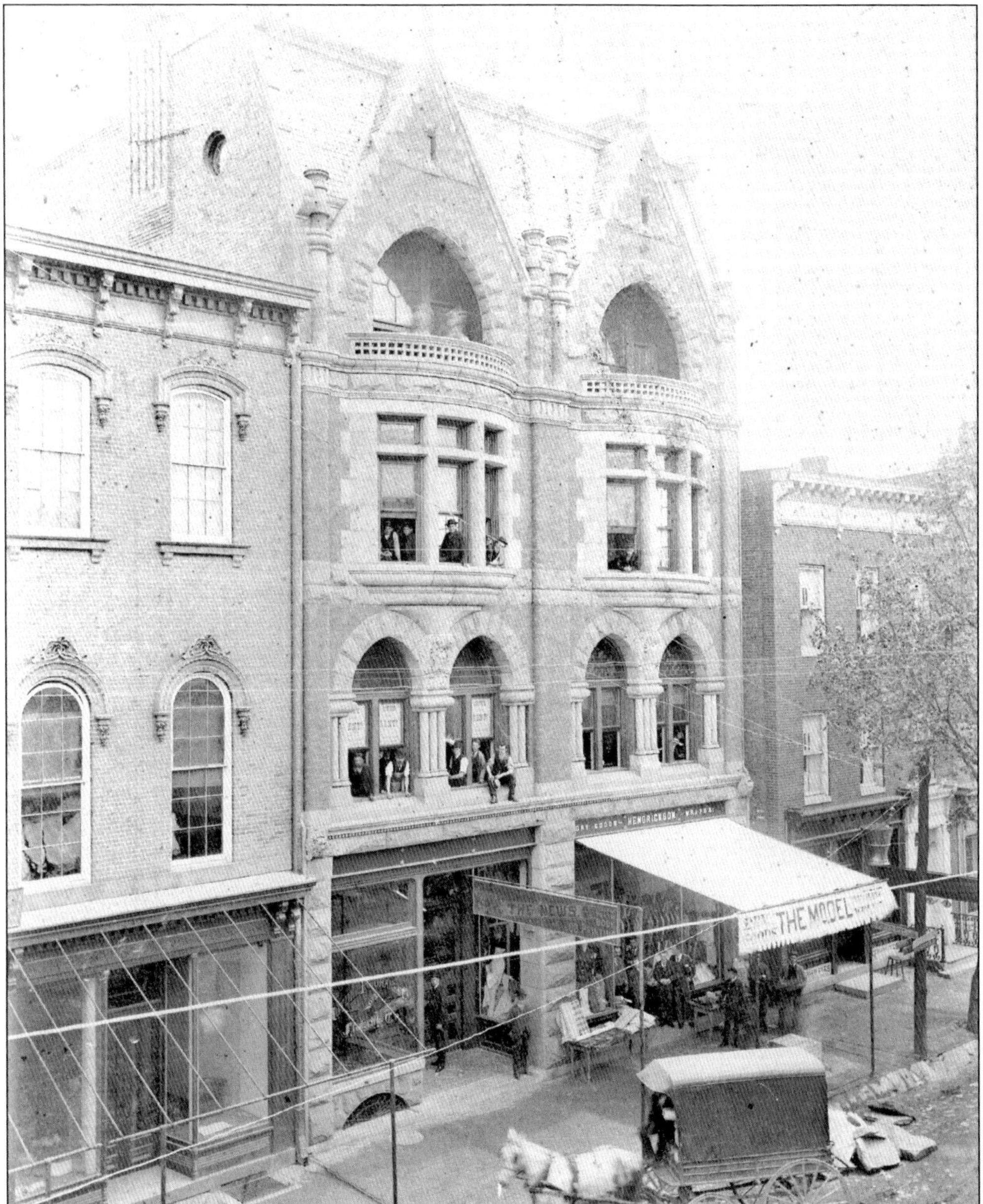

John D. Hendrickson established a dry goods store in Frederick in 1877, moving to this building on North Market Street in 1888. Initially called the Model Dry Goods House, the store's name was changed simply to Hendrickson's in the early 20th century. The store was known for its fine fashions and excellent service. In April 1912, Hendrickson advertised that an "expert corsetiere at your service for fittings" would be at his establishment for one week only. The *News* and the Frederick Mutual Fire Insurance Company occupied portions of the building in the early years, but by 1925, the store had taken over the entire building and an elevator had been installed. By 1954, customers could shop in air-conditioned comfort. The building was restored to its 1888 appearance amid much acclaim in 1977. The oldest family-owned store in downtown Frederick closed in 1980.

Pictured on the right in this *c.* 1890 photograph is John H. Markey's shoe store on North Market Street in Frederick. Markey purchased the store in 1863 from George Tyler after the death of Tyler's partner, Henry Steiner. The facade seen here was the result of improvements made in 1881. After Markey's death in 1899, the family carried on the business into the 1920s.

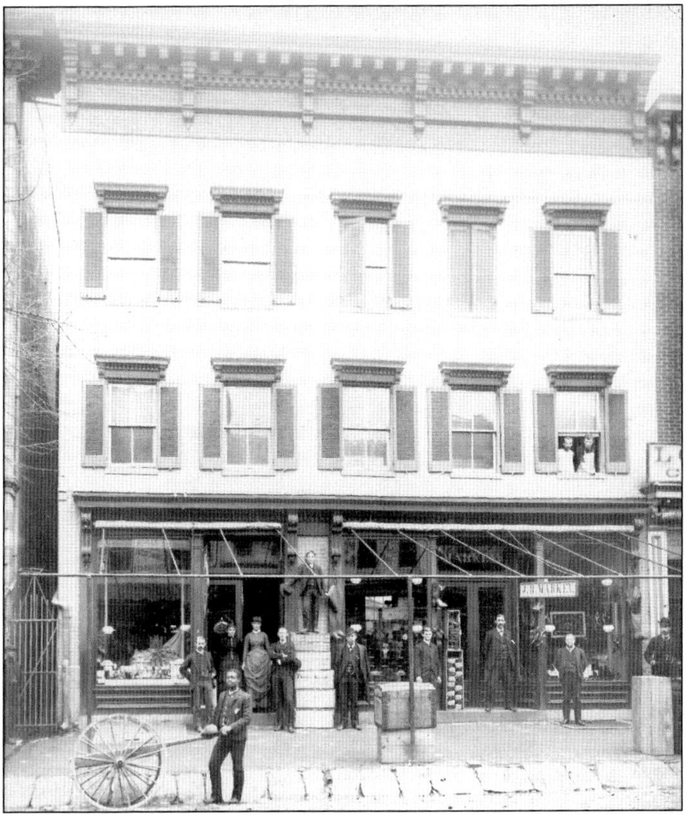

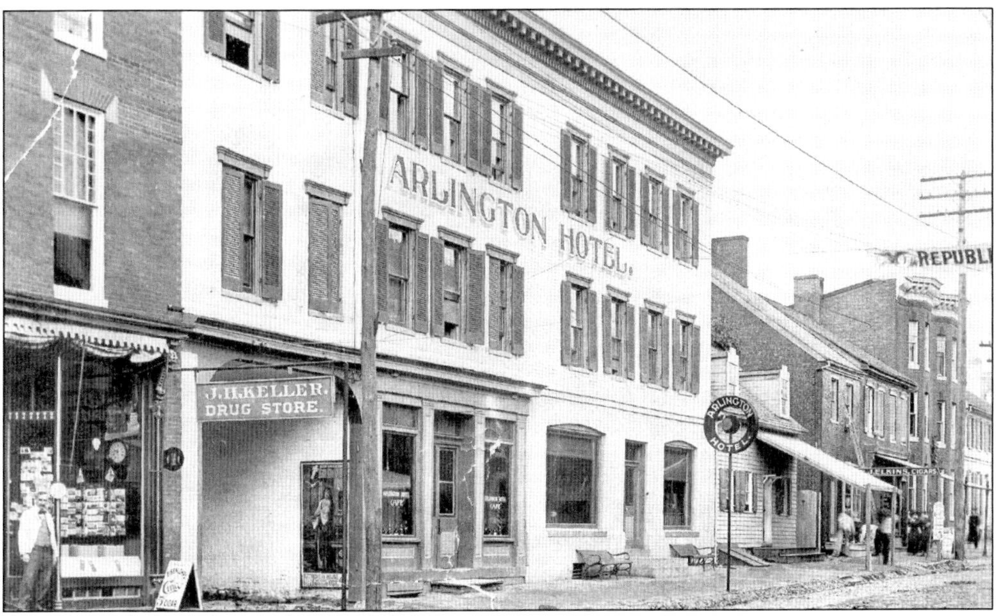

The J. H. Keller Drugstore on North Market Street was established *c.* 1906 by the druggist J. Heisley Keller, who is captured here standing outside his shop waiting for customers. The Arlington Hotel, established about 1909, was adjacent to the drugstore. The Arlington was among the several large, downtown Frederick hotels that accommodated tourists and other visitors.

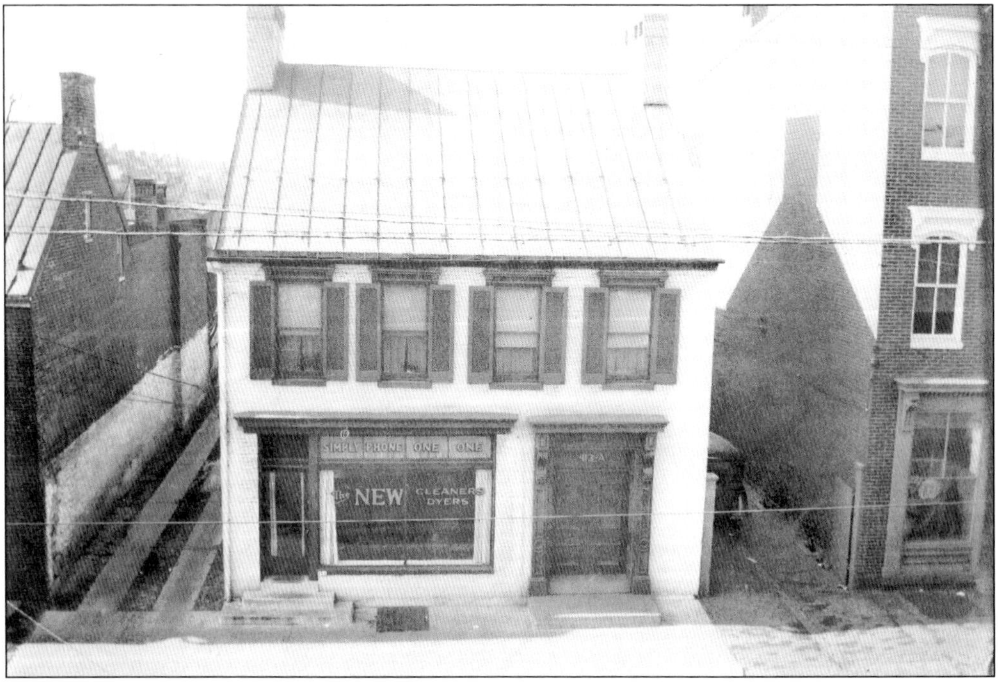

The New North End Cleaners, shown here, was located at 413 North Market Street in Frederick. Marcus W. Simmons started the business in the late 1920s. When his business outgrew the building, he built a dry-cleaning plant at the corner of Military Road and Seventh Street in 1945. Later Marcus Simmons opened another cleaning business at 111 West Patrick Street called Marcus Cleaning.

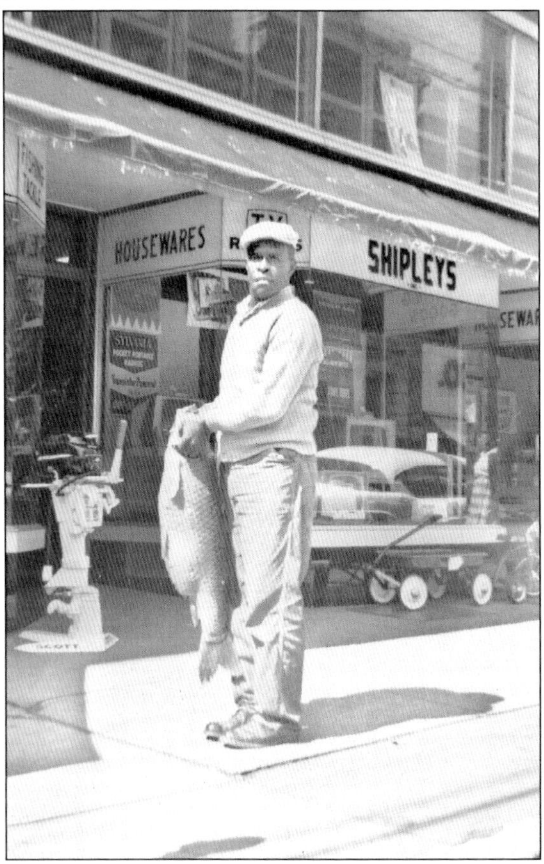

Evidently, the big one did not get away. This proud angler stands in front of Shipley's sporting goods store on Market Street in Frederick in 1959. Shipley's began in 1897 as Shipley and Bopst general merchandise store. In 1915, in a new location, it was Shipley's Temple of Fancy. Over the years, Shipley's moved several times and specialized in office supplies, then housewares, then athletic equipment, and, finally, home electronics.

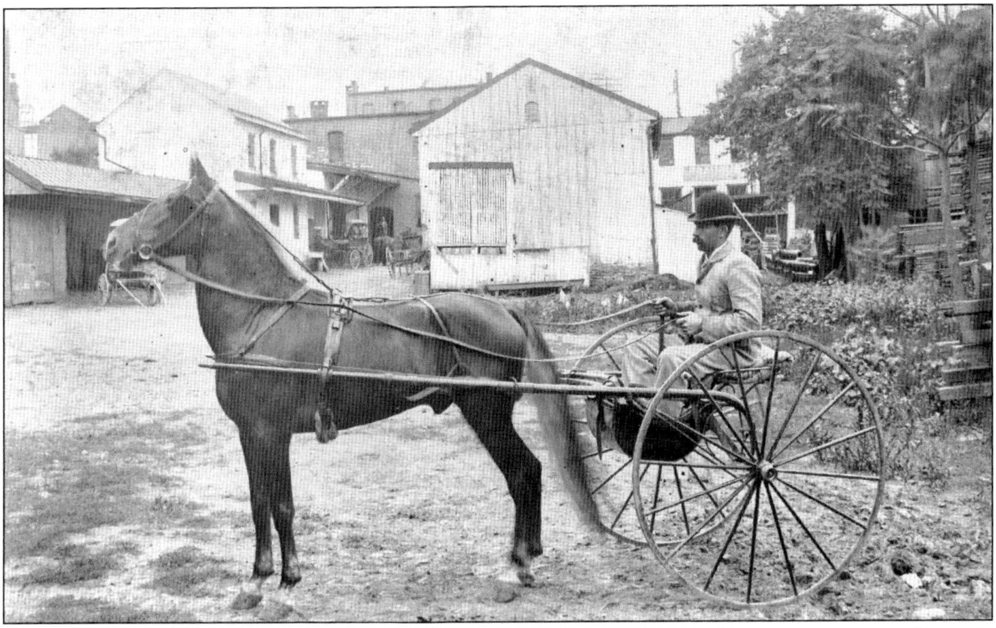

Pictured is Dr. Robert V. Smith, a Frederick veterinarian, about 1892. He is sitting upon a Brengle gig. After Samuel Brengle's stable was destroyed by an arson fire in 1874, he became a local carriage dealer and sold rigs like this one. Gigs—light, two-wheeled, one-horse carriages—likely got their name from the spinning action of their wheels.

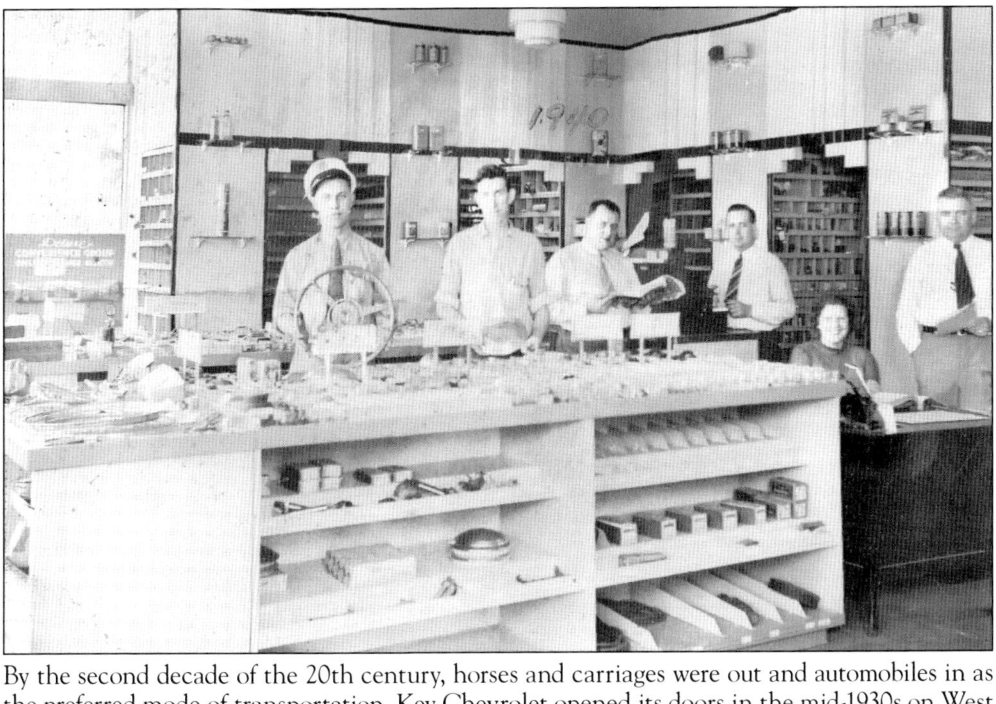

By the second decade of the 20th century, horses and carriages were out and automobiles in as the preferred mode of transportation. Key Chevrolet opened its doors in the mid-1930s on West Patrick Street in Frederick. The company moved to Baughman's Lane in the 1970s, the current site of Fitzgerald's Auto Mall. This 1940 image shows the company's employees, including Darrell Phebus and Deets Warfield.

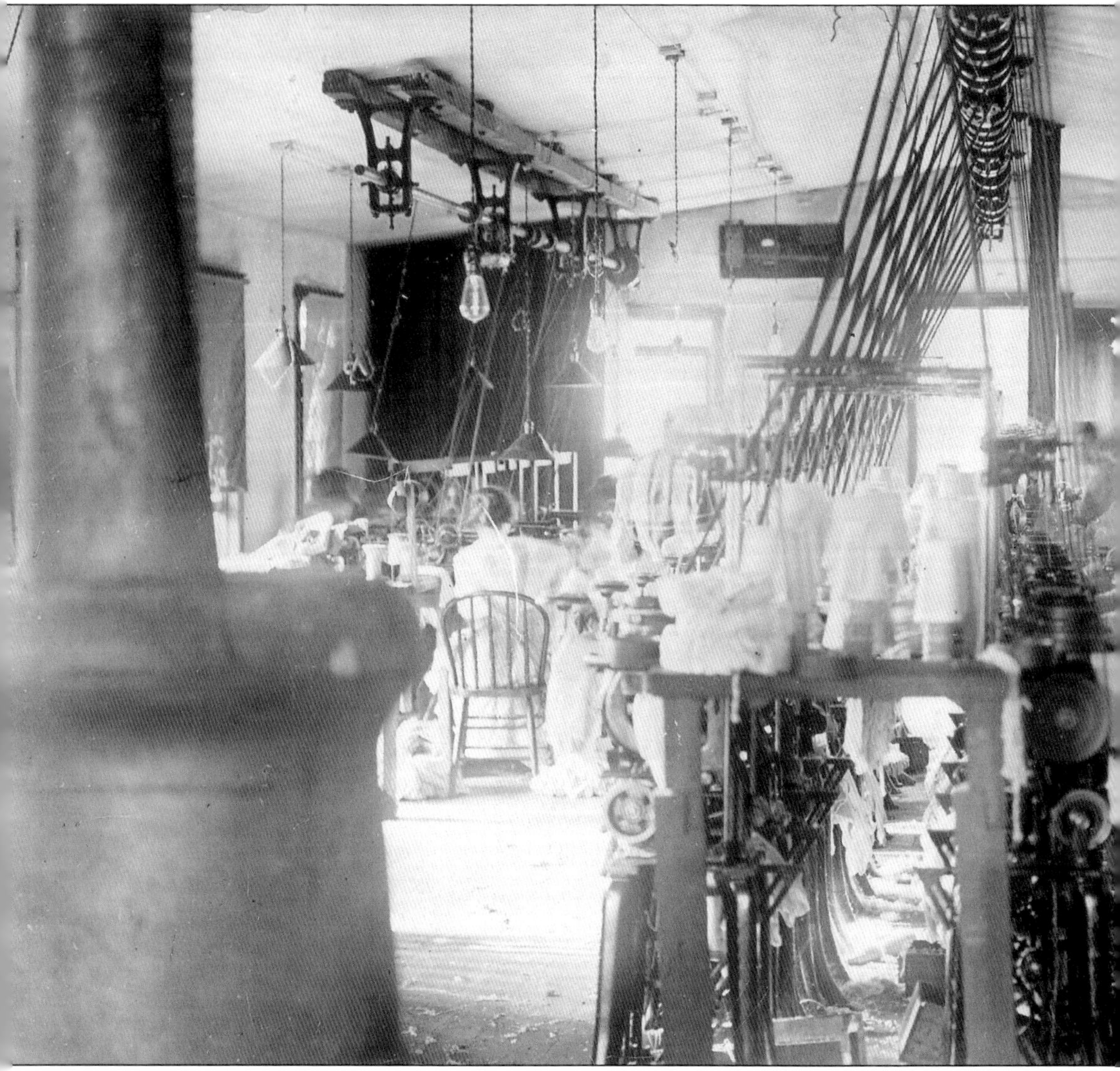

This interior view of a factory is a rare image enabling one to get a glimpse of working conditions nearly 100 years ago. It documents the Emmitsburg branch of the Union Manufacturing Company, a Frederick-based business that produced hosiery. The company purchased a former shirt factory located on Green Street in Emmitsburg and installed 30 knitting machines in 1912. The branch was not the first of its kind; Union Manufacturing had already established a workshop in Thurmont that housed 60 machines. When asked why they were setting up small knitting mills in other parts of the county instead of expanding their large facility on East Patrick Street, superintendent John L. Johnson replied that the shortage of "girls" in Frederick led them to take the work to the women living in other parts of the county.

This machine is attributed to the Ox Fibre Brush Company of Frederick. At one time, "OXCO," was a large employer, first appearing in 1887 as the Palmetto Fibre Company. The company originally made brushes by hand. Later McClintock Young created a machine that could manufacture the brushes more efficiently. In 1912, the company foiled a plot to place a spy among its workers and steal plans for its patented machines. The company left the area in the late 1960s.

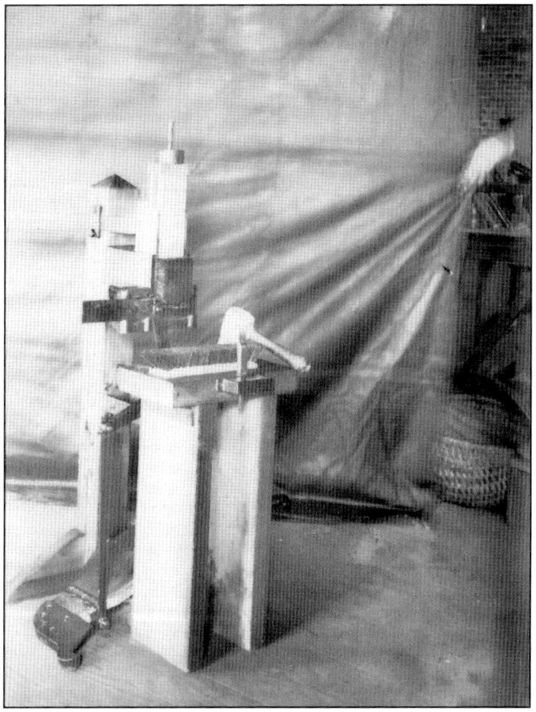

In 1920, the Lebherz brothers—William, Robert, and Harry—did not have an inkling that their hardware and home wares company would be turning out war manufactures in the space of 20 years' time. At the onset of World War II, the Everedy Company retooled to turn out navy floats and army grenade parts at a record pace, earning the Army-Navy "E" award in 1943. The Everedy Company closed its doors locally in 1977.

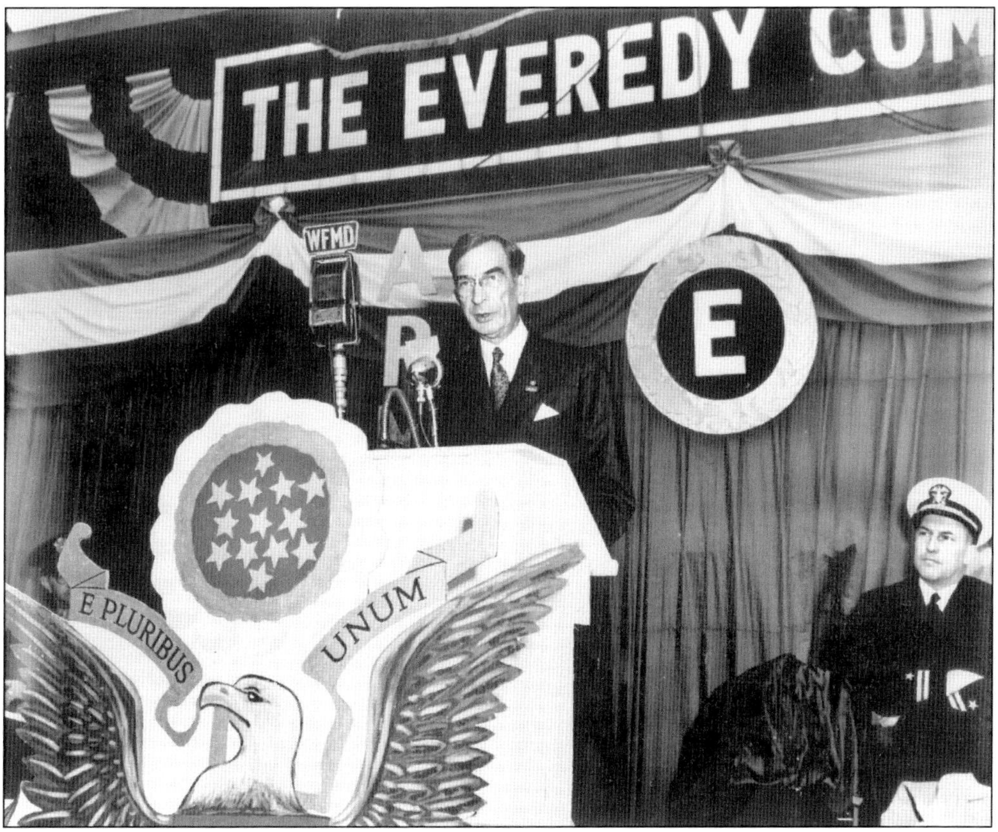

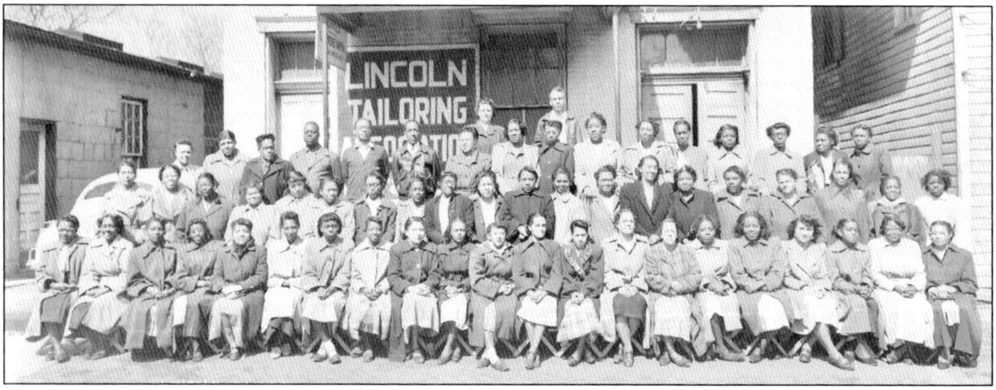

The Lincoln Tailoring Association was located at 111–113 West All Saints Street in Frederick, in the Pythian Castle building. The Colored Knights of Pythias, a fraternal organization, had at one time utilized the building. In 1945, Lincoln Tailoring advertised its "Opportunity for Colored Women." It promised a 40-hour, five-day workweek and a "clean, warm factory" in which to work. The company manufactured men's clothing from about 1944 to 1954.

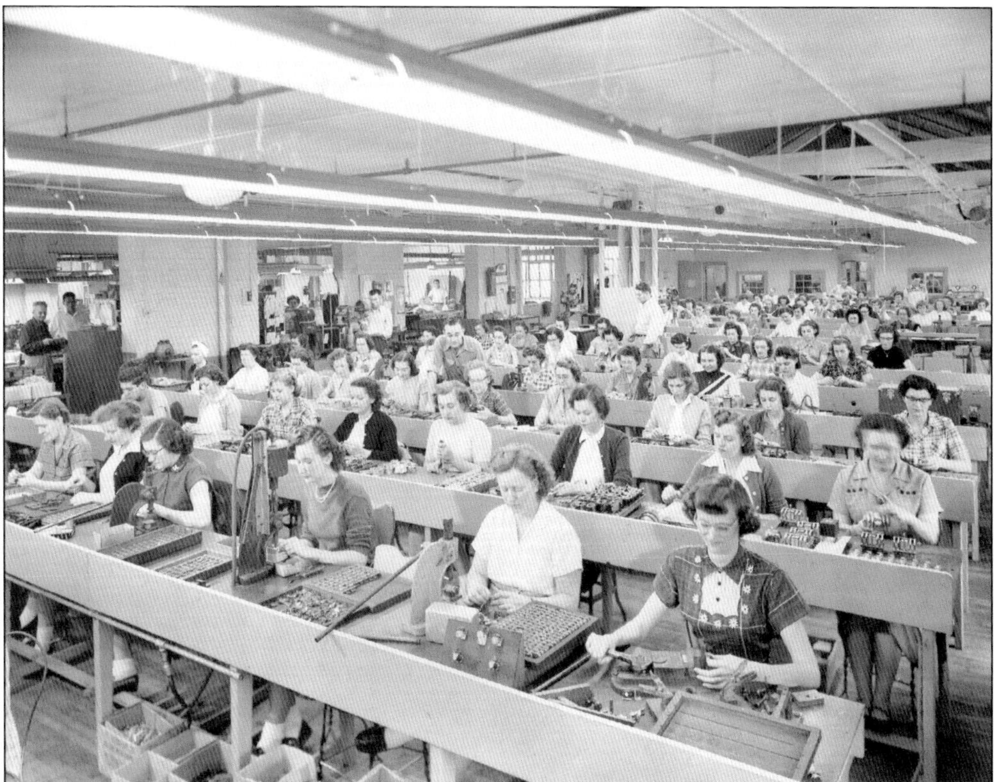

These workers are assembling electronics at Price Brothers Electric in Frederick about 1950. The company was started in 1914 by Joseph B. Price Sr. and Osborne Price. The company had prime contracts with the military and was awarded the Army-Navy "E" award in 1944. The company maintained several plants throughout the county but consolidated its operations to Frederick in 1955. Its trademark was Wolf, a Siberian husky owned by Osborne Price.

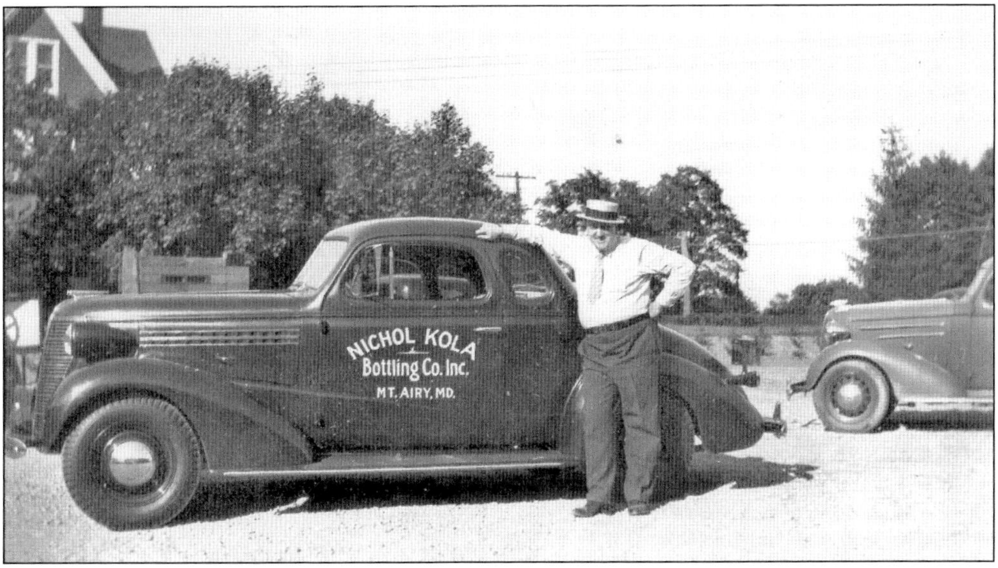

Nichol Kola was a popular beverage developed in the 1930s by Henry R. Nicholson in Baltimore. Though it was originally bottled by Canada Dry, a new bottling plant was built in Mount Airy in 1938. However, "America's Taste Sensation," as it billed itself, couldn't find its market. Today the H. R. Nicholson Company primarily packages and distributes fruit juices.

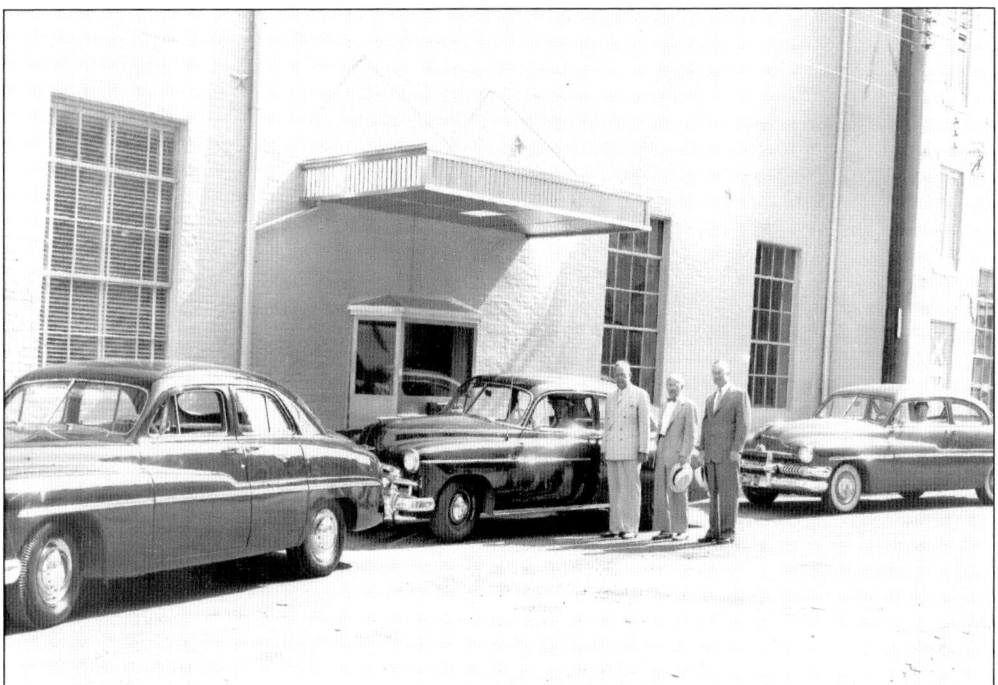

In August 1952, Farmers and Mechanics National Bank proudly announced the opening of its new drive-in banking window at their Frederick North Market Street location. The advertisement touted quick, convenient banking with no parking problem and no walking. Over the next several decades, the bank drive-through window would go from novelty to ubiquity throughout the county. F and M Bank president Robert E. Delaplaine is pictured on the left.

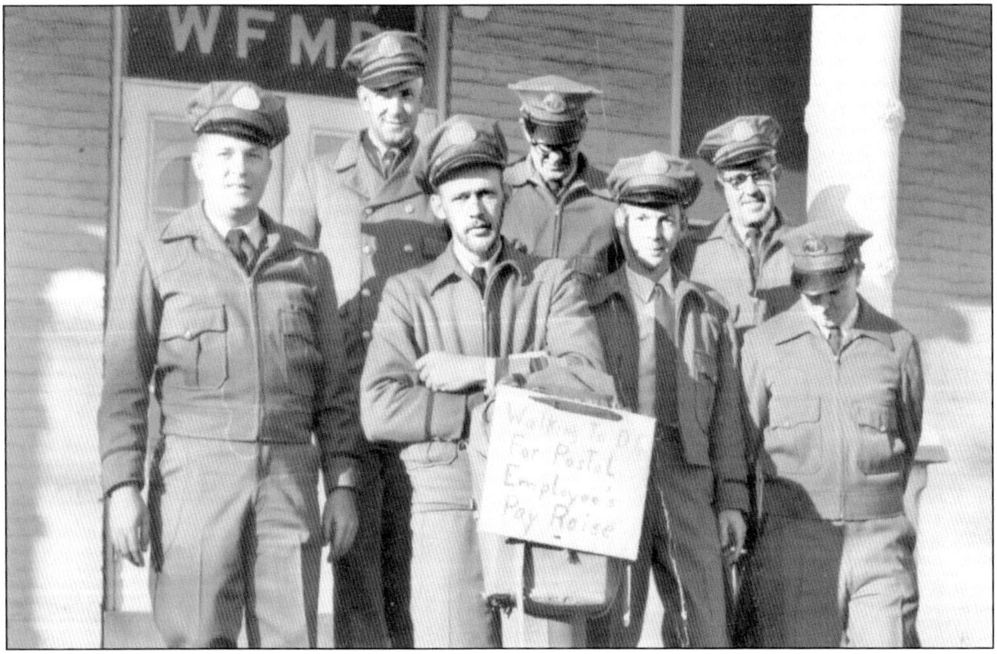

Dwight Eisenhower's first presidential term included a contentious Congressional debate about pay increases for postal workers. These seven mailmen, posing on the steps of the WFMD radio station, then located at Seventh and Market Streets in Frederick, participated in a walk to the nation's capital to highlight their need for more money. They got their wish when Eisenhower signed a bill in June 1955 giving them an eight-percent raise.

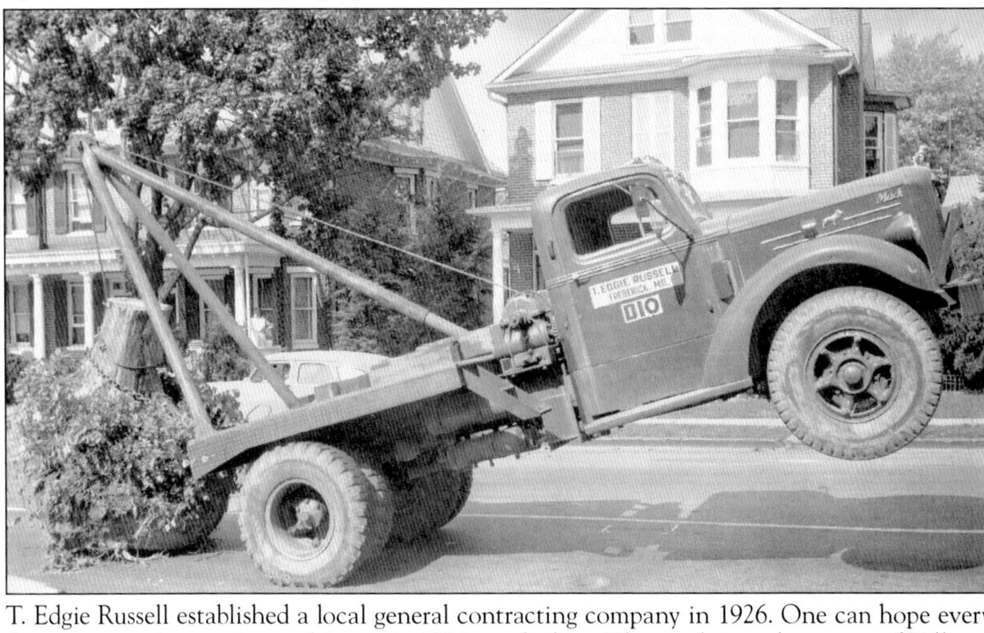

T. Edgie Russell established a local general contracting company in 1926. One can hope every day was not as interesting as this one in 1956 was for him. The truck is at the corner of Dill and Bentz Streets in Frederick. Russell's son, Robert, took over the family business in 1959 after his father died. The company continued to serve county airports, roads, bridges, farms, and private residences until 1964.

Seven

The Great Outdoors

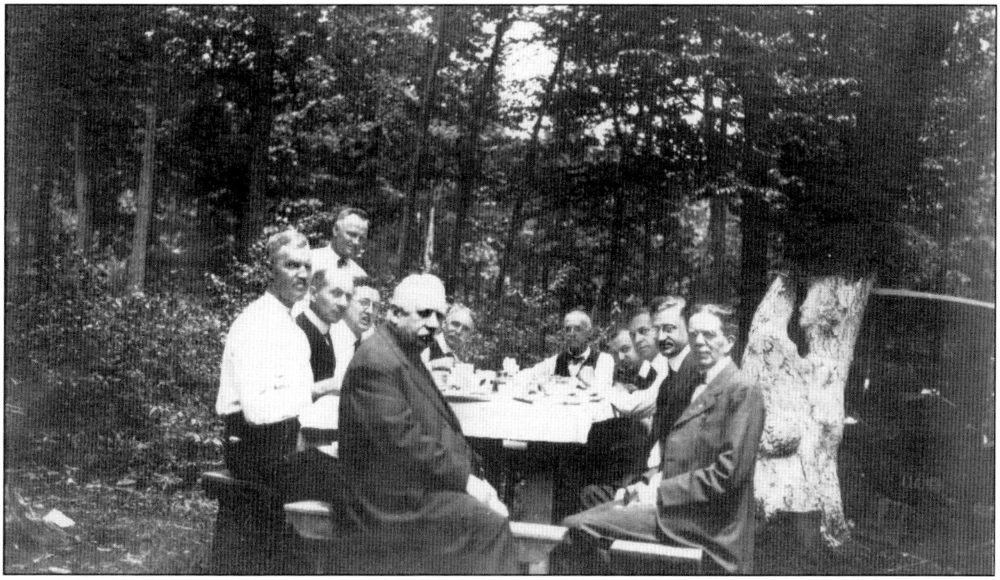

In a literal illustration of an open meeting, Frederick mayor Gilmer Schley, elected in 1919, brought the Board of Aldermen—Thomas Zimmerman, James Doub, Samuel Gregg, Lorenzo Mullinex, and Elmer Phebus—and several others to the woods for lunch. An avid sportsman, the mayor was perhaps indulging his love of the outdoors while seeing to city business.

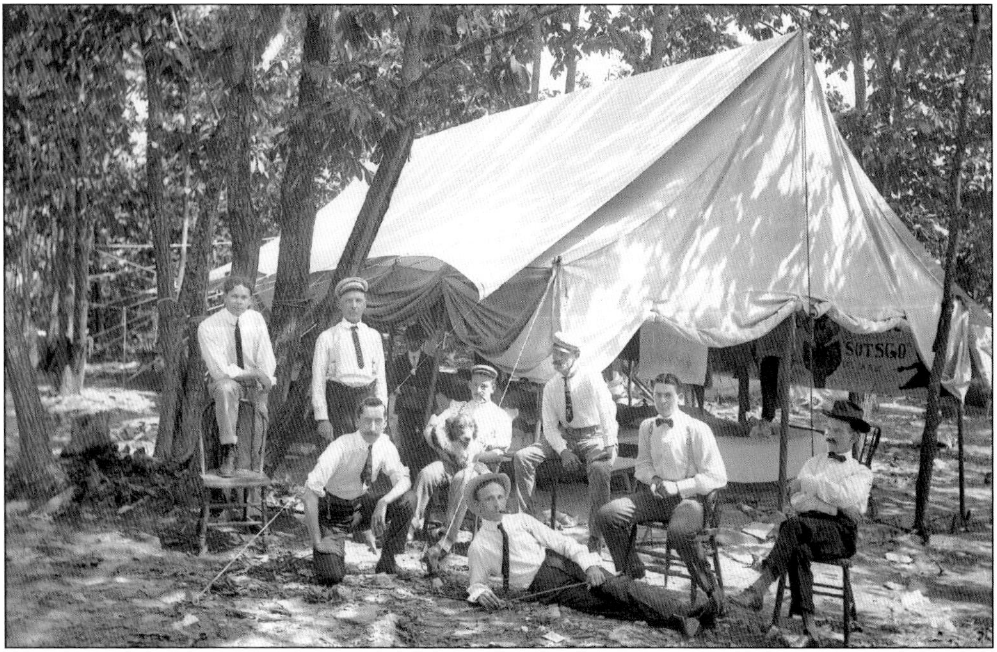

These casually dressed men are camped near the Monocacy River in Frederick County c. 1900. The Monocacy was a favorite place for camping, fishing, religious camp meetings, military encampments, and picnics throughout the 19th and early 20th centuries. This image is one of four of this particular camp known to exist. In this view, sleeping cots can be seen. Not evident is the full-size cook stove, dishes, clothes racks, and other "necessities" of camp life.

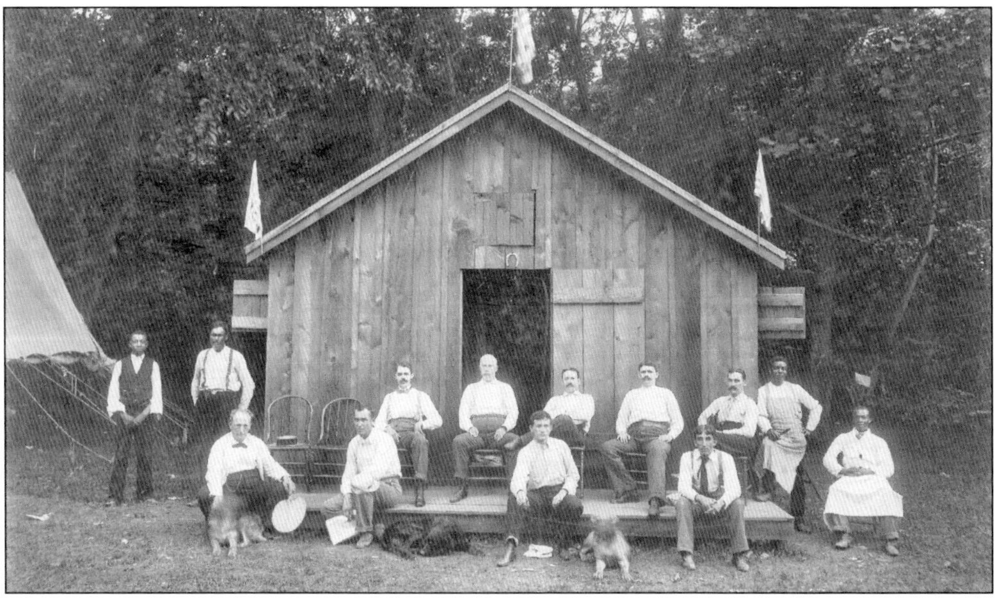

If it were not for the dogs, one would be hard-pressed to identify this photograph as one of a hunting camp. With shirts buttoned up to their necks, some even with ties, this group of well-fed fellows set up camp in Gilded Age style along the Monocacy River, off Gas House Pike, bringing along with them four African American servants to make sure that their rustic abode was as comfortable as possible.

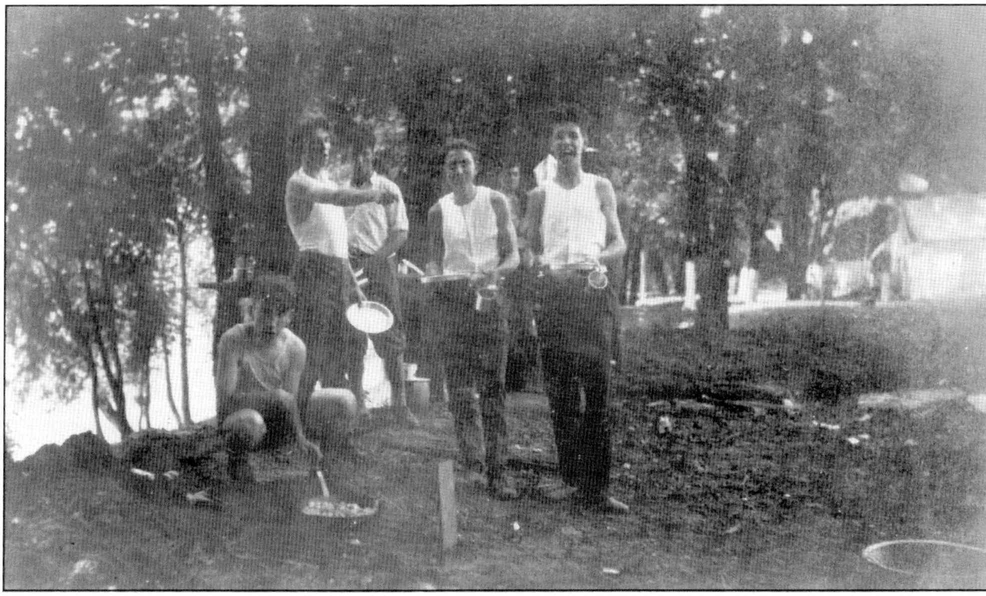

These Boys Scouts from Frederick get ready to enjoy a campfire meal at their camp—this photograph bears the affectionate appellation, "Camp Canoodle"—along the Potomac River near Licksville *c.* 1925. The Scouts enjoyed swimming, boating, fishing, pitching quoits (a game played much like horseshoes using a heavy disk), and other activities. Evidently, the boys also made periodic raids on a nearby store, cleaning it out of candy and pop.

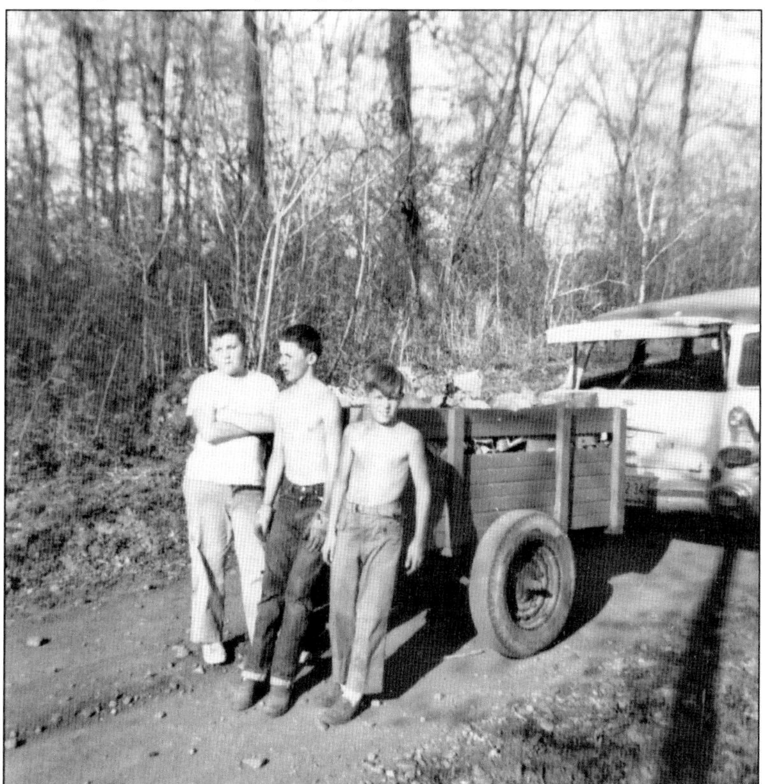

A kerchief-less Bobby Hartman (left), Kevin Loucks (center), and Bobby Clevenger of Scout Troop 279 worked outdoors as part of the handful of boys who picked up two trailer loads of trash along roadways near Point of Rocks on April 23, 1960. They continued a cleanup effort begun in April 1955 when 625 adults, Scouts, and 4-H club members collected 244 loads of trash in a one-day, county-wide cleanup campaign.

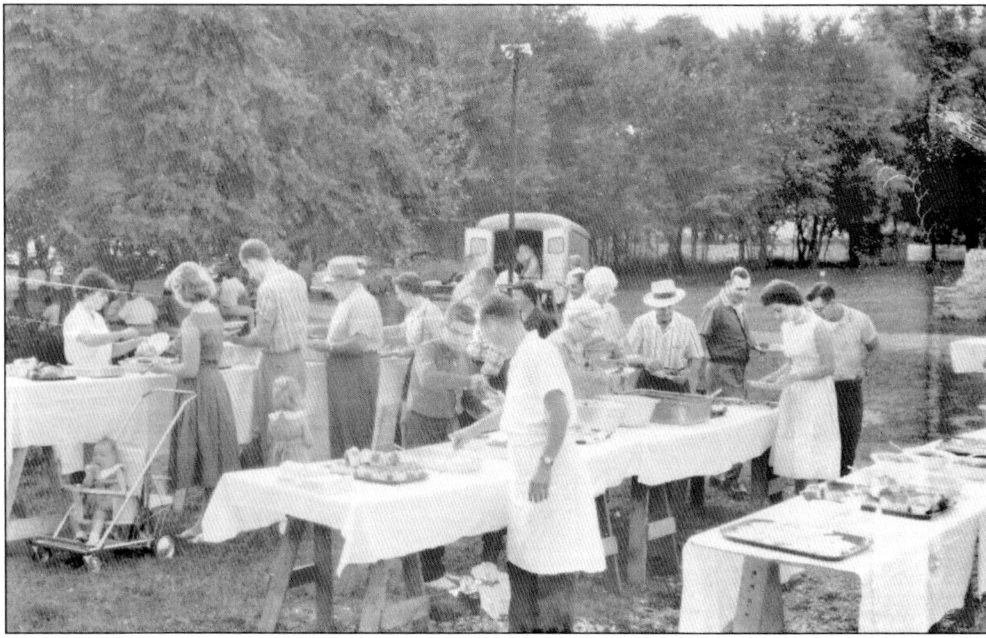

Employees and families of the Ox Fibre Brush Company enjoyed a fried chicken picnic at Husky Park in Frederick on August 11, 1960. Husky Park was originally created by Price Electric in 1954 and opened to local businesses, sports leagues, organizations, and employees. At one time, it was equipped with baseball diamonds, brick grills, a horseshoe pit, and a pistol range.

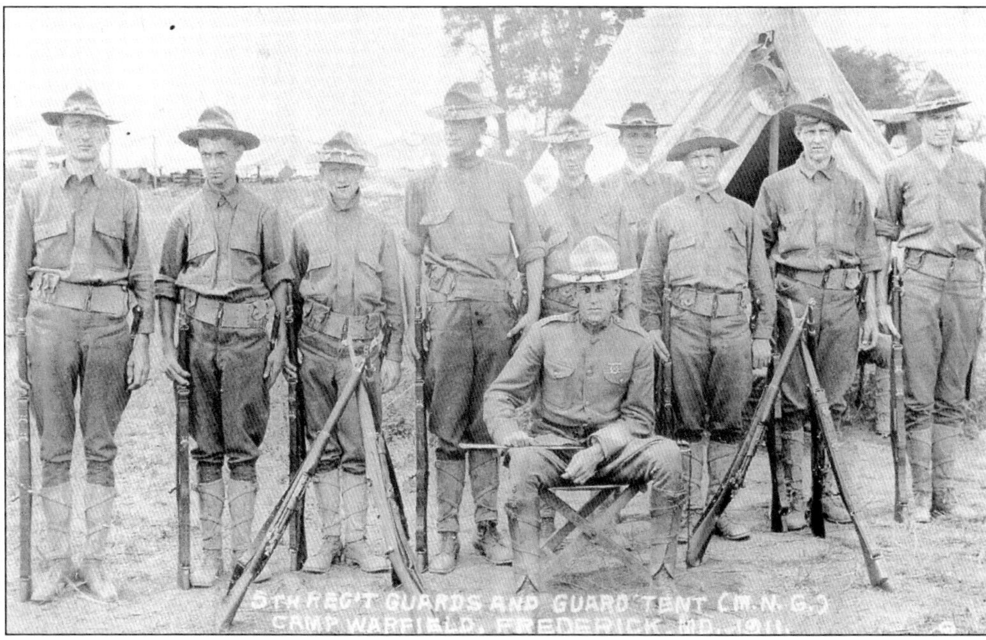

Not all camping is fun. Members of the Maryland National Guard gathered at the Kemp Farm near Frederick from July 13 to July 23, 1911. The 5th Regiment, members of which are seen here, were among three regiments of the 1st Brigade who participated in the exercises. In addition to daily drills, Camp Warfield culminated in a large maneuver on July 21. The camp was named for the state's adjutant general.

Nicholas Yinger loved photography and hunting and combined these two passions for this photograph taken in November 1955. His talent and eye for composition is evident in the many photographs he took in and around Frederick. Here in a photograph he set up and took using a timer, Yinger crouches beside the game he bagged using his Winchester 12-gauge at Summers Quarry.

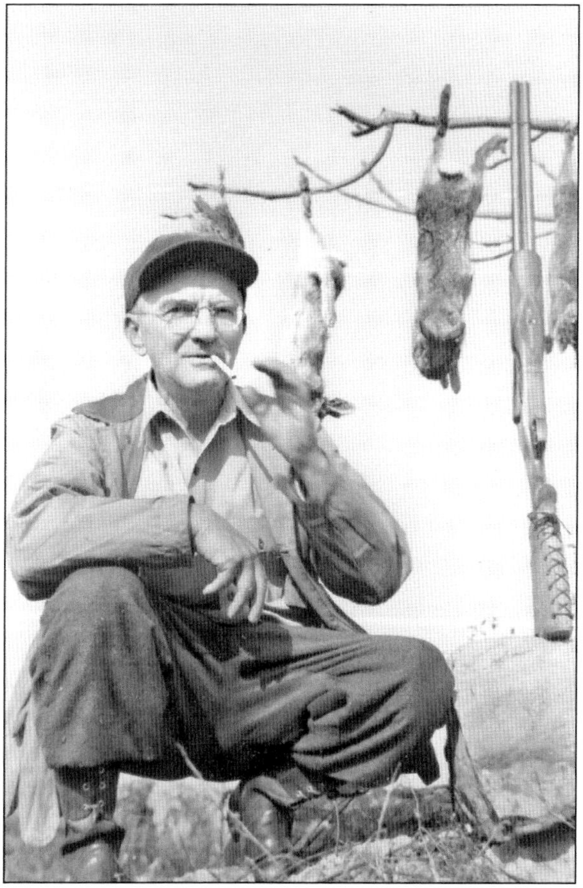

Nick Yinger wrote, "Happy Days are Here Again!" on the reverse of this May 1962 snapshot. Hanging from the Swinging Bridge over Carroll Creek in Frederick's Baker Park are, in unknown order, Pierre Bell and Arthur Hall. The challenge was to go hand over hand from one end to the other without getting wet. Yinger noted that "he and the gang" had done it 50 years before when the bridge was at its original location over Bentz Street. The footbridge was reconstructed at this location in 1930.

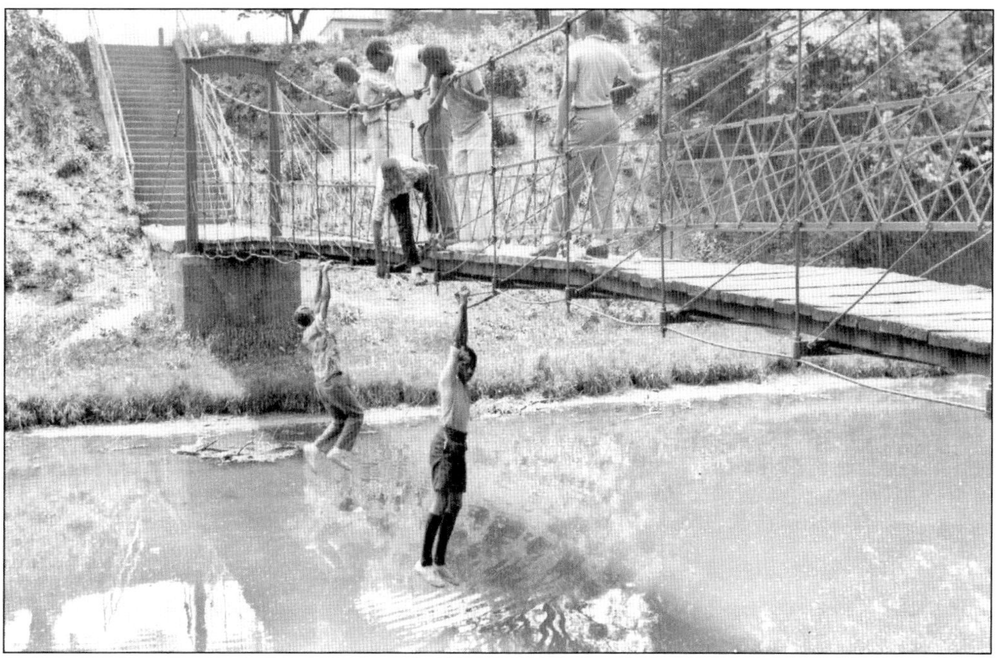

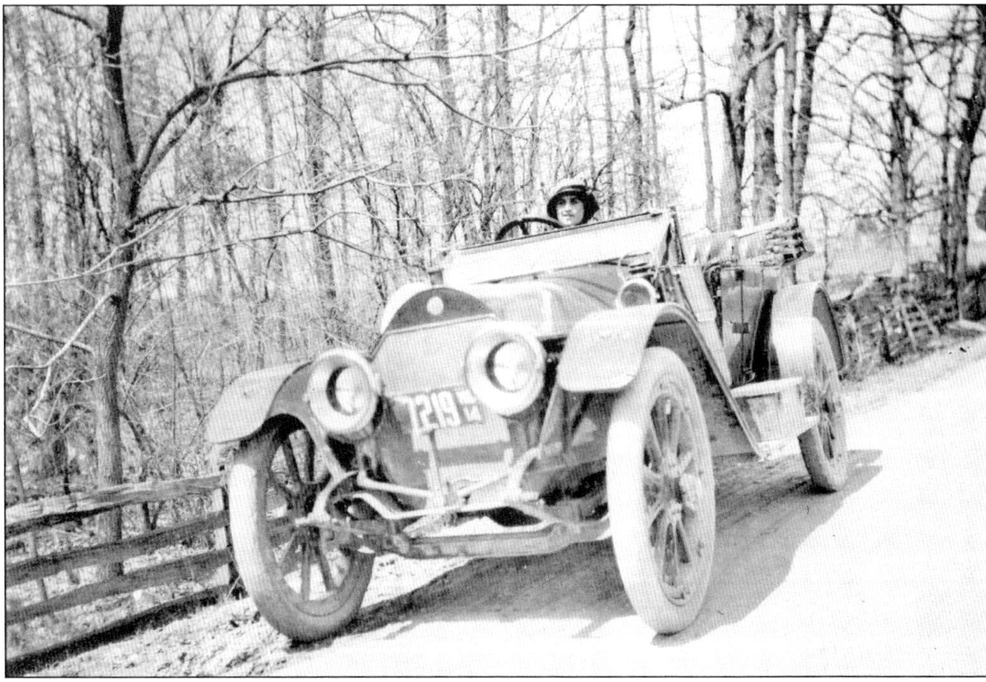

Motoring became all the rage with the advent of the automobile. Feeling the wind in her hair is Alice Dean McCain, probably not long after her marriage in 1915. Born in Harmony Grove in 1889, she graduated from Girls' High School in Frederick and attended Wilson College in Chambersburg before settling down with Elmer Dwight McCain. Their wedding announcement reported that they left on their wedding tour in Elmer's "machine."

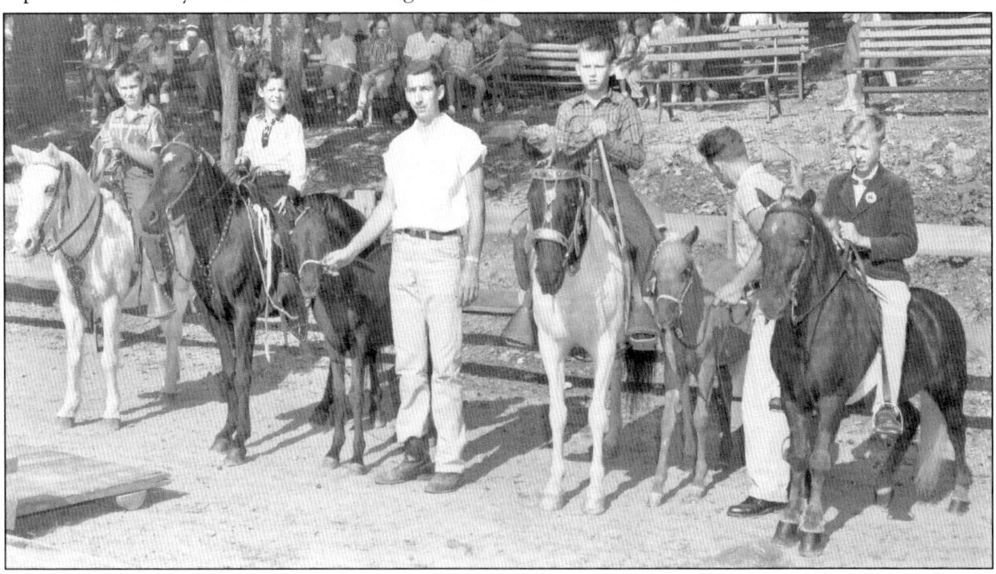

Originally conceived as a resort community, Braddock Heights was the home of the popular Braddock Heights Amusement Park. Many other entertainments also could be found there, including pony shows and pony rides. The first annual pony show at Braddock Heights was in 1957. My Golden Toy, a grand champion, and Trigger, "the world famous trick horse," were special guests at the show.

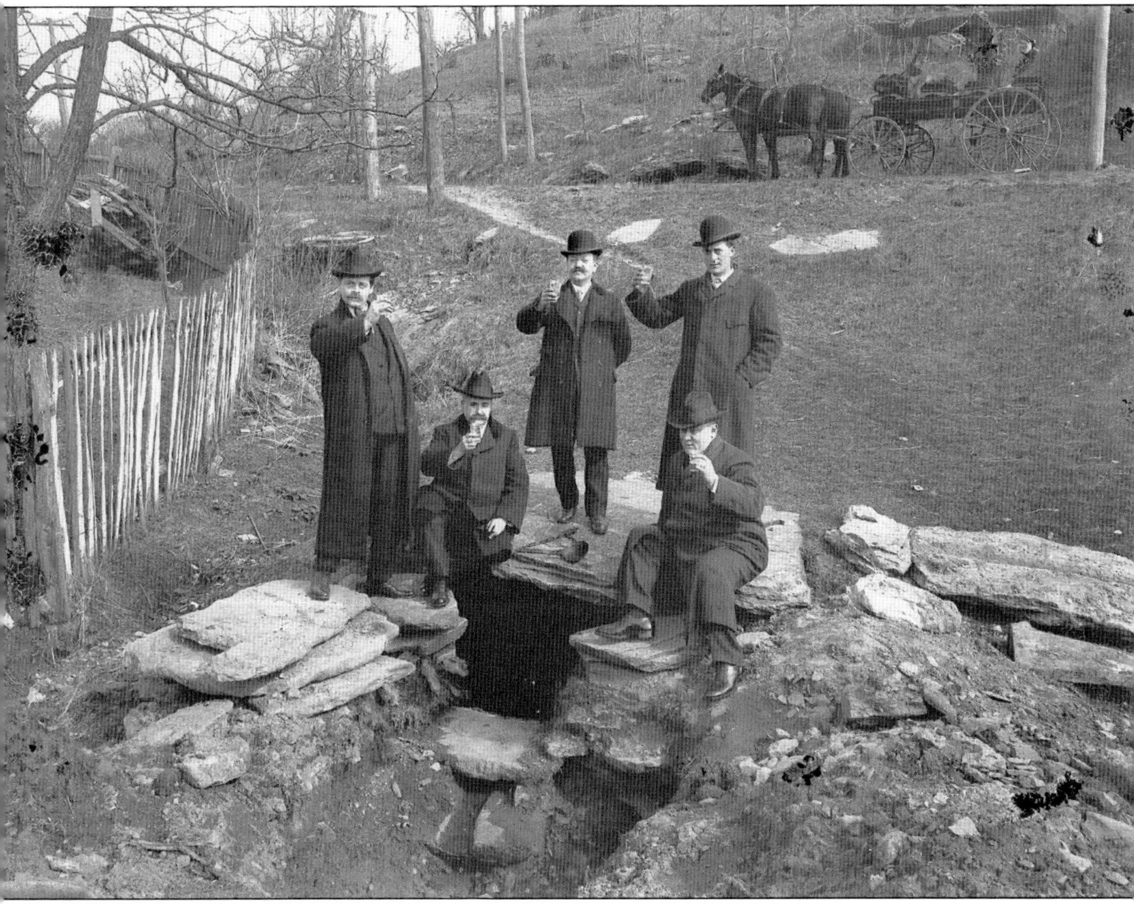

These gentlemen have disembarked from their touring wagon to drink from Braddock Springs as many other travelers along the National Road and pilgrims to the spring had done. In fact, for many years, the humble-looking spring was regarded as a refreshing shrine. Located near Braddock Heights, the spring was famous for reputedly quenching the thirst of Gen. Edward Braddock in 1755 during the French and Indian War. Braddock, with a young George Washington as his aide-de-camp, established the route on his way to capture Fort Duquesne from the French. However, the general was killed in the Battle of the Wilderness, punctuating a disastrous British defeat. Because of its historical connection, the spring reached a status enjoyed only by a few other county historical tourist destinations in the early 20th century. In addition to satisfying passersby, the spring served as the main source of water for Braddock Heights for many years.

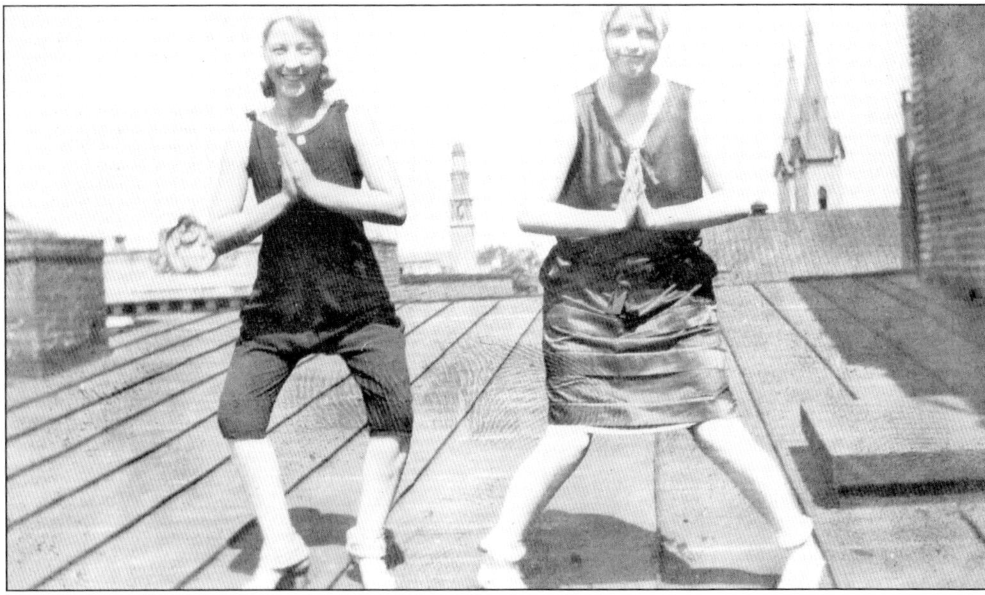

The outdoors can be enjoyed in unlikely places. Clowning on the roof of H. F. Shipley's Market Street store in Frederick on a July day in 1930 are Pauline Victoria "Polly" Shipley, daughter of the store's owner, and Alesa "Sue" Wisner, a store clerk. The person behind the camera may have been Charlotte Shipley, Polly's sister and a classmate of Sue. By the end of the following year, all three young women were married to local boys.

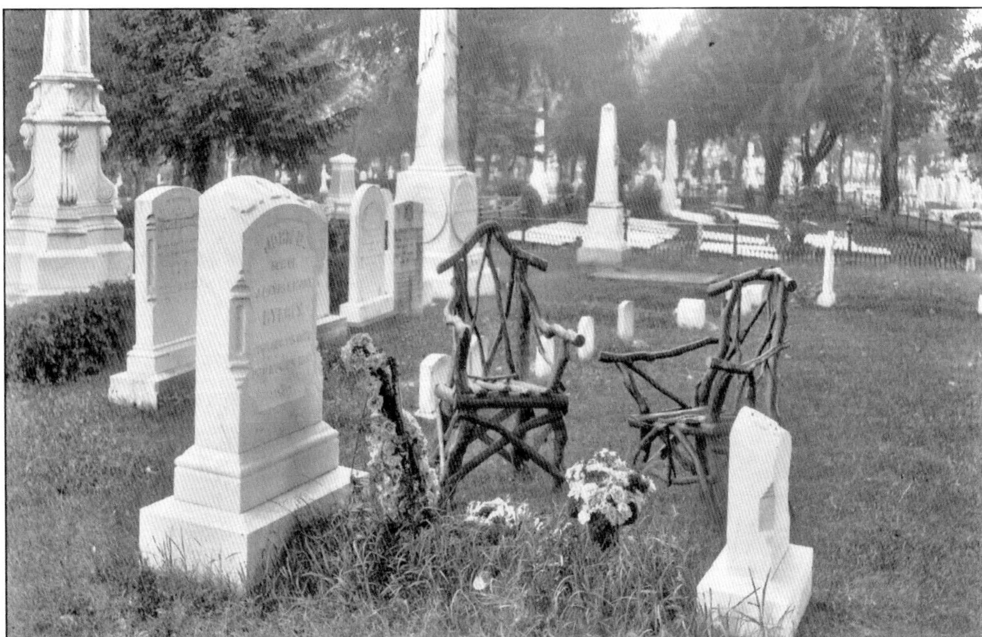

This photograph was taken by Charles Byerly about 1905 at his brother's Mount Olivet Cemetery grave site. John D. Byerly died in 1891, at age 19. While the photograph today may seem a bit odd, it would not have been when it was produced. At the time, public cemeteries, with their mixture of natural and monumental, were considered pleasant and respectable places for picnics and other informal gatherings.

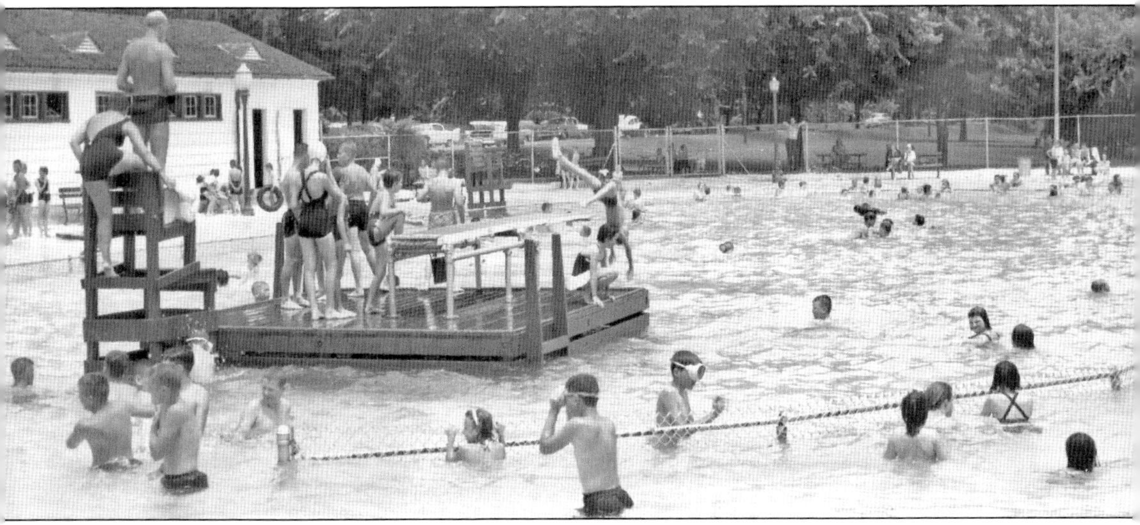

There's nothing quite like a cool dip on a hot summer's day, as this group of young people at the Frederick city pool in Baker Park about 1960 would affirm. Public swimming pools became popular in the early 20th century. In 1911, the *News* reported that 828 men had utilized the YMCA's pool that year—as had 12 women. The opening of Frederick's municipal pool in June 1928 was highly anticipated, with the local newspaper running a series of articles on regulation, hygiene, and management issues associated with public pools. Within two weeks of the pool opening, over 3,500 people had taken a plunge. None of them were black; the pool, like the park, was for whites only. Two decades later, a pool designated for the city's black residents was dedicated at Mullinix Park. The William R. Diggs swimming pool was built by members of the Joseph D. Baker family and named to honor their longtime family friend and employee. Frederick's pools were finally integrated in the early 1960s.

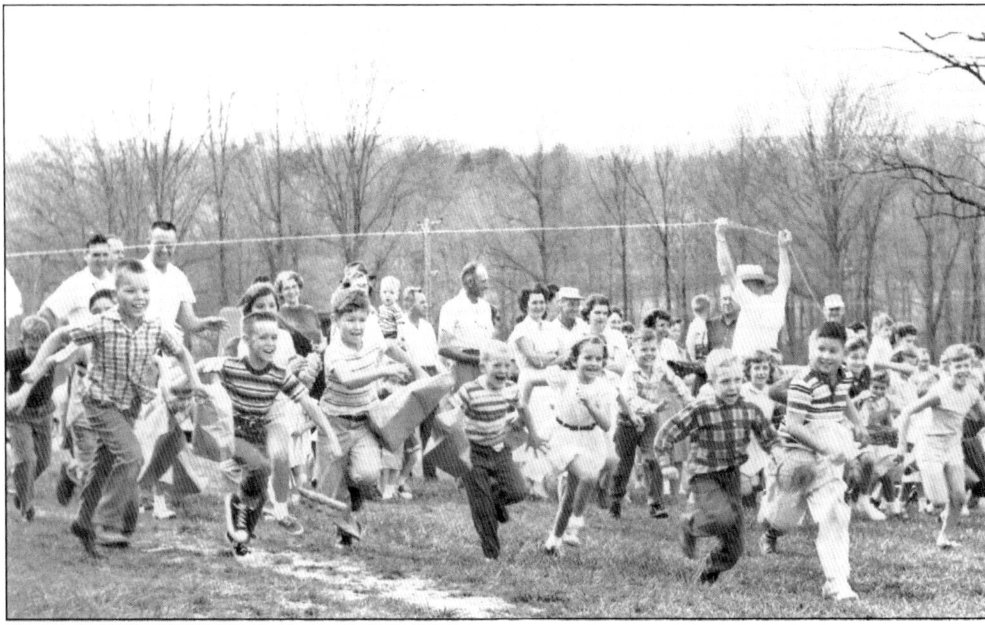

Many organizations throughout Frederick County have had annual Easter egg hunts as a rite and welcome of spring for local children. Civic organizations such as the Kiwanis, 4-H clubs, and others held the popular egg hunts each year. The children pictured here have just begun their frantic hunt at a Lions Club event in the early 1960s.

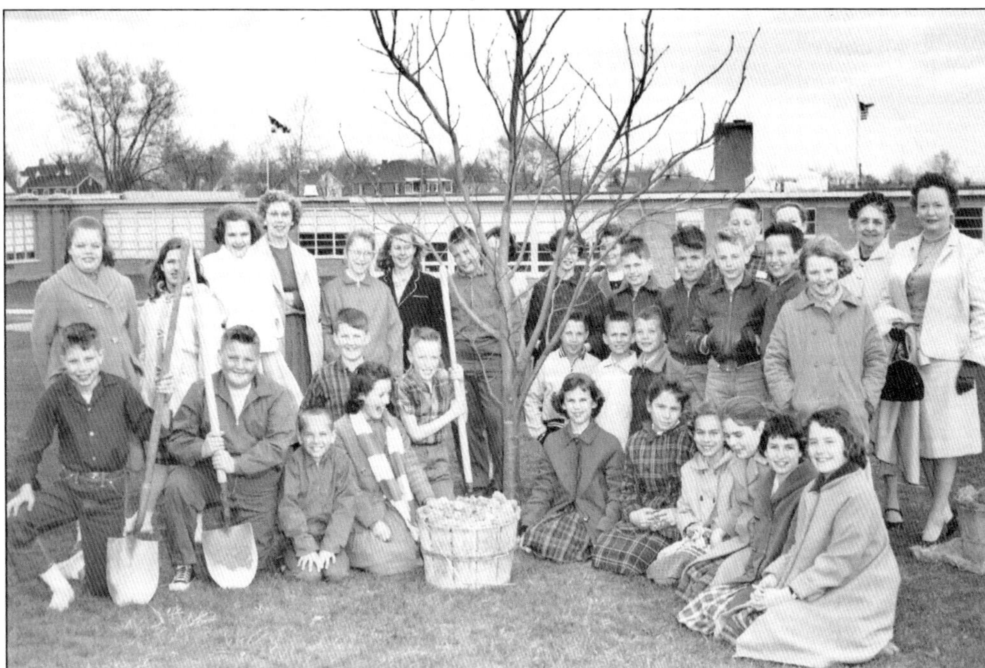

The first Arbor Day observance took place in Nebraska on April 10, 1872, when as many as one million trees were planted in that state. Members of the Junior Garden Club of Frederick—North Frederick Elementary School fifth-grade students known as the "Dirt Dobbers"—continued that tradition at a tree-planting ceremony sponsored by the Garden Club of Frederick in April 1961.

Eight

Good Times and Bad

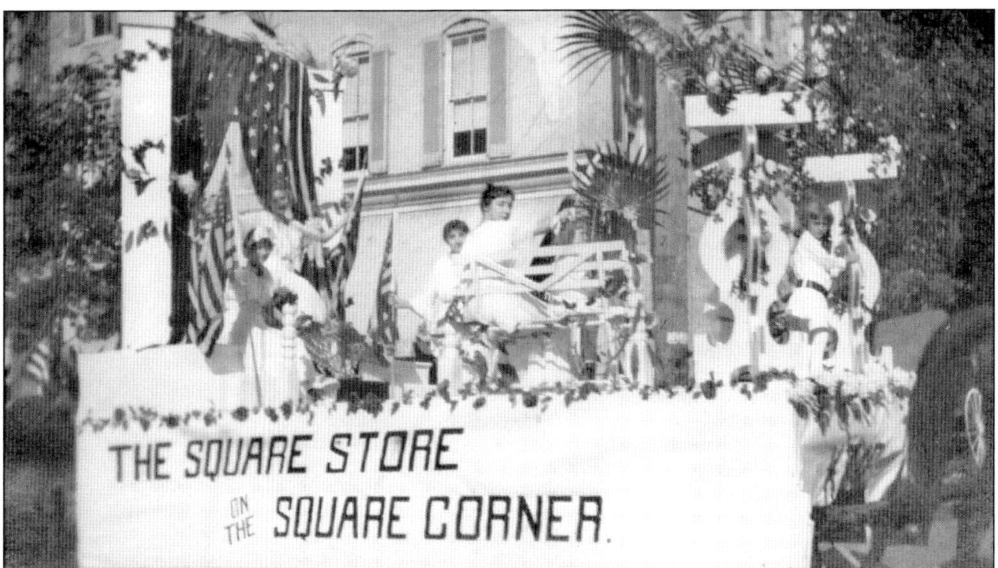

The 1914 celebration of the Frederick County Star Spangled Banner and Home Coming Week was centered in Frederick for a week of parades, concerts, addresses by honored guests, and other special events. On September 10, a parade of floats representing county businesses wended its way down through downtown. C. Thomas Kemp's dry goods store entered this float, which was supposed to represent youth and beauty.

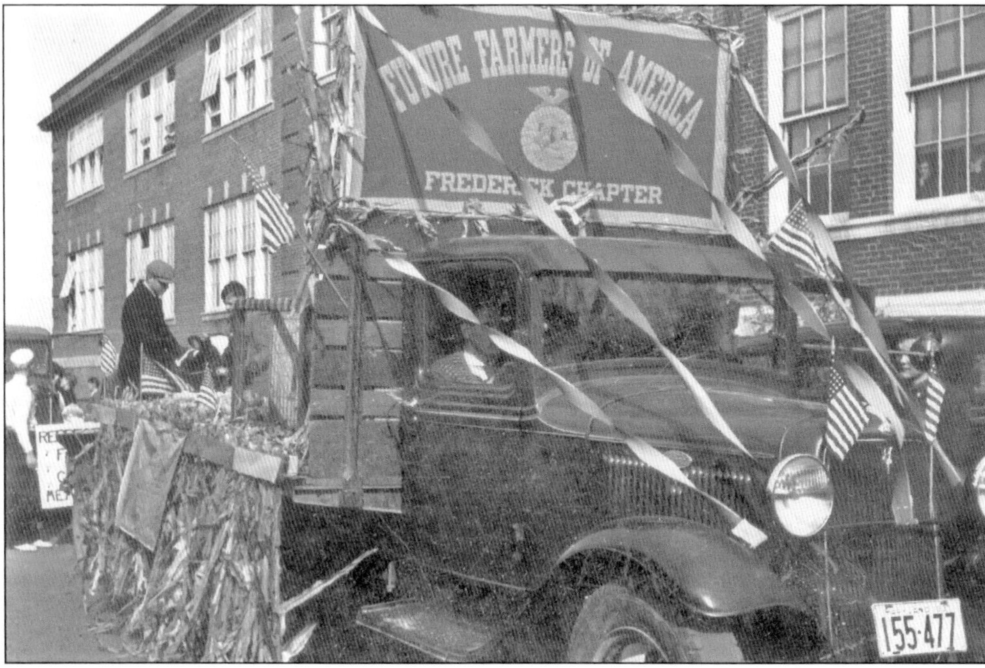

Frederick High School's Future Farmers of America won a best float award of $7.50 for their entry in Frederick's annual Armistice Day celebration on November 11, 1937. The float featured various products raised throughout the county, including a young heifer, pigs, and chickens. Another series of floats created by high school students featured scenes meant to suggest that the "war to end all wars" most likely was not.

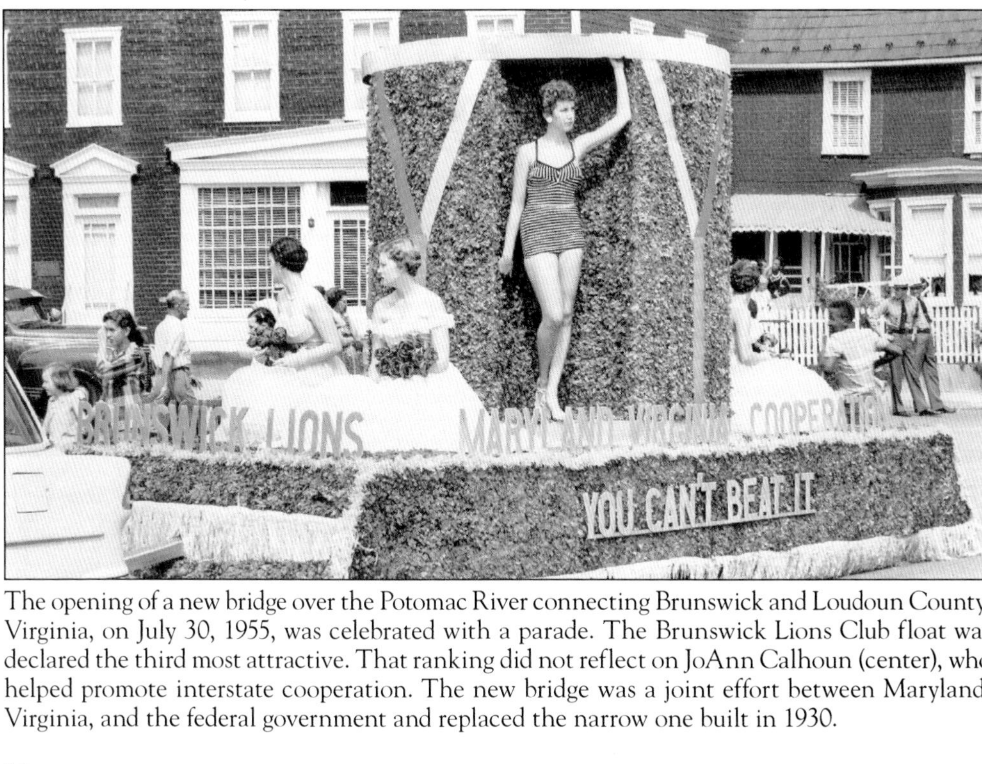

The opening of a new bridge over the Potomac River connecting Brunswick and Loudoun County, Virginia, on July 30, 1955, was celebrated with a parade. The Brunswick Lions Club float was declared the third most attractive. That ranking did not reflect on JoAnn Calhoun (center), who helped promote interstate cooperation. The new bridge was a joint effort between Maryland, Virginia, and the federal government and replaced the narrow one built in 1930.

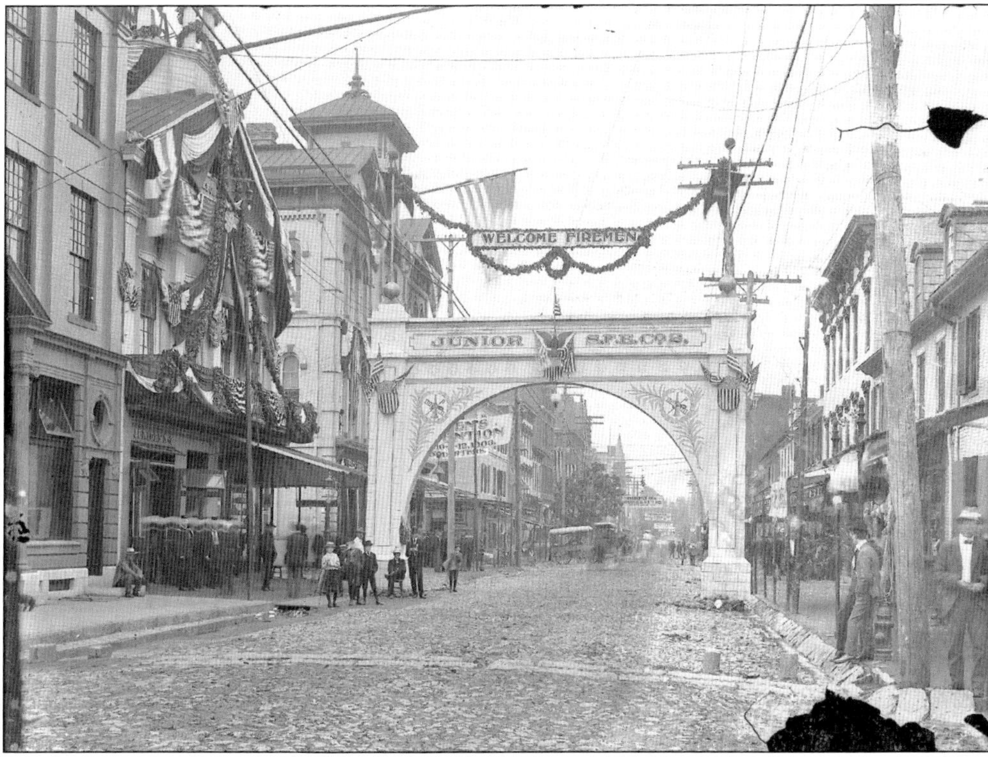

Fire bells rang all day and restaurants stayed open all night for the State Firemen's Convention held June 9–11, 1903, in Frederick. Local fire companies erected arches, including one by the Junior Fire Company (above). The Junior's firehouse was an attraction for visiting firemen who admired its horses and up-to-date equipment. The Independent Hose Company also constructed an arch, which was topped by an eagle adorned with electric lights (right). Many houses and businesses were decorated with flags, bunting, and signs. Locals eagerly cheered on firemen competing in hook-and-ladder contests, fire-hose races, and other competitions throughout the convention. The *News* reported, "Even the children have the fever," with boys decorating their bicycles and girls having dresses of red, white, and blue bunting.

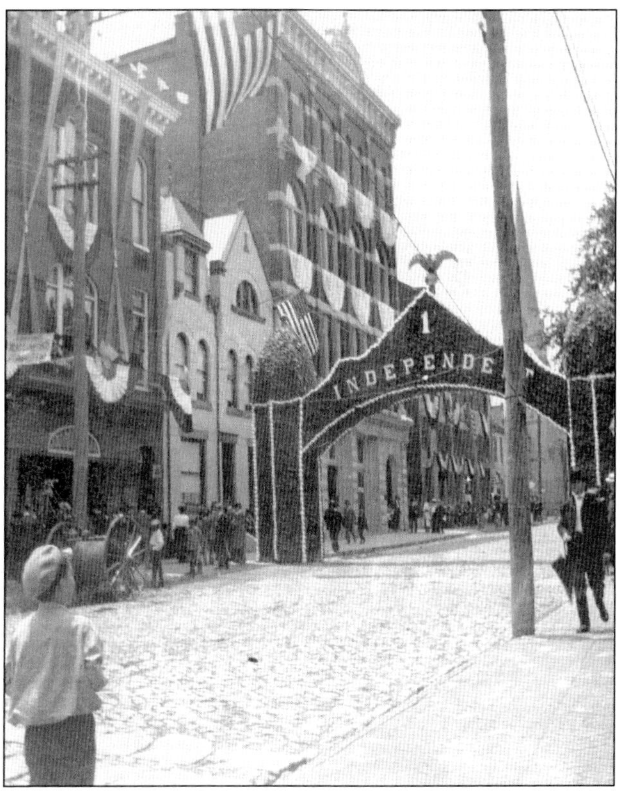

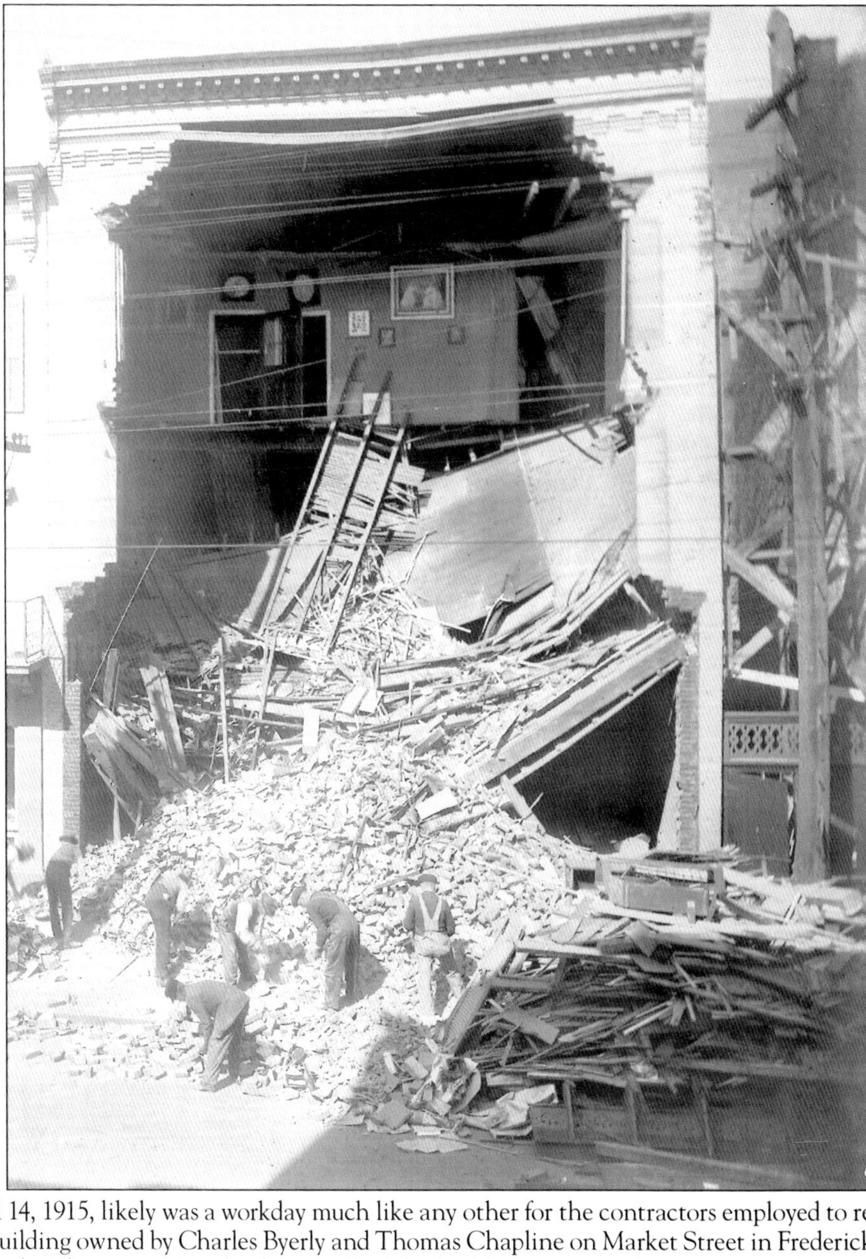

April 14, 1915, likely was a workday much like any other for the contractors employed to remodel the building owned by Charles Byerly and Thomas Chapline on Market Street in Frederick. That is, until without warning the front wall of the building came crashing down to the pavement. Thankfully, cuts and bruises were about the worst injuries suffered by the workmen in the building at the time. The building had housed Dutrow's confectionery on the first floor and Byerly's photographic studio on the third. Byerly suffered the loss of all his photographic equipment, and it perhaps was this that spurred his early retirement from the profession. The *Frederick Post* reported that by nightfall, fellow photographer L. R. Dertzbaugh had prints of the collapsed building for sale in the windows of nearby shops. The newspaper also reported that a large mahogany desk belonging to Barbara Fritchie, local Civil War heroine, fell from Byerly's studio but landed with little damage on the wreckage below. The desk is now part of the Historical Society of Frederick County's collection.

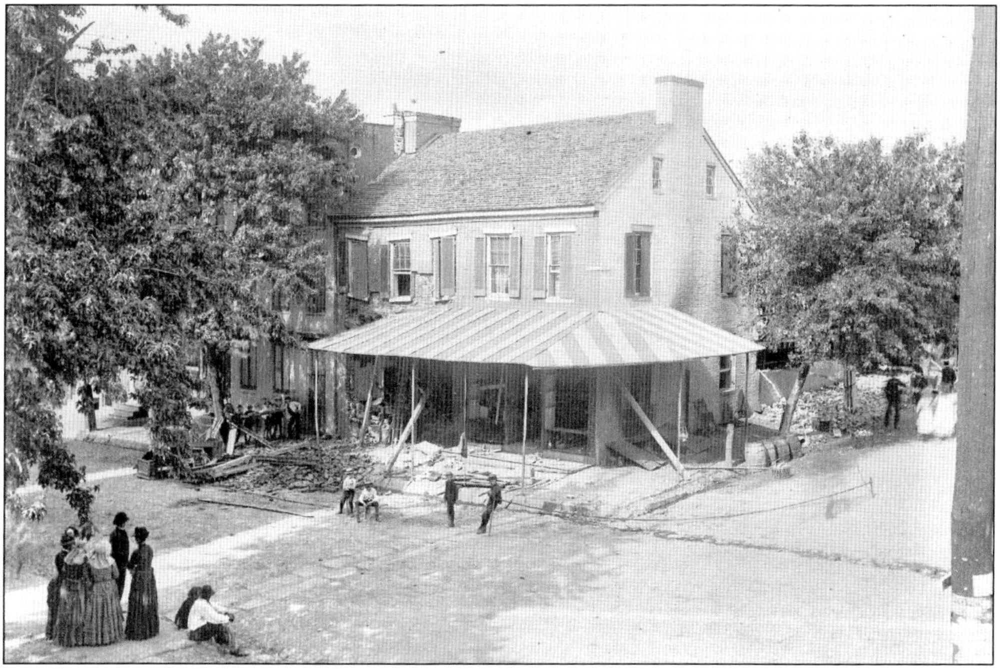

On the evening of May 28, 1888, the shriek, "Fire! Fire! Fire!" went out on South Market and East South Streets in Frederick. An employee's lantern had ignited a fire at Zeller's Grocery in a storage room filled with barrels of gasoline, coal oil, and whiskey. Even before the firemen arrived with their steam pumper, a large crowd had gathered. An explosion of gasoline surprised them, sending out shrapnel that injured more than 70 people. One curious onlooker, Charlie Poole, age 12, was killed. For the next few days, people from all over came to view the wreckage.

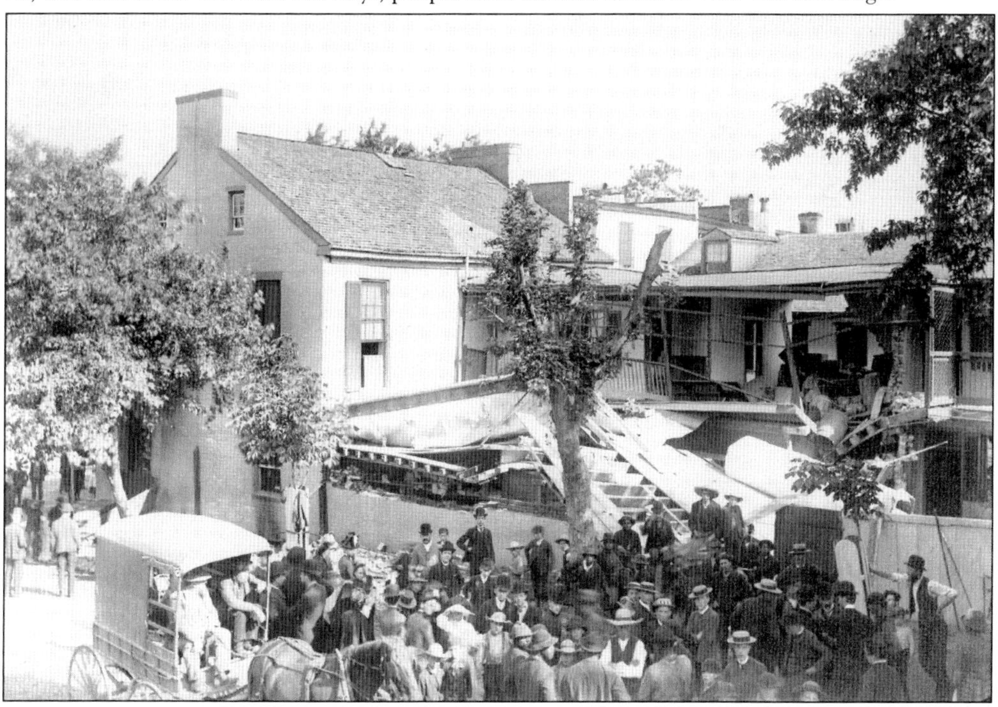

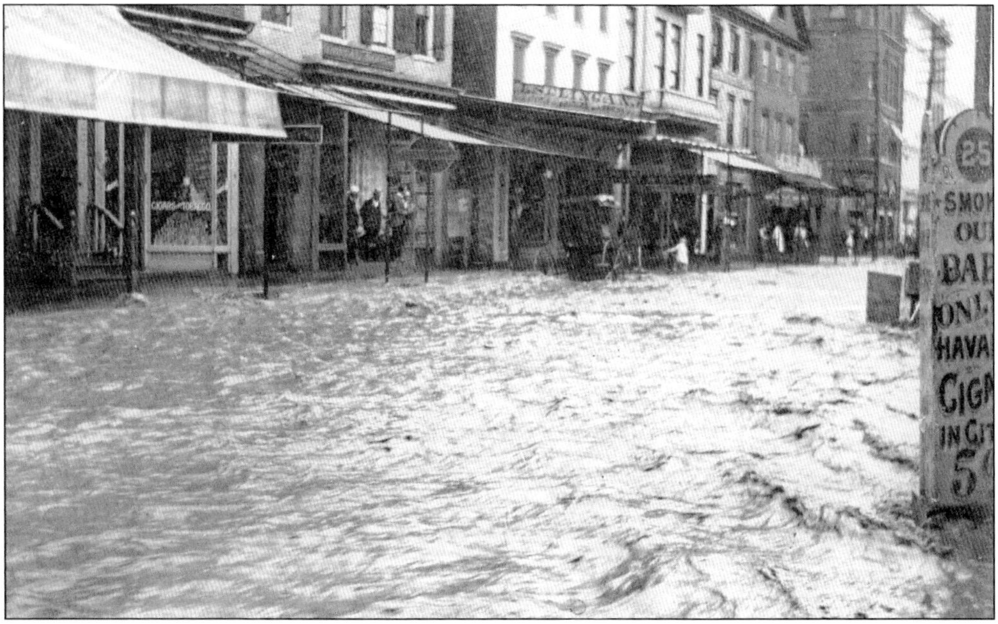

The "heaviest rain in years" caused streams, sewers, and gutters to overflow into the streets of Frederick in the afternoon of August 18, 1898. The downpour lasted just half an hour. According to the *Daily News*, unsecured boxes and barrels were swept down Market Street. The newspaper also reported that a lady from Myersville was fortunate enough to capture a photograph of the scene, likely the image shown here.

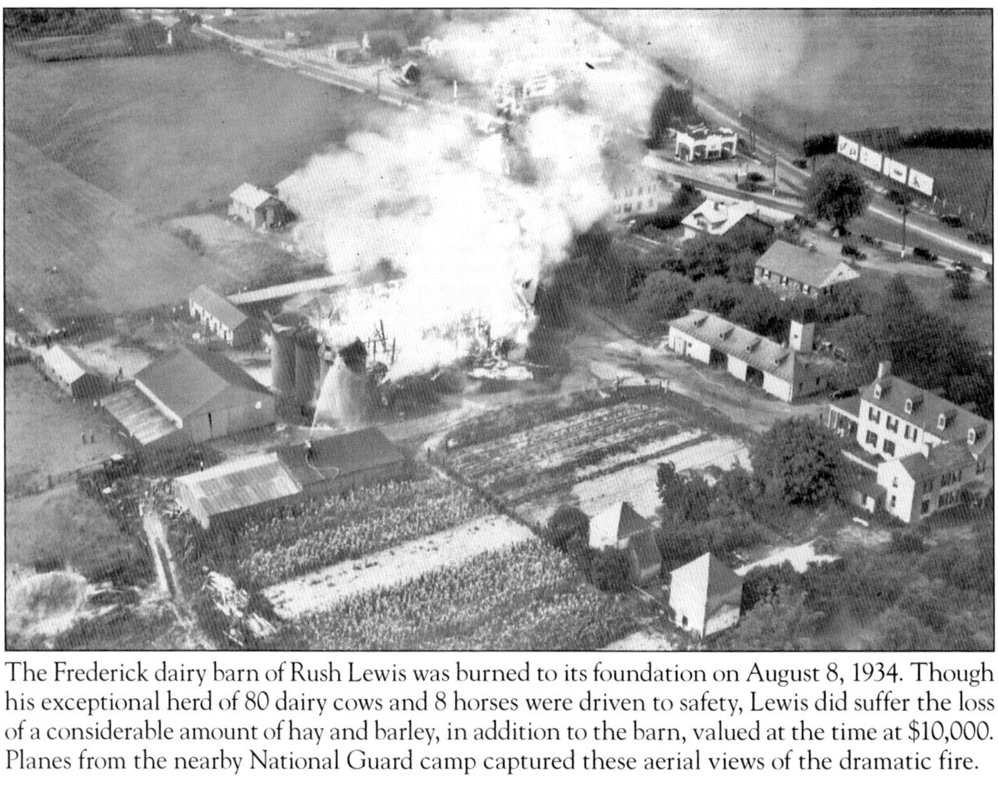

The Frederick dairy barn of Rush Lewis was burned to its foundation on August 8, 1934. Though his exceptional herd of 80 dairy cows and 8 horses were driven to safety, Lewis did suffer the loss of a considerable amount of hay and barley, in addition to the barn, valued at the time at $10,000. Planes from the nearby National Guard camp captured these aerial views of the dramatic fire.

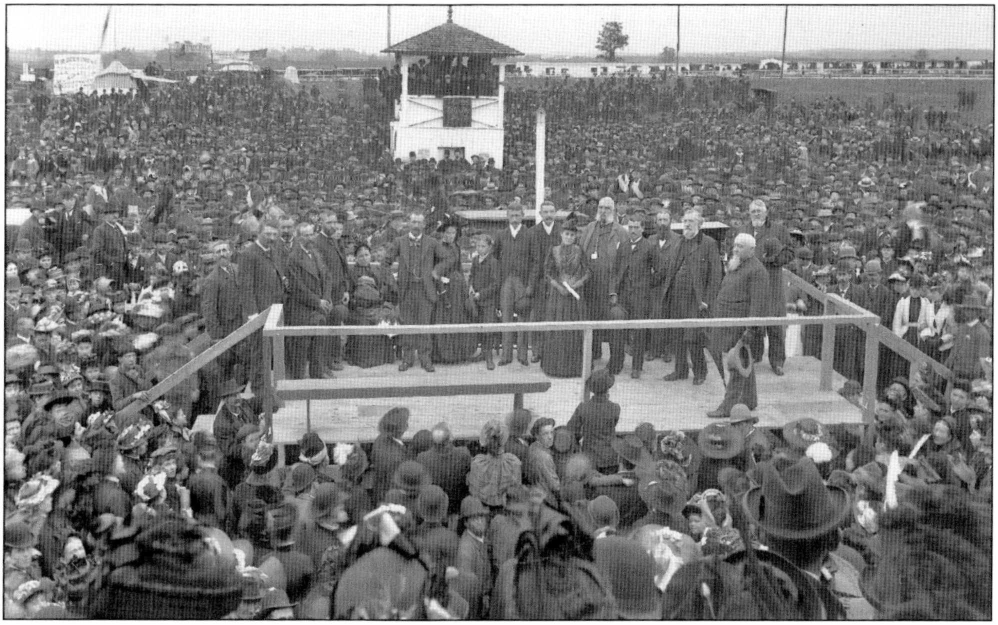

On October 16, 1890, an estimated 30,000 people witnessed the nuptials of Ella Graser and Jacob Kanode at the Frederick Fair. The *News* noted that the bride looked "very pretty and charming" in a dress furnished by J. D. Hendrickson and that the groom was "in the full bloom of manly glory." After the ceremony, it reported, "The immense crowd cheered lustily, steam whistles blew and the small boy wasted the strength of his lungs on the inevitable tin horn."

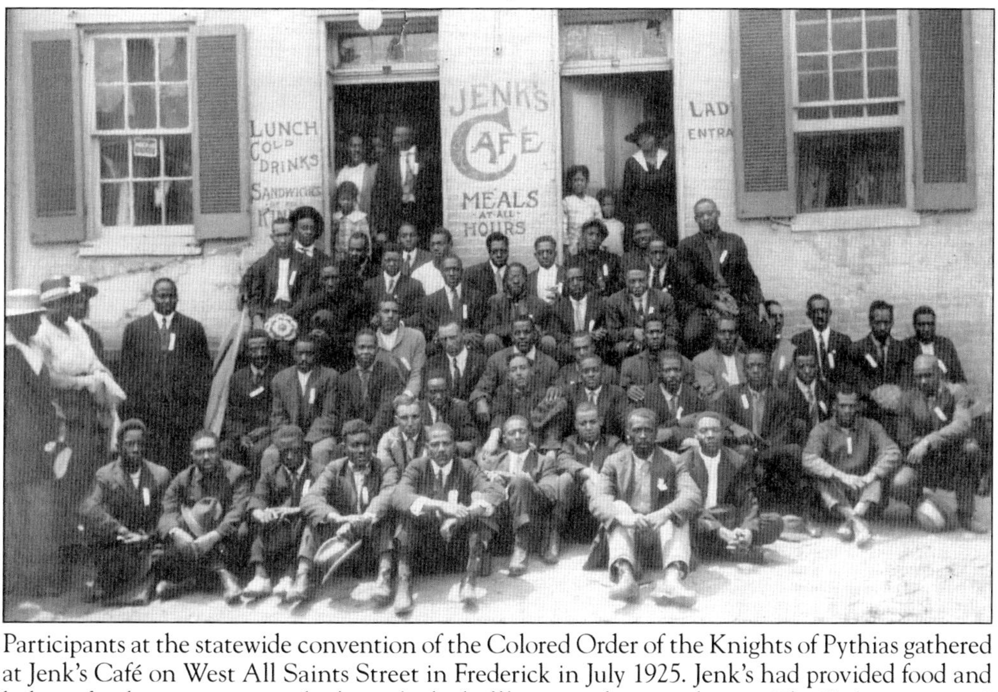

Participants at the statewide convention of the Colored Order of the Knights of Pythias gathered at Jenk's Café on West All Saints Street in Frederick in July 1925. Jenk's had provided food and lodging for the convention, which was kicked off by a parade around town. The "ladies entrance" may have been used by the women of the Grand Court of Calanthe, which also was meeting in town.

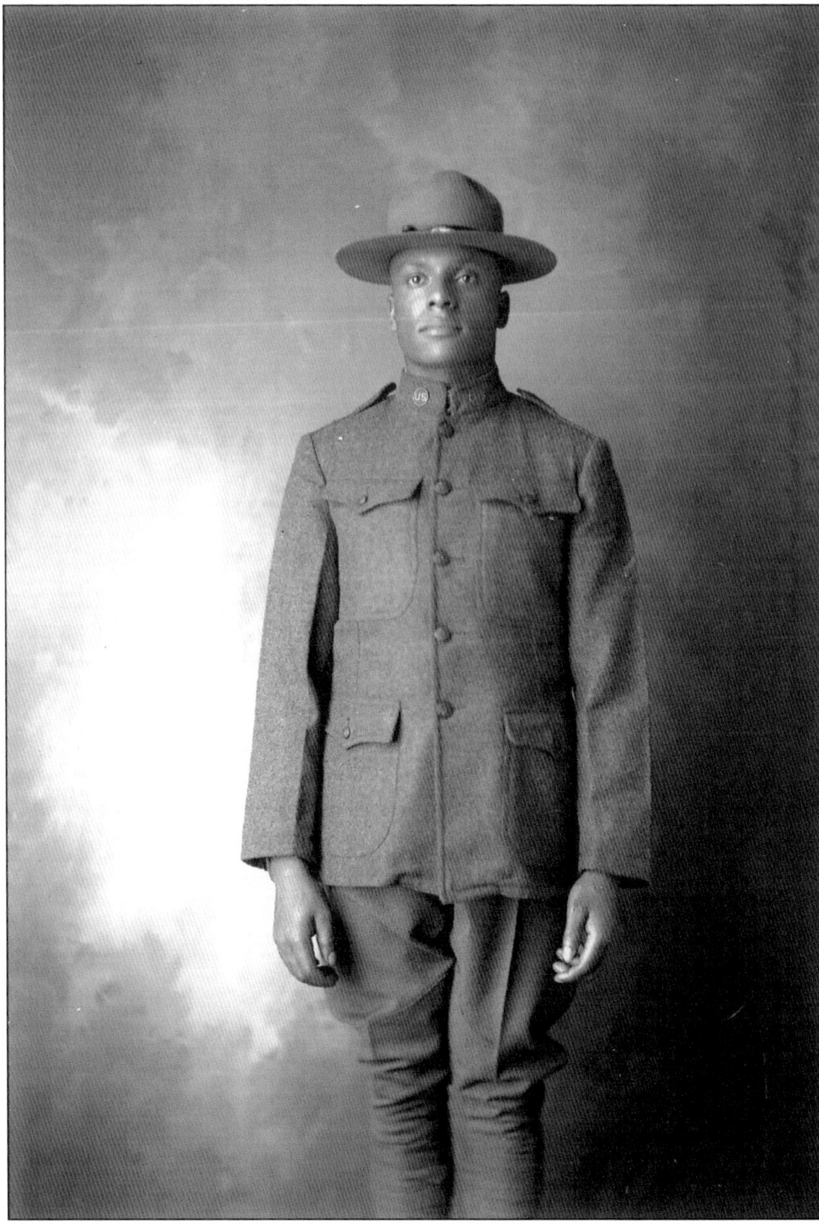

The rumblings of a world war in local 1914 newspapers illustrates why many locals may have been torn in their sympathies early on. In August, at least three local men, recent German émigrés, were anxiously awaiting a call from "their Emperor" to do their duty for the Fatherland. Other Frederick Countians, many of German stock, worried over the safety of friends and family living or traveling abroad. By 1917, county men were going off to war, a number of them black. This unidentified soldier was photographed at the Byerly studio in Frederick likely before going off to serve during World War I. Racial barriers in the armed forces meant that black servicemen served primarily in supporting roles. After the war, local veterans also were honored separately: as part of the first Armistice Day celebration on November 11, 1919, white veterans were treated to a banquet—"one of the biggest functions ever held in the city," according to the Frederick *News*—at the City Hotel, while their black comrades-in-arms supped at the Asbury Methodist Church.

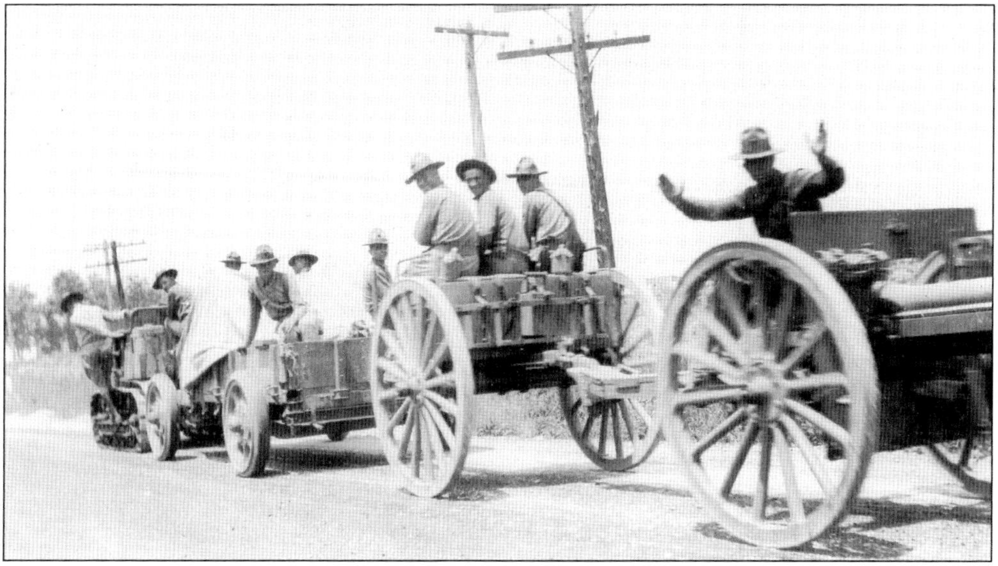

In an anachronistic twist, 5,000 U.S. Marines equipped with modern artillery and tanks traveled through Frederick County on their way to and from their reenactment of the Civil War battle of Gettysburg on July 4, 1922. On their return to their Quantico, Virginia, base, the marines stopped in Emmitsburg, where they enjoyed a moving picture of the baseball game they had played against locals a week earlier. In Frederick on July 8, the marines were reviewed in front of City Hall on Market Street by a delegation that included Maryland governor Albert Ritchie (in top hat), Mayor Lloyd Culler, and Acting Secretary of the Navy Theodore Roosevelt Jr. One dignitary who was not in attendance was Pres. Warren G. Harding, who was unable to make it to Frederick in time. Harding did greet the troops later as they bivouacked at the Frederick fairgrounds.

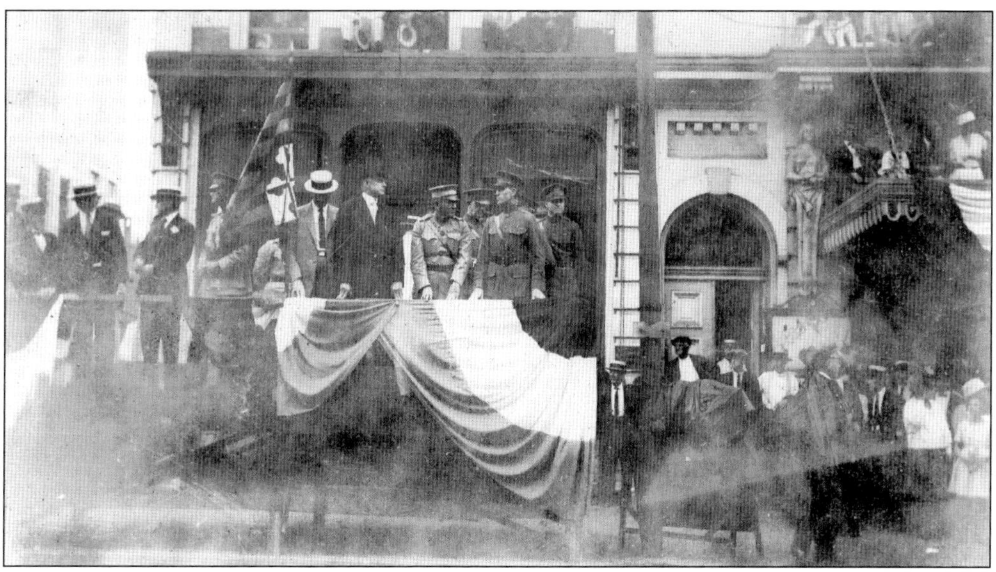

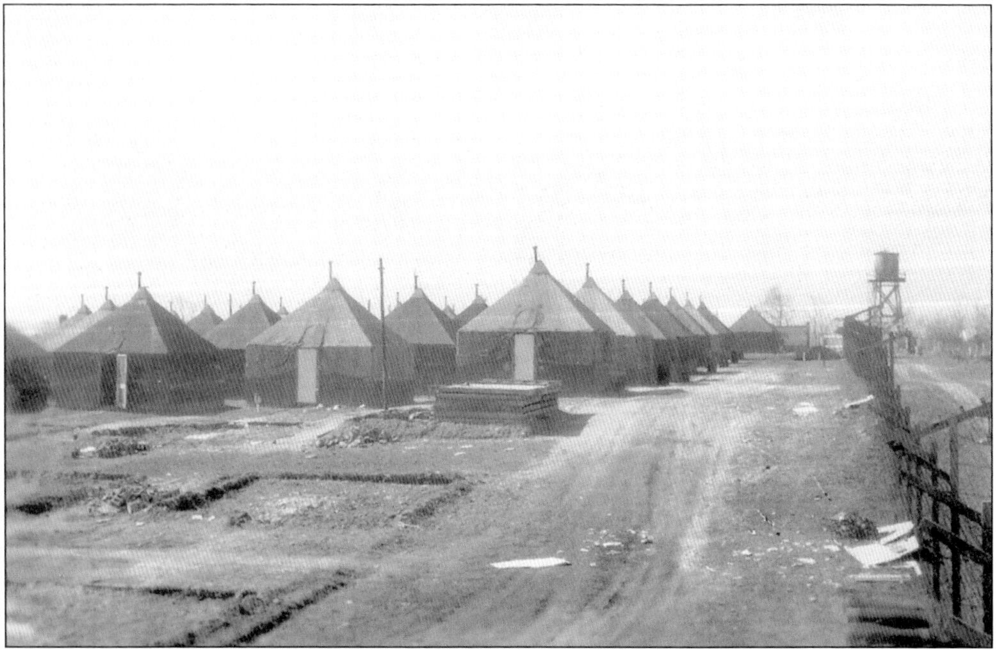

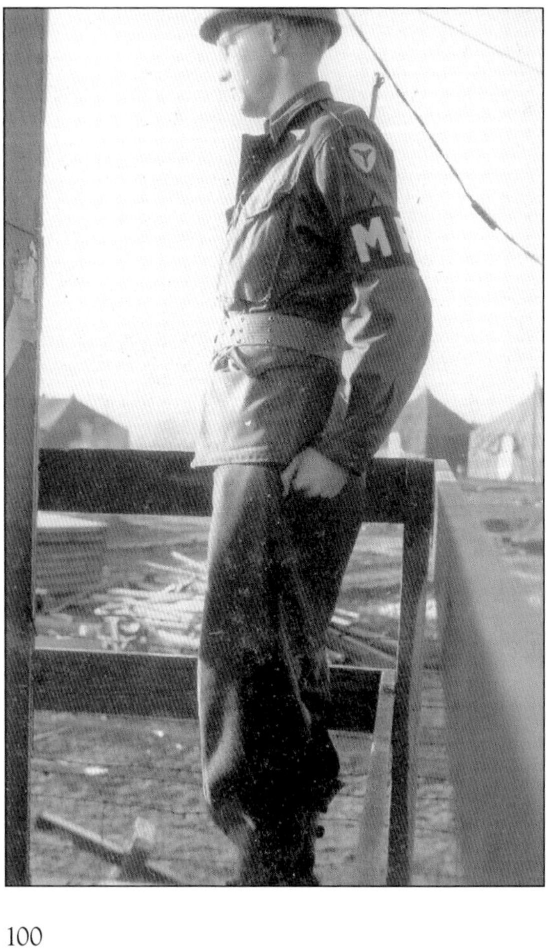

During World War II, prisoners of war lived in camps like the one pictured above, P. W. Branch Camp No. 6, located on Old Camp Road west of Frederick. Here German prisoners were guarded by young American soldiers. The prisoners worked on local farms, in factories, and in canneries, sometimes unguarded. This photograph was taken in March 1946 and shows the remaining prisoners' tents (the removal of some tents is evident in the foreground), the outer stockade fence, and, in the distance, the camp's water tower. The camp's prisoners were "Class A," meaning they claimed to be anti-Nazi and volunteered to work. Pfc. Charles P. Wales of Bethesda snapped these photographs during the time he was assigned to duty at the camp, from September 1945 to June 1946, when it was closed. He took the photograph of himself using a timer while on guard duty.

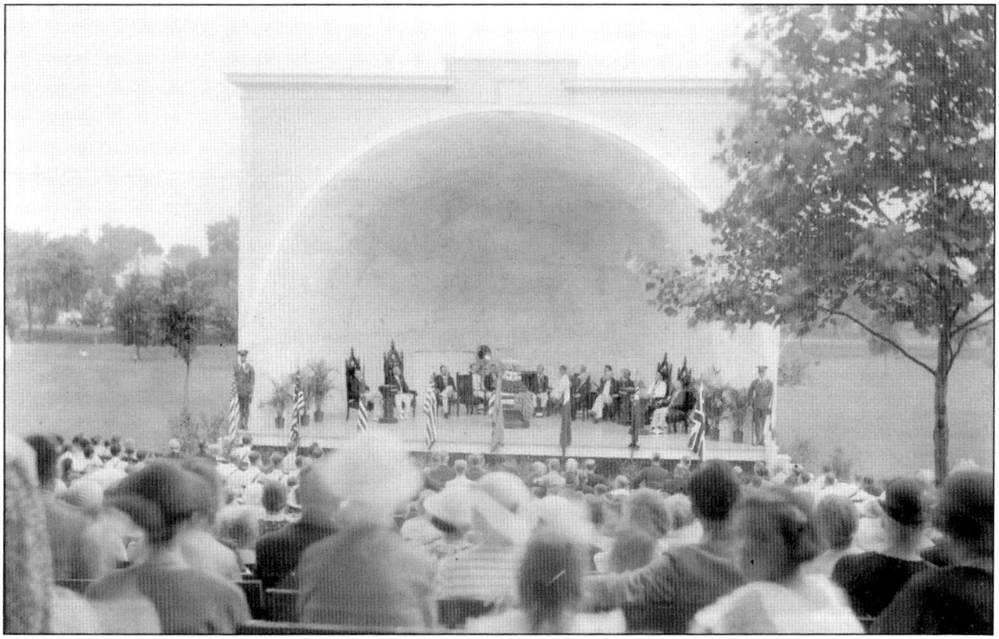

Flag Day ceremonies, like the one pictured, were celebrated annually at Frederick's Baker Park for many years. In fact, the first event to take place in the band shell was a Flag Day ceremony organized by the B.P.O. Elks. The band shell was constructed in 1935, the decision to build it coming shortly after the measure was passed to create an amphitheater in the park.

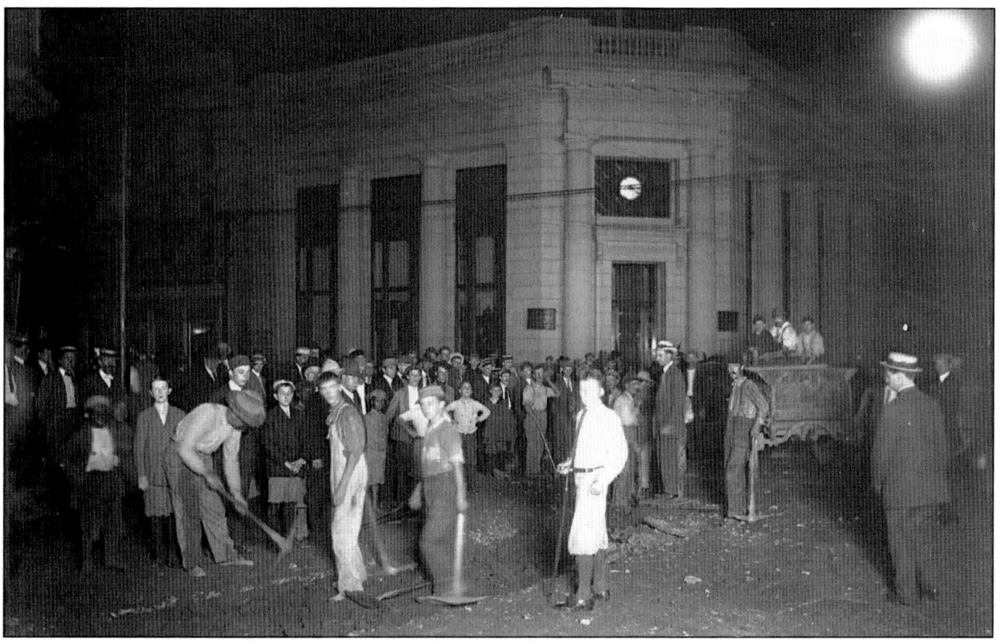

Crews worked through the nights in summer and early autumn 1910 to prepare the roadbed and lay the track for the Frederick Railroad Company's trolley line on North Market and several other downtown Frederick streets. The city's aldermen set the speed limit on Market Street at six miles an hour and the fare for all passengers over age five at 5¢. The first run on the completed loop took place on October 23, 1910, and lasted about 45 minutes.

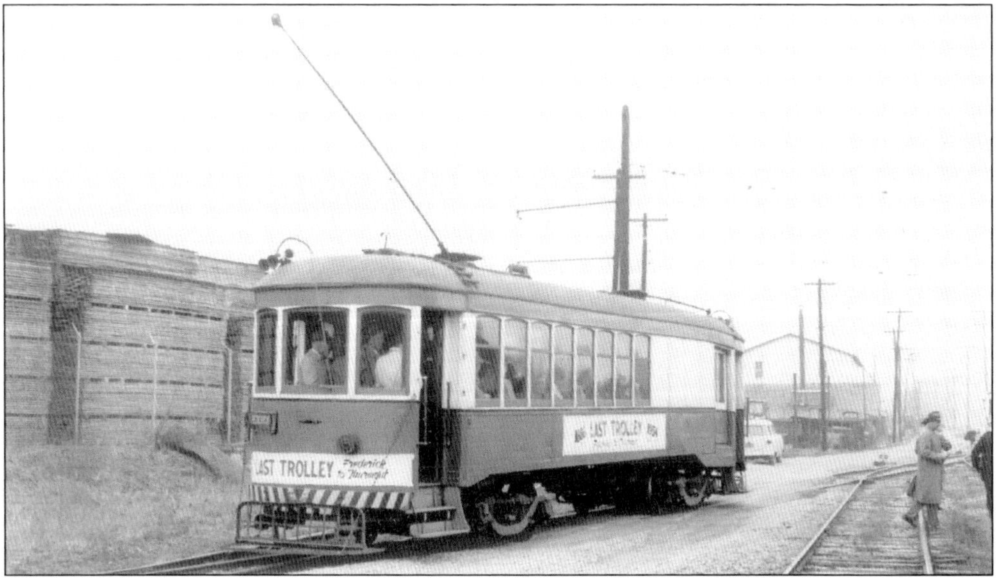

By the early 1950s, automobiles had supplanted electric railways as a preferred mode of travel. On February 20, 1954, the Hagerstown and Frederick Railway made its final passenger trolley runs from Frederick to Thurmont. One of those runs by Car No. 171 is pictured above. The trolley enthusiasts, media representatives, and Potomac Edison officials on board the trolley cars witnessed the end of the trolley era in Frederick County. Five years later, in spring 1959, crews from the City of Frederick began removing sections of track from the abandoned Hagerstown and Frederick Railway along Fifth Street and the Hood College cross streets. Tracks had been removed from the Hood College campus the previous year. Passenger service on the trolley line ceased in 1954; freight service ended in 1958.

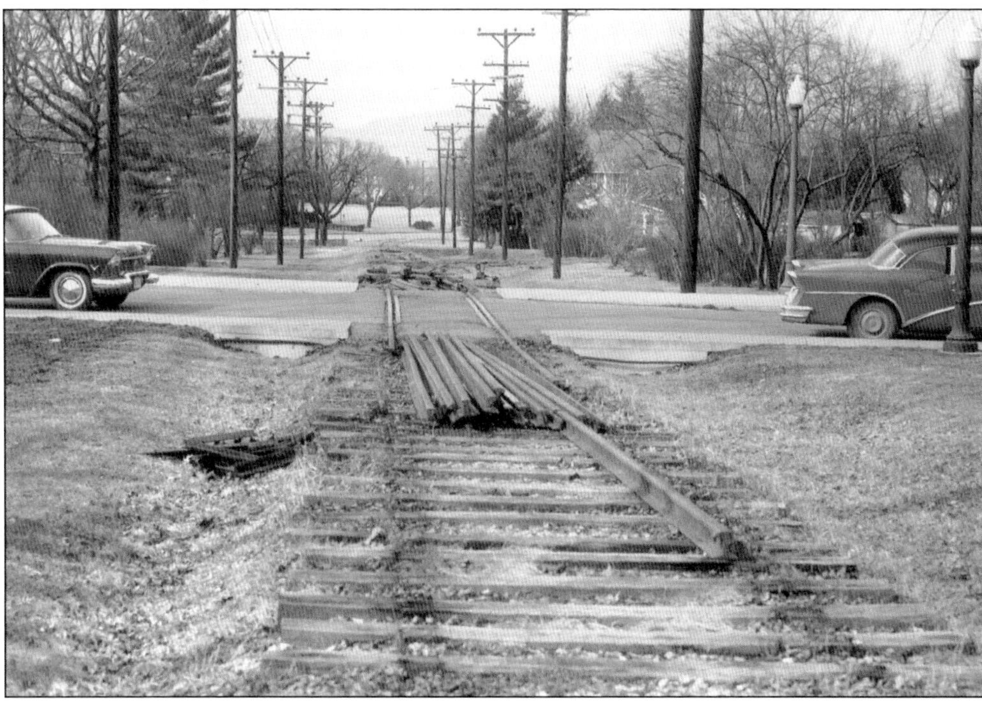

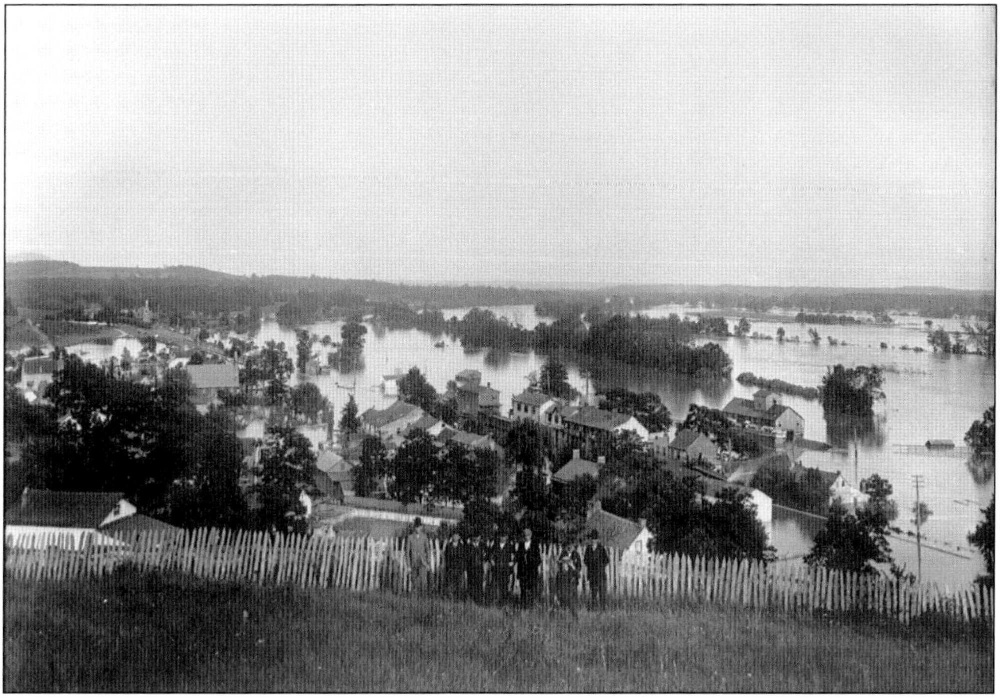

These gentlemen gathered on the high ground above Point of Rocks on June 2, 1889, to get a better view of the rampant flood damage in the town below. The railroad station can be seen in the distance at left. In May 1889, more than 21 inches of rain fell in the area. On May 31, another six inches came down and the Monocacy River flooded its banks, washing away most of the bridges. The weather system was the same that caused the tragic Johnstown, Pennsylvania, flood.

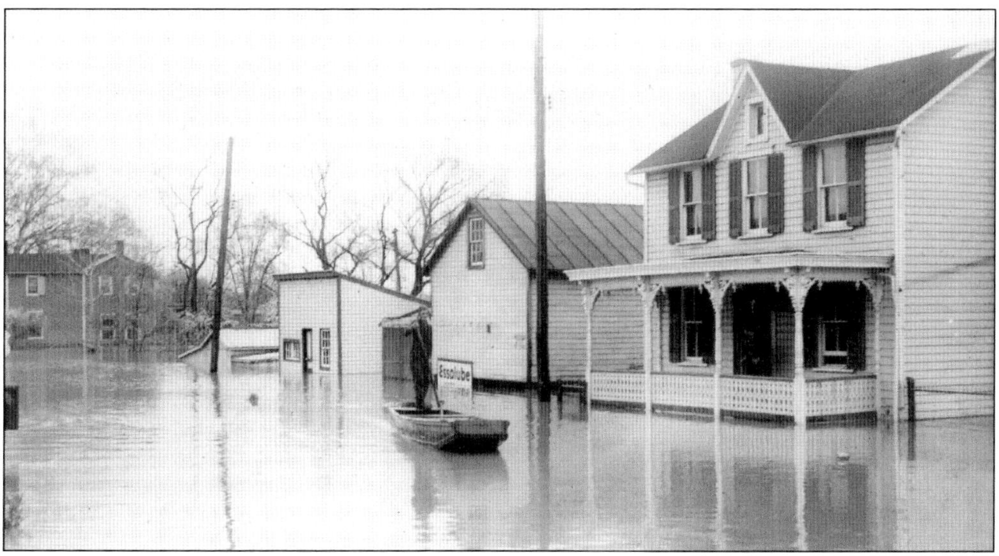

Boats were the preferred mode of transportation through the streets of Point of Rocks following another flood in March 1936. Its location along the Potomac River made the town particularly vulnerable to flooding. The 1936 flood was the most severe on record in the town.

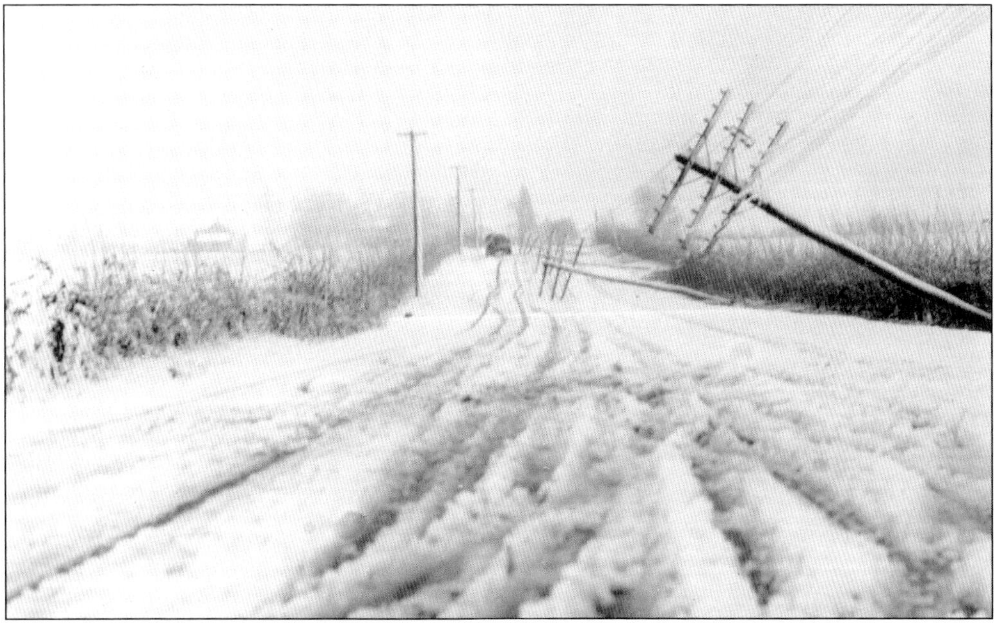

On March 6 and 7, 1932, a blizzard ravaged the area, leaving behind 3- to 4-foot snowdrifts throughout the county. Extensive damage was done to telephone and electric lines, as can be seen in this photograph taken along Jefferson Road in the storm's aftermath. Hundreds of motorists were stranded, and many more were left isolated in the worst storm of the decade.

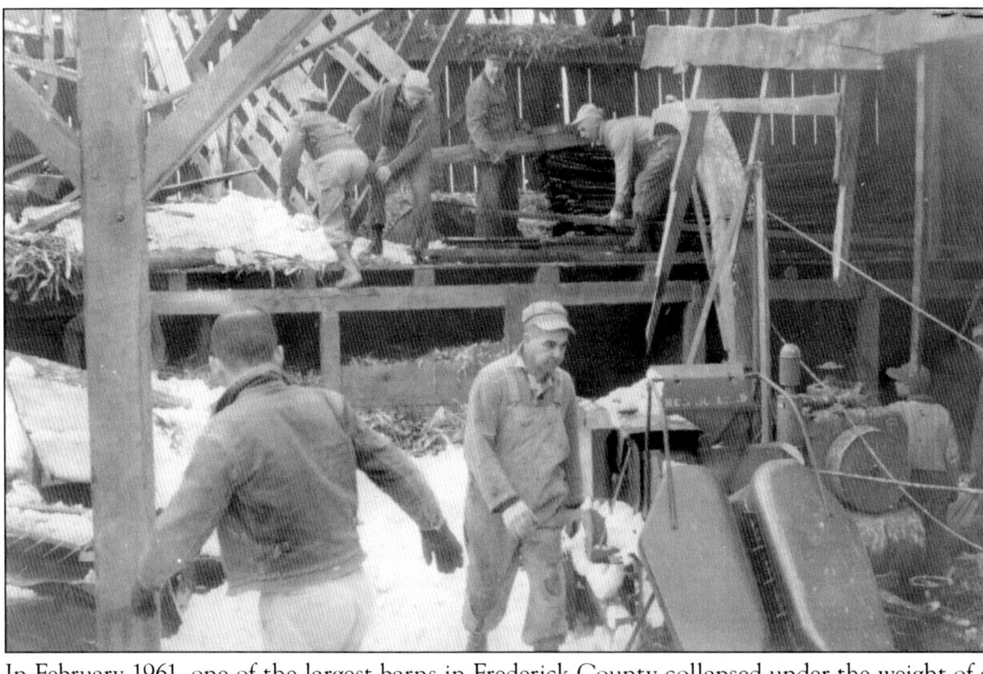

In February 1961, one of the largest barns in Frederick County collapsed under the weight of a heavy snowfall. The 50-by-150-foot barn near Creagerstown was owned by Edgar Emrich. Paul Beale captured this photograph of local good Samaritans assisting with cleanup. In the foreground are Robert Valentine (with his back to the camera) and William Baker, Thurmont High School agricultural instructor.

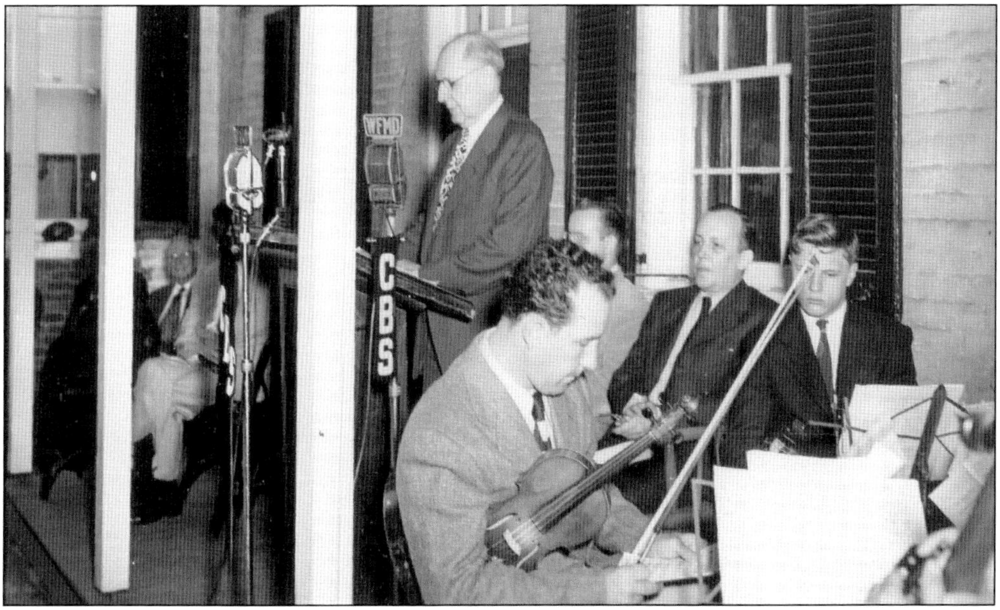

The Historical Society of Frederick County dedicated its first museum and headquarters facility, the Steiner House, on September 3, 1945. WFMD broadcast the ceremonies as part of Frederick's bicentennial celebration. The dedication featured guest speaker Sen. George L. Radcliffe. Historical Society president Marshall Etchison is seated directly behind him. After the Historical Society purchased its current Church Street property in 1959, the Steiner House was acquired by the Frederick Women's Civic Club.

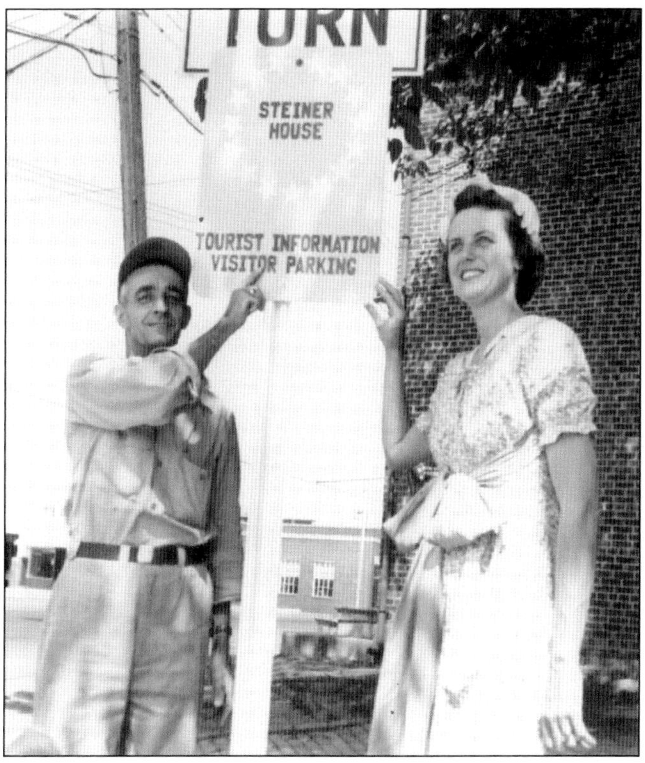

In 1962, the Frederick Women's Civic Club had big plans for the Steiner House, their newly acquired headquarters. Located on busy West Patrick Street (Route 40), they opened a tourist information center and gift shop featuring items made by local crafters. The center closed around 1968, but the house continues to serve as the club's meeting place today.

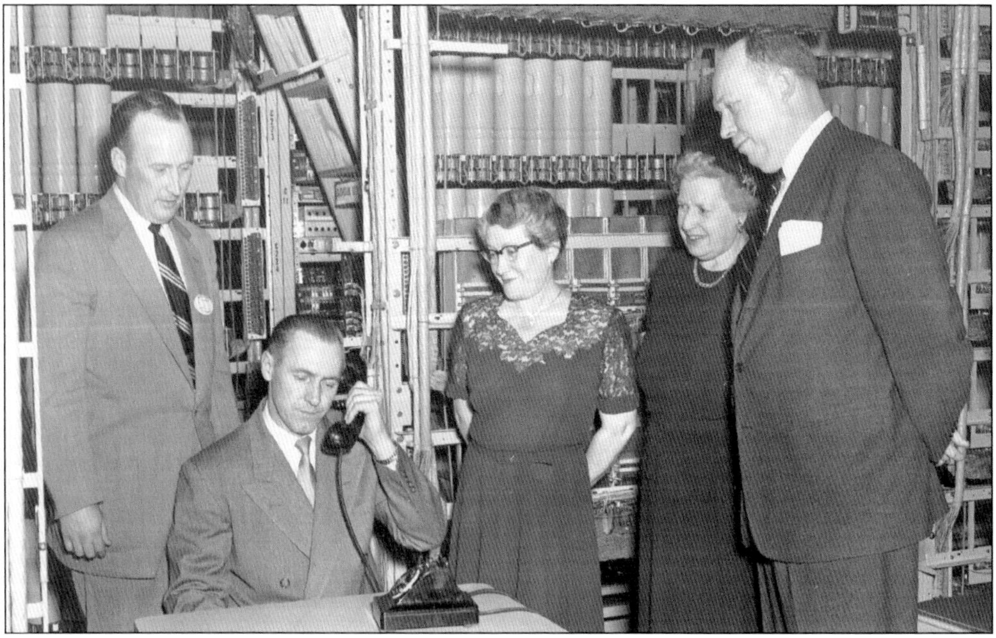

Photographer Frank Keefer captured the first telephone call over Frederick's new dial system in the wee hours of March 1, 1953. The original midnight changeover from the manual switchboard was postponed because of an emergency call on the system. Pictured from left to right are Walter Landus, C&P Telephone's local manager; Mayor Donald Rice making the call; Mrs. Paul I. Payne, whose late husband was local manager; Margaret Hartman, retired local operator; and W. Griffin Morrel, C&P vice president.

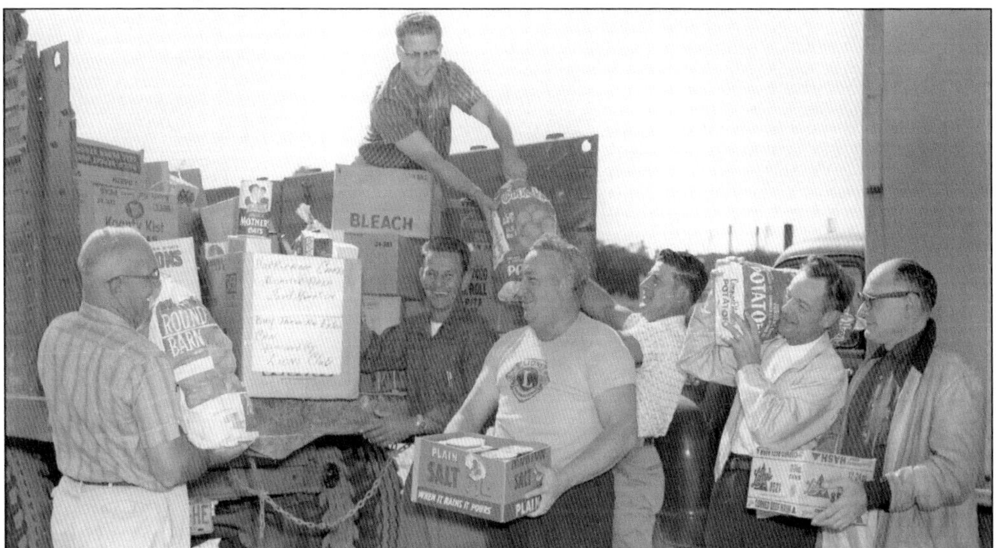

More than four decades before Hurricane Katrina swept across the Louisiana and Texas coastline, Hurricane Carla struck. The storm was the first dangerous and the deadliest to hit the United States in 1961, killing about 50 people and doing over $400 million in damage. In response, the Lions Clubs of Frederick County organized an emergency relief food drive. Here members of the Frederick Lions load relief supplies bound for Texas.

Ricky Tregoning happily received his first haircut in 1959 at the North End Barbershop on North Market Street in Frederick. The barber, Charles Schultz, wielded the clippers, following in the footsteps of such early Frederick barbers as Godfry Koontz, who advertised his sweet scented soap and keen razor in the local newspaper in 1824, and Evan Hopkins, who published his appreciation for his customers in 1830.

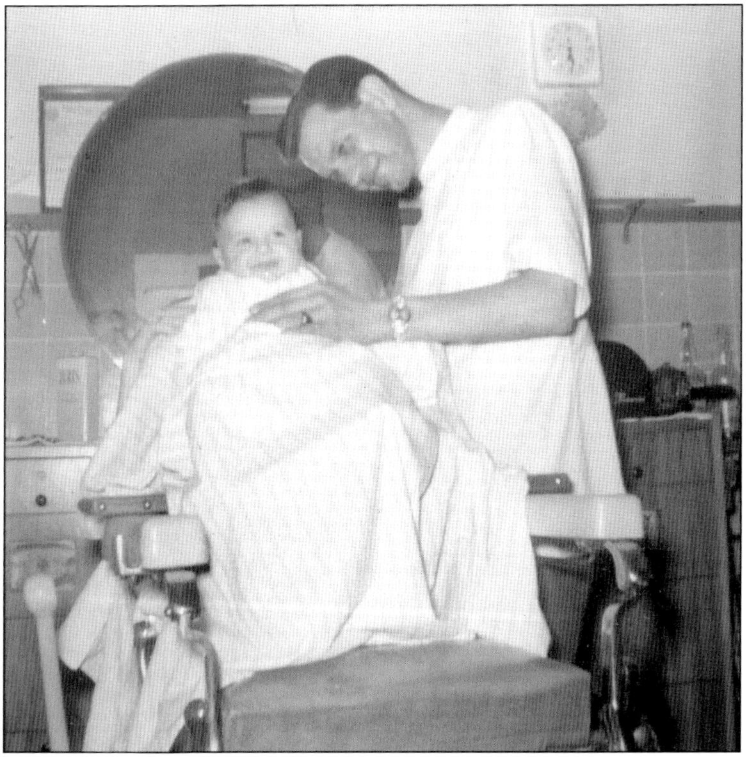

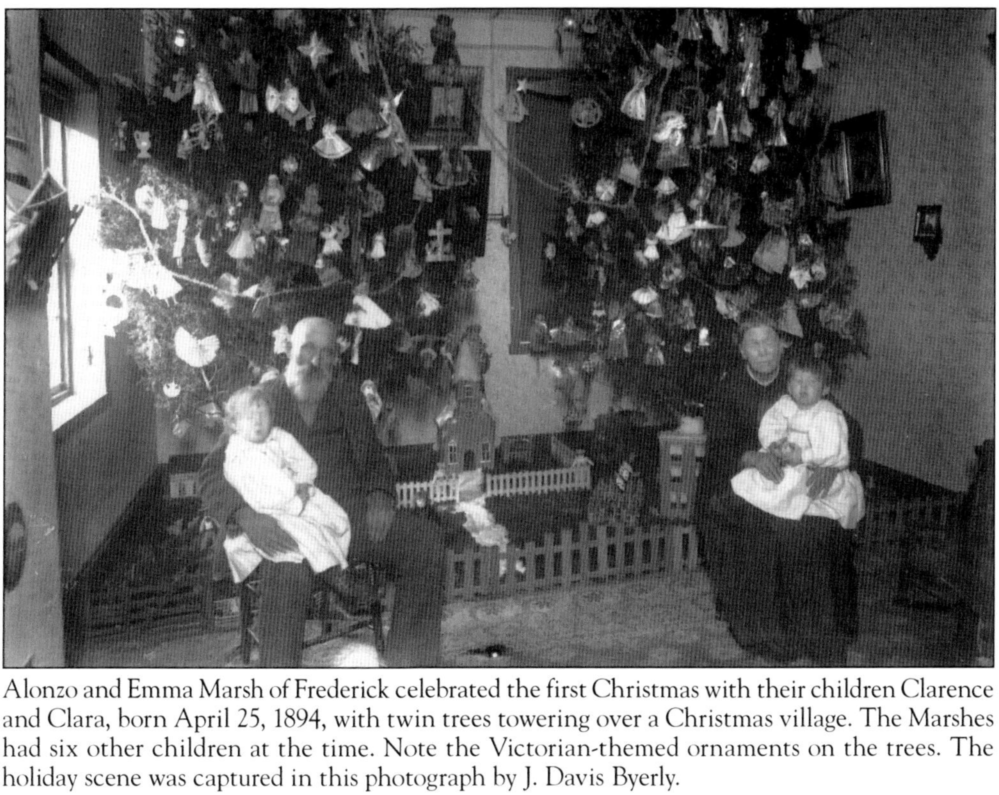

Alonzo and Emma Marsh of Frederick celebrated the first Christmas with their children Clarence and Clara, born April 25, 1894, with twin trees towering over a Christmas village. The Marshes had six other children at the time. Note the Victorian-themed ornaments on the trees. The holiday scene was captured in this photograph by J. Davis Byerly.

Although Santa Claus is beloved by children the world over, parents can attest that their initial reaction at meeting the jolly old man sometimes is like the one pictured here. Timmy Lee Wachter is not as pleased as his sister, Teresa K. Wachter, to have his photograph taken on Santa's lap at the Sears in Frederick *c.* 1960. In this case, Kris Kringle was portrayed by Augustine Wickless.

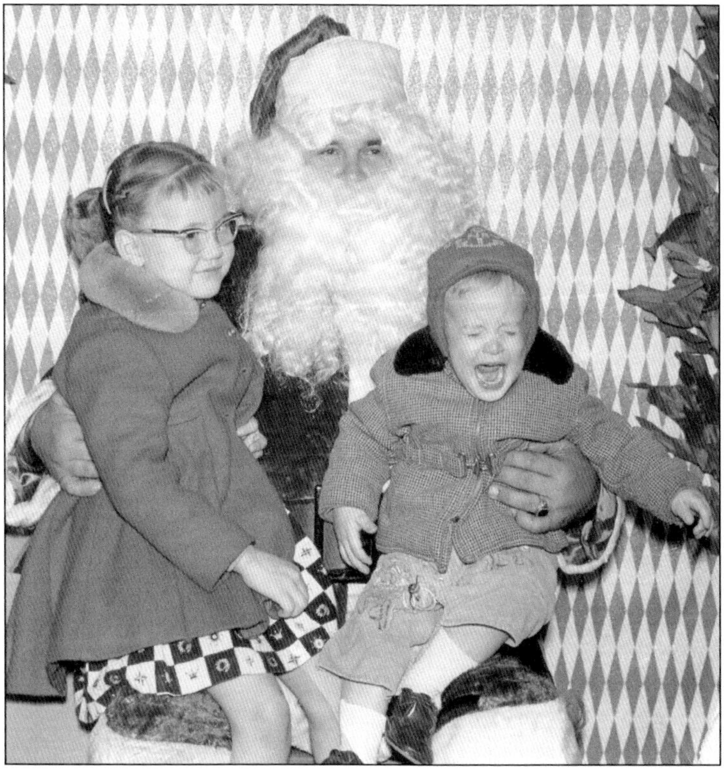

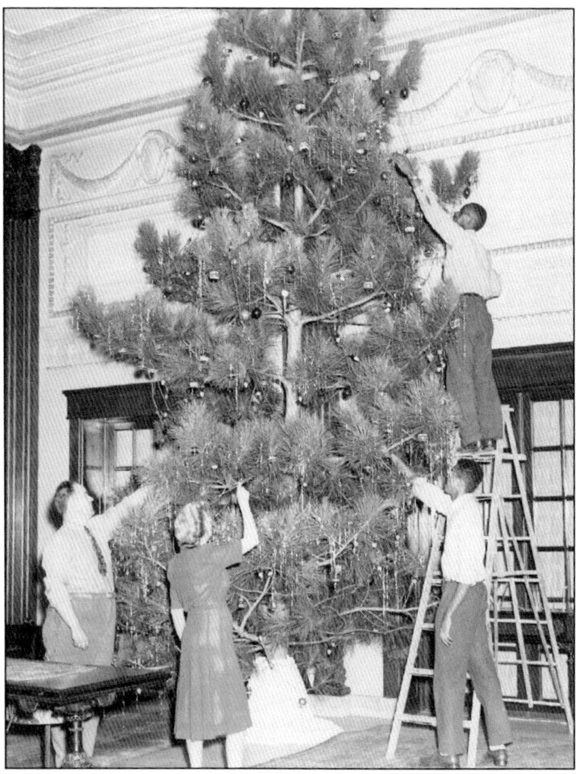

The Francis Scott Key Hotel in downtown Frederick hosted guests from the early 1920s to 1970s. Its lobby often was extravagantly decorated for Christmas, setting the mood for the many parties held there. Hotel housekeeper Hazel White (in foreground) once noted that each year some new decorations were added to the collection of decorations used in previous years. Helping her decorate are Raymond Skipper (left), George Jenkins (center), and John Hamilton.

Nine

PEOPLE AND PLACES

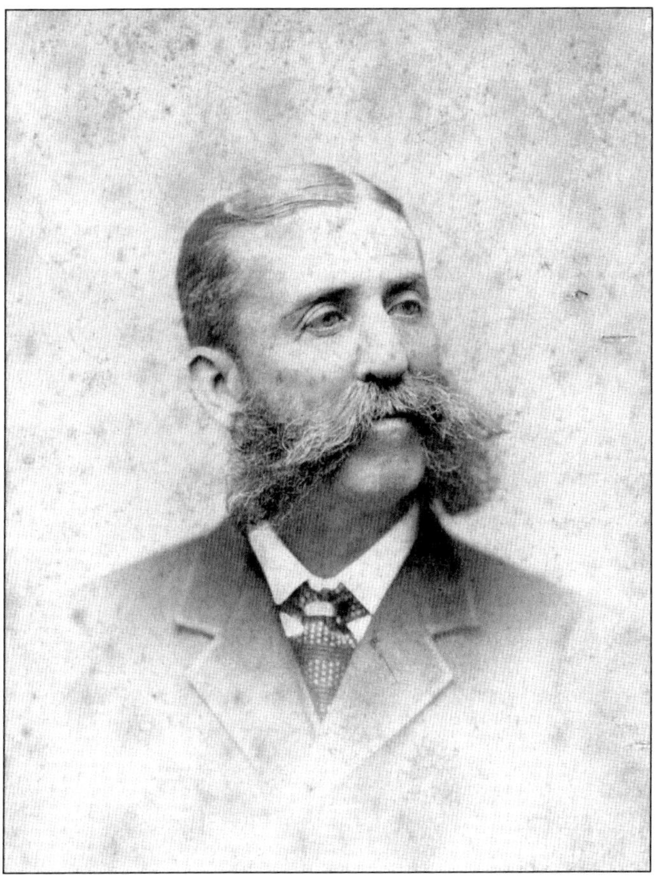

In 1861, during the Civil War, Luke Tiernan Brien served as the chief of staff for Gen. J. E. B. Stuart and, after one year of service, was elected lieutenant colonel of the 1st Virginia Cavalry. In 1864, he served as chief of staff for Gen. W. H. H. Lee. By 1882, Colonel Brien was husband to Mary V. Wilson and father of six children and had settled at the "Tyrone" homestead in Urbana district.

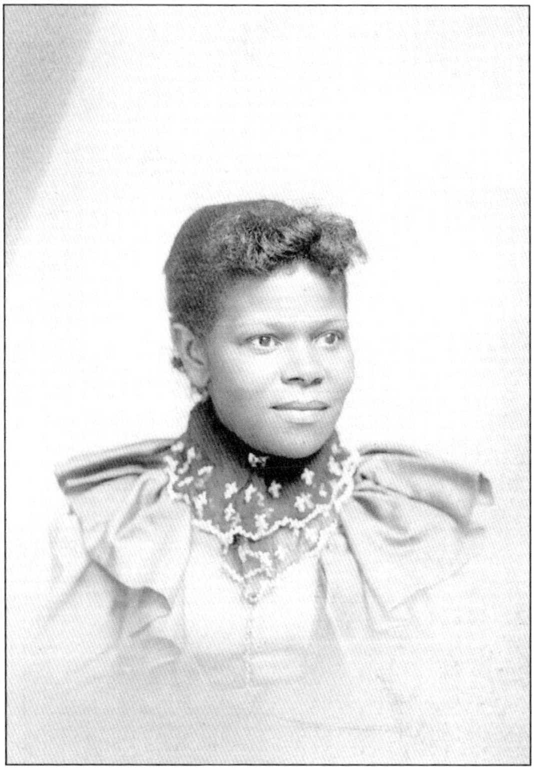

Young, attractive Pinkey Taylor of Frederick is pictured here in a portrait taken at the Byerly studios. Born in 1868, she earned her living working in the home of George Z. Best, a conductor on the Pennsylvania Railroad, and his wife. Taylor was a member of the Asbury Methodist Church, not far from the home she shared with her husband, Lewis W. Taylor, on West All Saints Street.

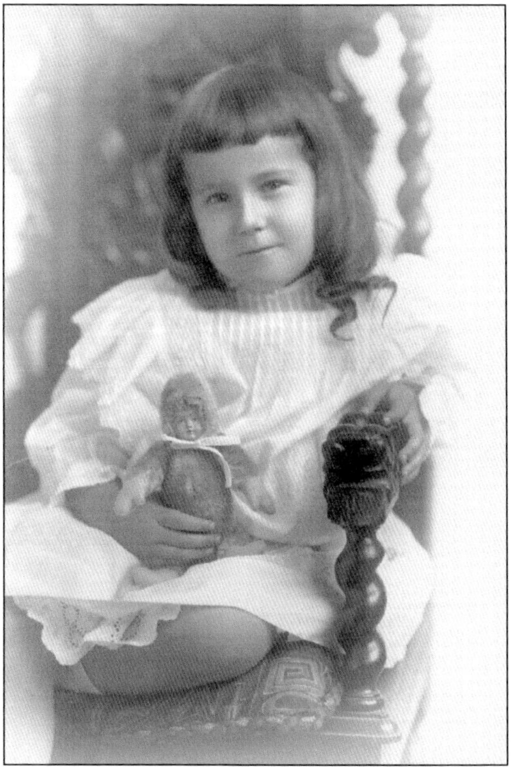

Little Josephine Etchison is proudly holding her snow baby in this 1908 photograph. The doll was inspired by a book written about Marie Peary, the daughter of Adm. Robert and Josephine Peary who was born on an Arctic expedition. Books figured large in Josephine Etchison's life; she would go on to Drexel University in Philadelphia for a degree in library science. She returned to Frederick to be the first director of the C. Burr Artz Library when it opened in 1937.

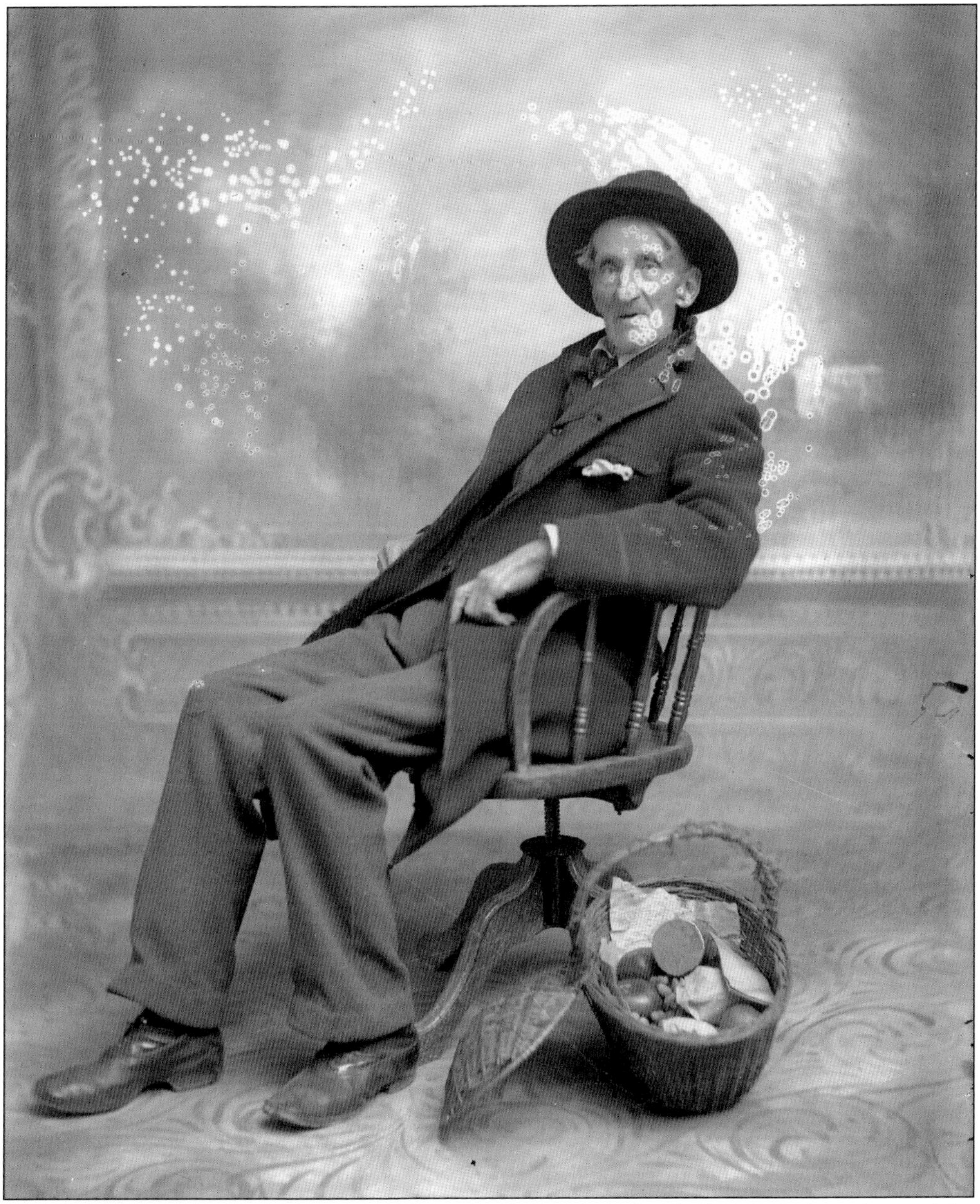

William H. Hilton, known as "Uncle Billy," was a beloved Frederick character. A graduate of the mathematics department at Frederick College, a local boys' school, Hilton opened a barbershop in the United States Hotel on Market Street in 1861. In his later years, he also became known as the "pretzel man" for selling pretzels and crullers on the streets of Frederick. A basket of his goods is seen in this Charles Byerly photograph. Sadly, Hilton died destitute at age 75 in 1914. His obituary stated, "Although he was never able to free himself from the gripping influence of Bacchus, 'Uncle Billy' was always a peaceful citizen, and his kindly manner, quaint knowledge and wise sayings made him a character of much interest, and he made friends with everybody." Frederick mayor Lewis Fraley and Leo Weinberg led a drive to raise funds—about $35—for Hilton's funeral and burial. Hilton's local celebrity was evident in 1910 when artist Jane Zimmerman rendered his likeness and had it printed on the top of calendars, which were wildly popular around town.

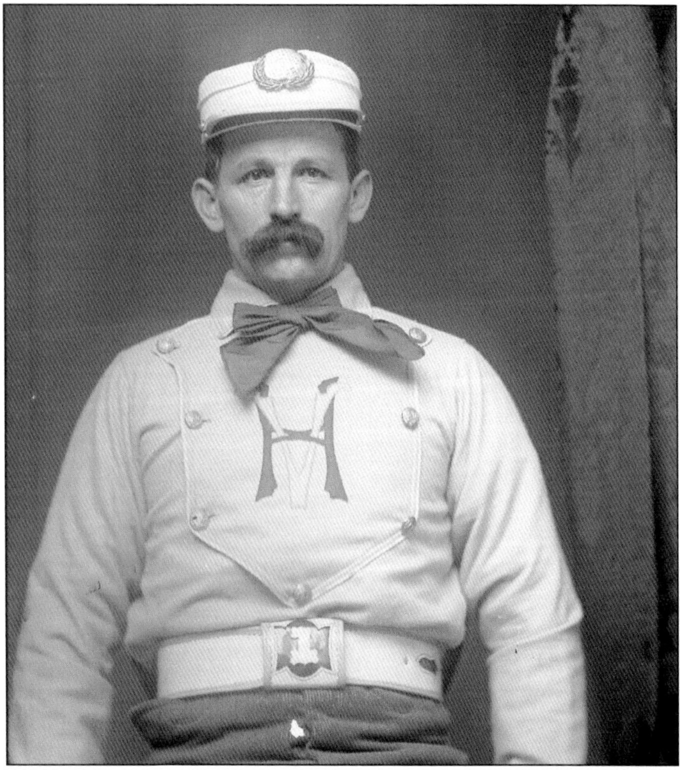

Edward Hoke Rowe, seen here in his parade uniform, was the first president of the Vigilant Hose Company in Emmitsburg. He was one of any number of dedicated men who helped establish the volunteer firefighting services throughout the county. The Vigilant Hose Company was founded in 1884 and still serves the Emmitsburg community to this day.

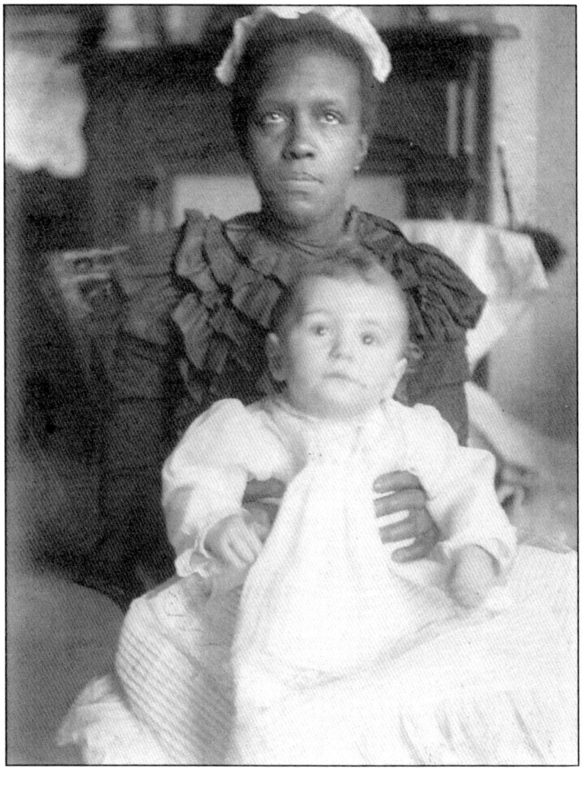

Charles Wertheimer Jr., pictured here with a young caretaker in 1901, was son of Fredericktonians Charles and Annie Wertheimer. Charles Sr. was a partner in the Lowenstein and Wertheimer mercantile house, vice president of the Central National Bank of Frederick, and owner of several farms, including Elmwood Dairy Farm. Charles Jr. ran Elmwood for a time before his death from tuberculosis at age 22 on January 21, 1924. His death was reported that evening on the front page of the Frederick *News*.

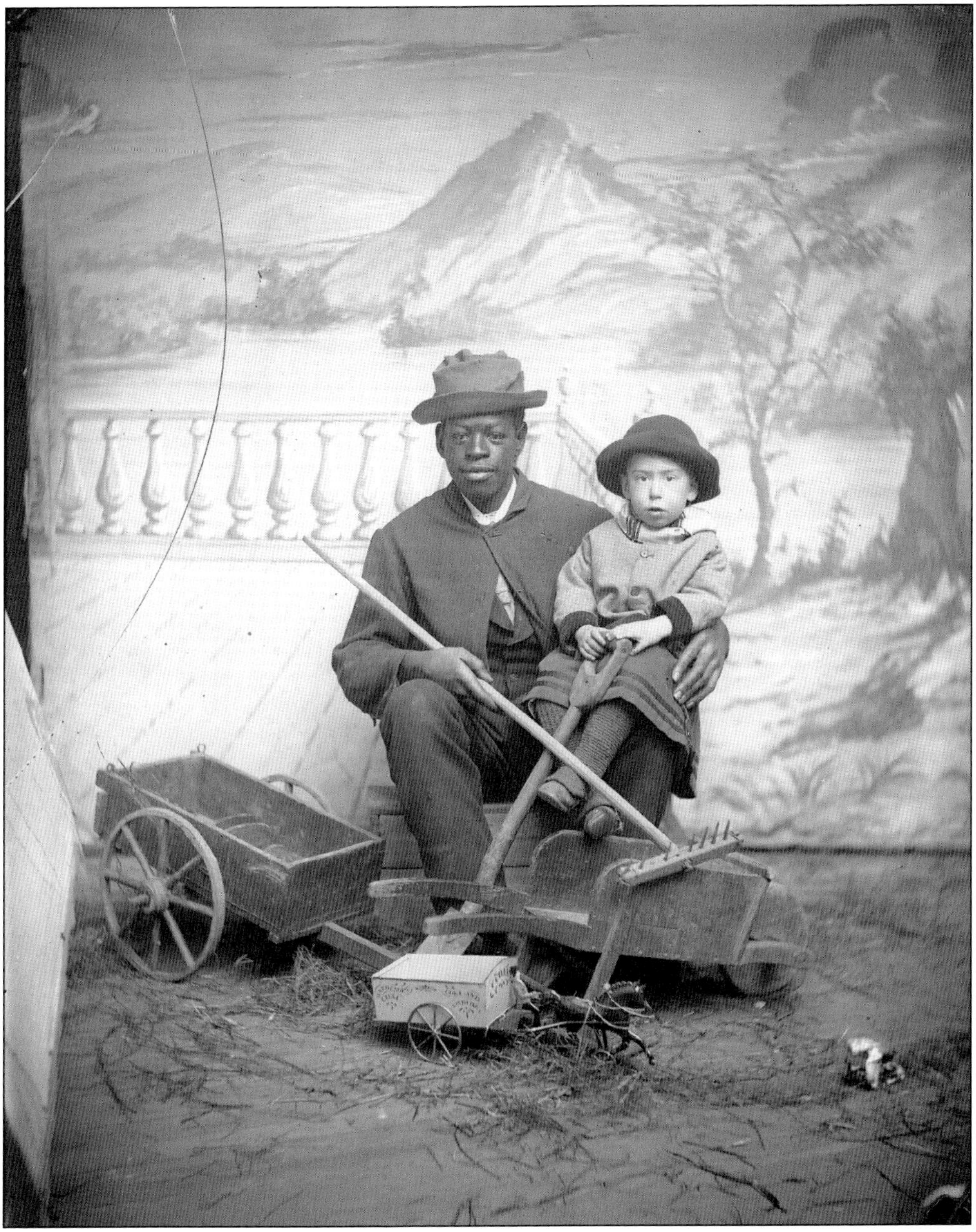

John Francis Byerly took this photograph of his son, Charles, and Luther Potts, the family's handyman, about 1880. Potts was an organizer against Frederick's registration law in the 1913 municipal election. The law required that only those males who owned more than $500 worth of property and were eligible to vote, or were male descendants of someone who was eligible to vote, in a state election before January 1, 1869, could register. The law was aimed directly at the local black community. It was challenged in court, and pending a decision, Potts and about 30 others tried to register but were refused because of the "grandfather clause." They believed that the law was in conflict with the 15th Amendment to the U.S. Constitution; city attorneys claimed that the amendment regarded only federal elections. On May 16, county judges disagreed and declared both clauses unconstitutional.

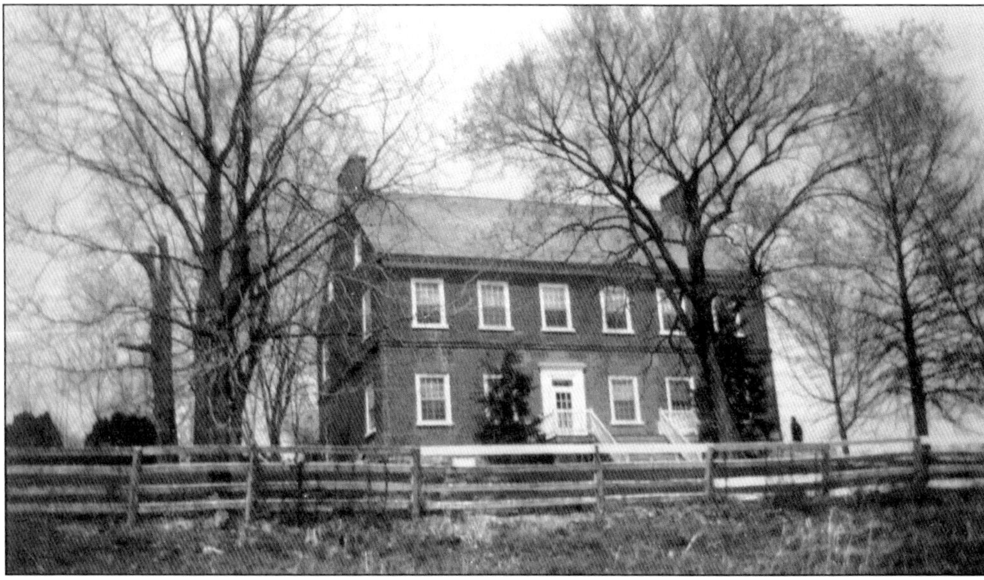

The Amelung home was built overlooking Bennett's Creek near Urbana in 1784 by John Friedrich Amelung, a German immigrant and glassmaker. His nearby glassworks employed over 300 people and produced window glass, bottles, presentation pieces, and tableware. Despite the quality of his glass, Amelung's venture failed and he was bankrupt by 1795. The "New Bremen" settlement he had created for his workers quickly disappeared. Today Amelung glass is sought-after and highly collectible.

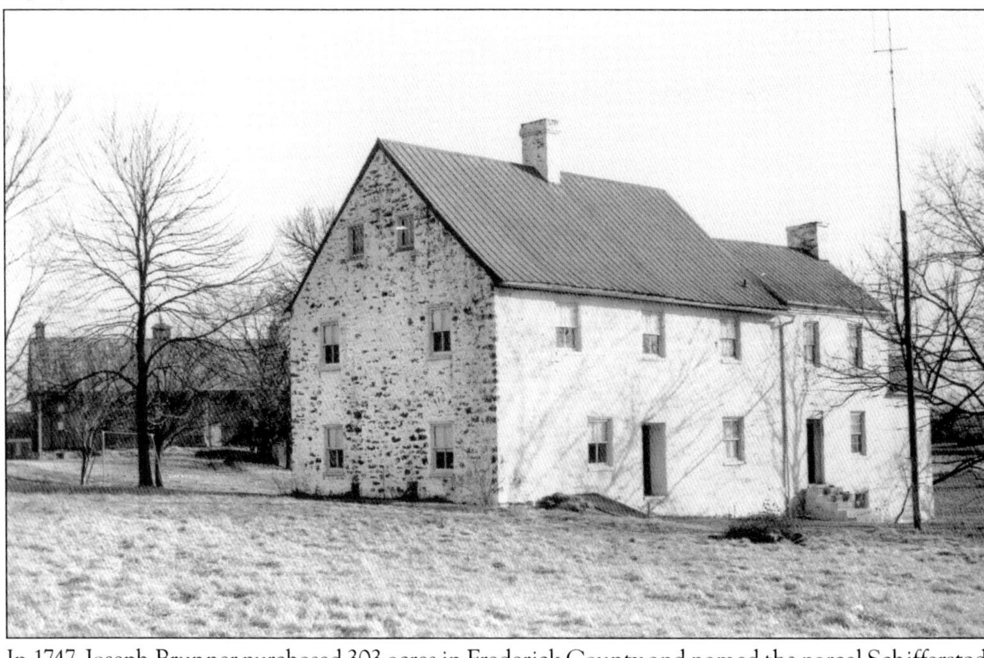

In 1747, Joseph Brunner purchased 303 acres in Frederick County and named the parcel Schifferstadt after his native home in Germany. Brunner's son, Elias, built the stone section of the house in 1756. The house was saved from demolition in 1974 by the Frederick County Landmarks Foundation and is now operated as Schifferstadt Architectural Museum, which shares information about the German architecture found inside the oldest extant house in Frederick.

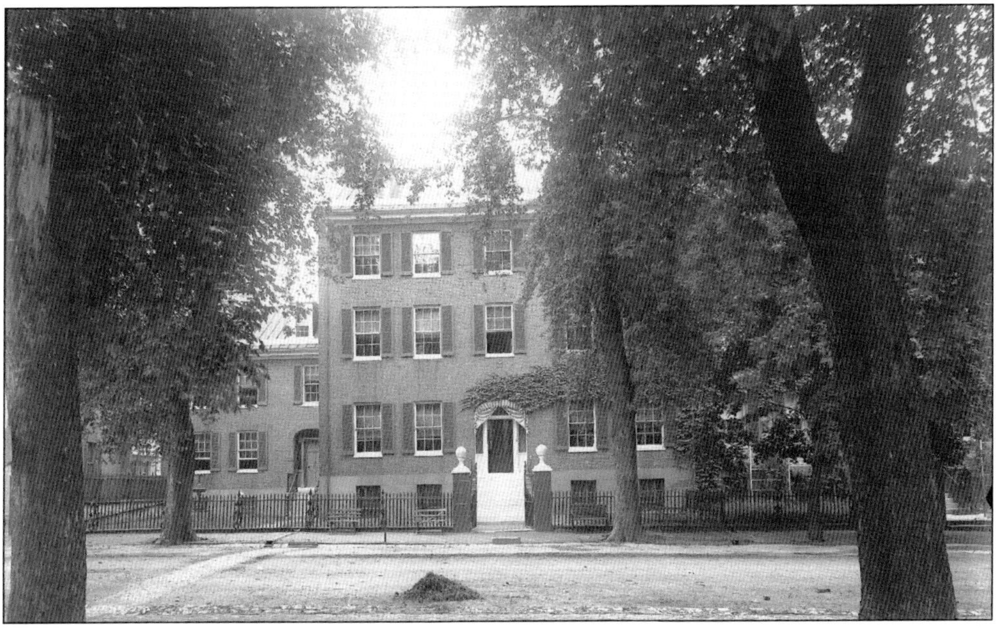

The pile of manure on the street in front of the Ross House on Council Street in Frederick hardly reflects its dignified history. The property was purchased in 1815 by Col. John McPherson, who owned Catoctin Furnace. The family entertained the Marquis de Lafayette at the residence during his 1824 visit to Frederick. John Brien, McPherson's partner and son-in-law, lived in an identical home next door. The iron fence was cast at the Catoctin Furnace.

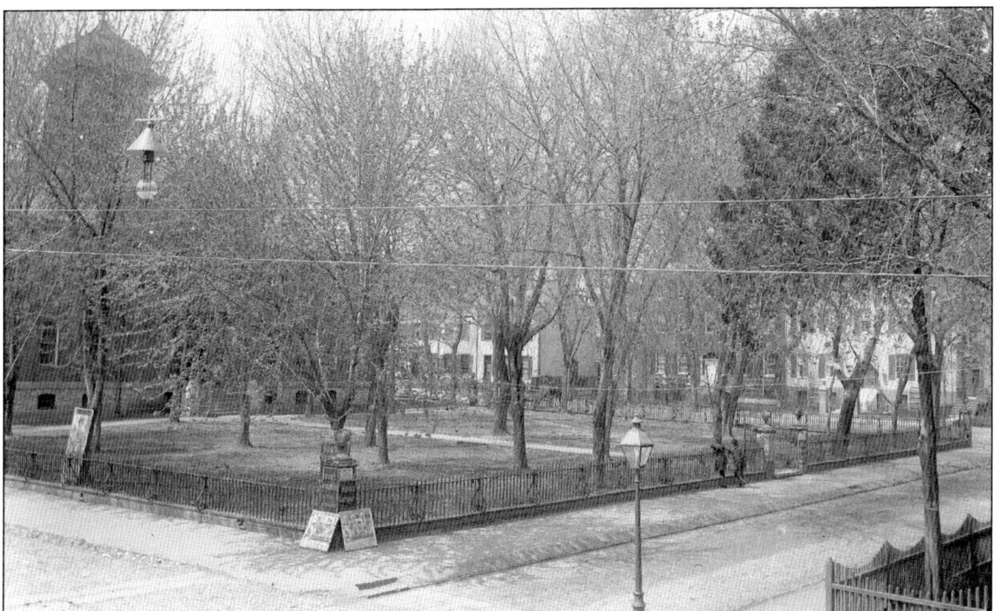

This view of Frederick's Courthouse Square was taken about 1900. The courthouse, Frederick County's third on the site, was erected in 1862 following a fire that destroyed the previous one. Controversy erupted when it was proposed to tear out the iron fence. In 1912, after the fence's removal, the futility of the opposition to such progress was used by the *Evening Post* to encourage citizens to vote for Frederick's new charter. The courthouse now is home to Frederick City Hall.

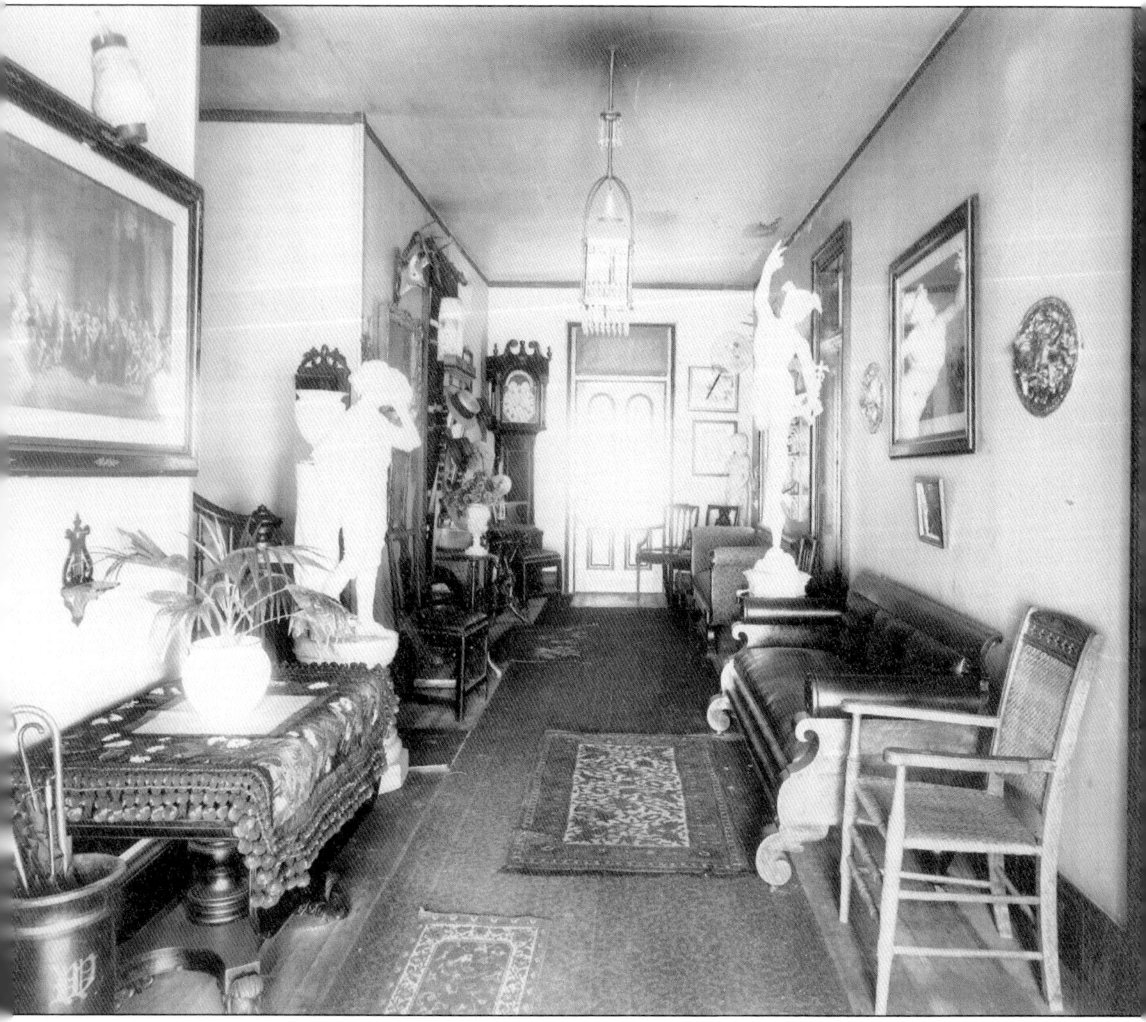

From this vantage point right inside the front door, Janet Williams's house at 22 South Market Street in Frederick is the epitome of a late-Victorian home. Decorating in the last half of the 19th century and first few decades of the 20th involved a great deal of layering: putting things on top of things, like the throw rugs on top of the hall carpet, or the plant on top of the doily on top of the throw, which covers the table at the left. Several generations of furniture are here as well, illustrating the owner's long-established ties to this country, an important distinction during an era of increased immigration. Williams lived in the house with her cousin, Eleanor Shriver, to whom she left the use of the property after her death in 1922. When Shriver died in 1930, the house became the headquarters of the Federated Charities Corporation of Frederick in accordance with Williams's will.

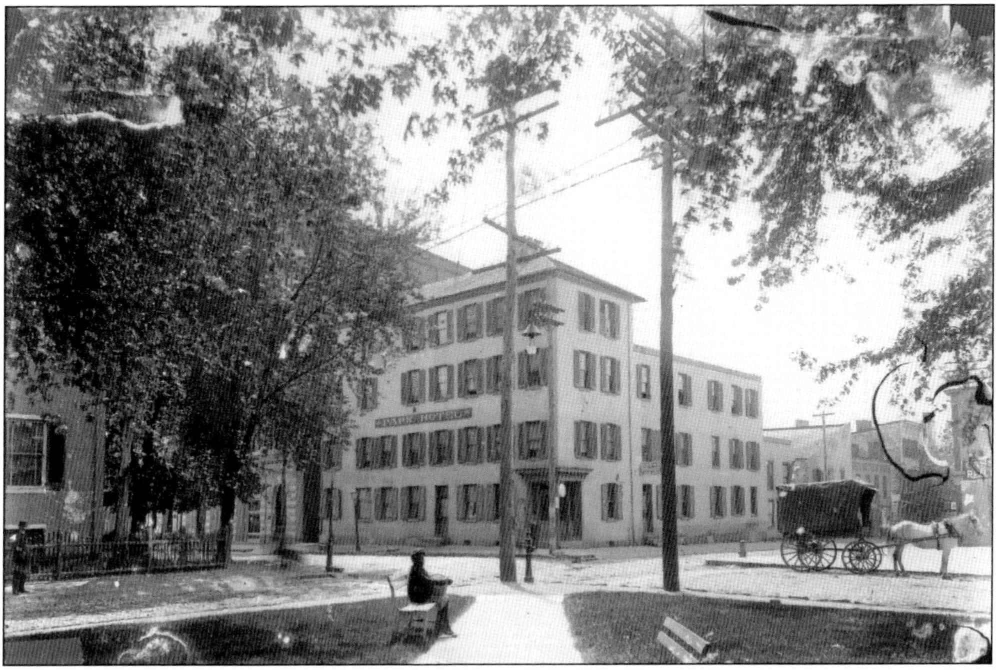

E. E. Steele, proprietor of the Park Hotel, celebrated the hotel's grand opening on Saturday, May 10, 1902, with music all evening. Once standing at the southeast corner of Church and Court Streets, the Park Hotel welcomed visitors to Frederick. The site had been home to many other hotels from the late 19th century. By 1906, a new YMCA building was constructed on the site. That building burned in 1974.

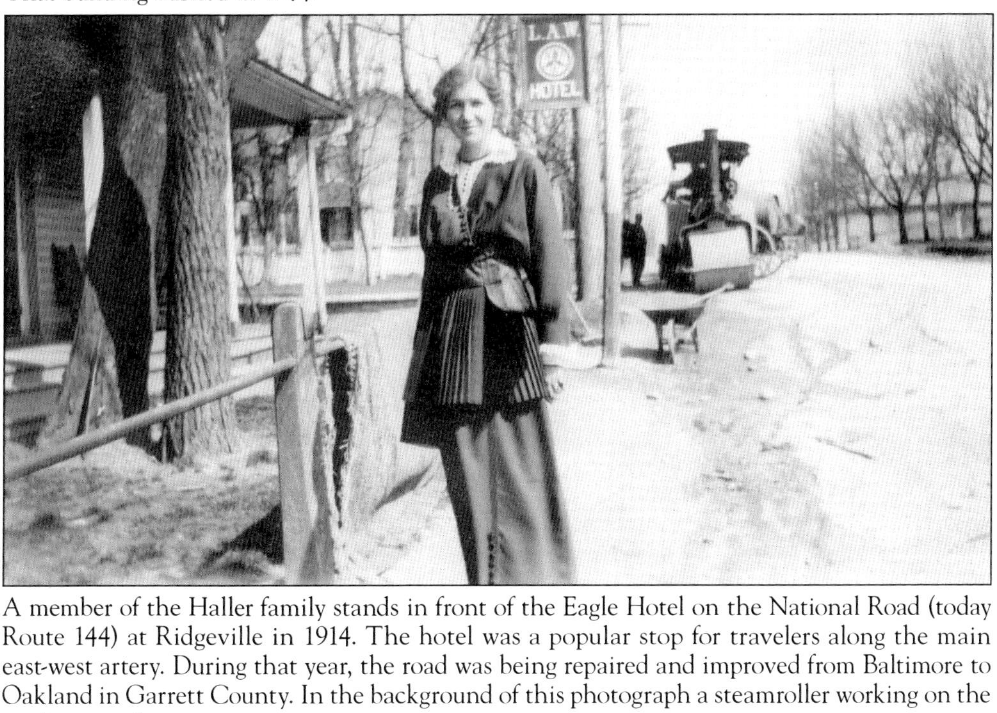

A member of the Haller family stands in front of the Eagle Hotel on the National Road (today Route 144) at Ridgeville in 1914. The hotel was a popular stop for travelers along the main east-west artery. During that year, the road was being repaired and improved from Baltimore to Oakland in Garrett County. In the background of this photograph a steamroller working on the roadway can be seen.

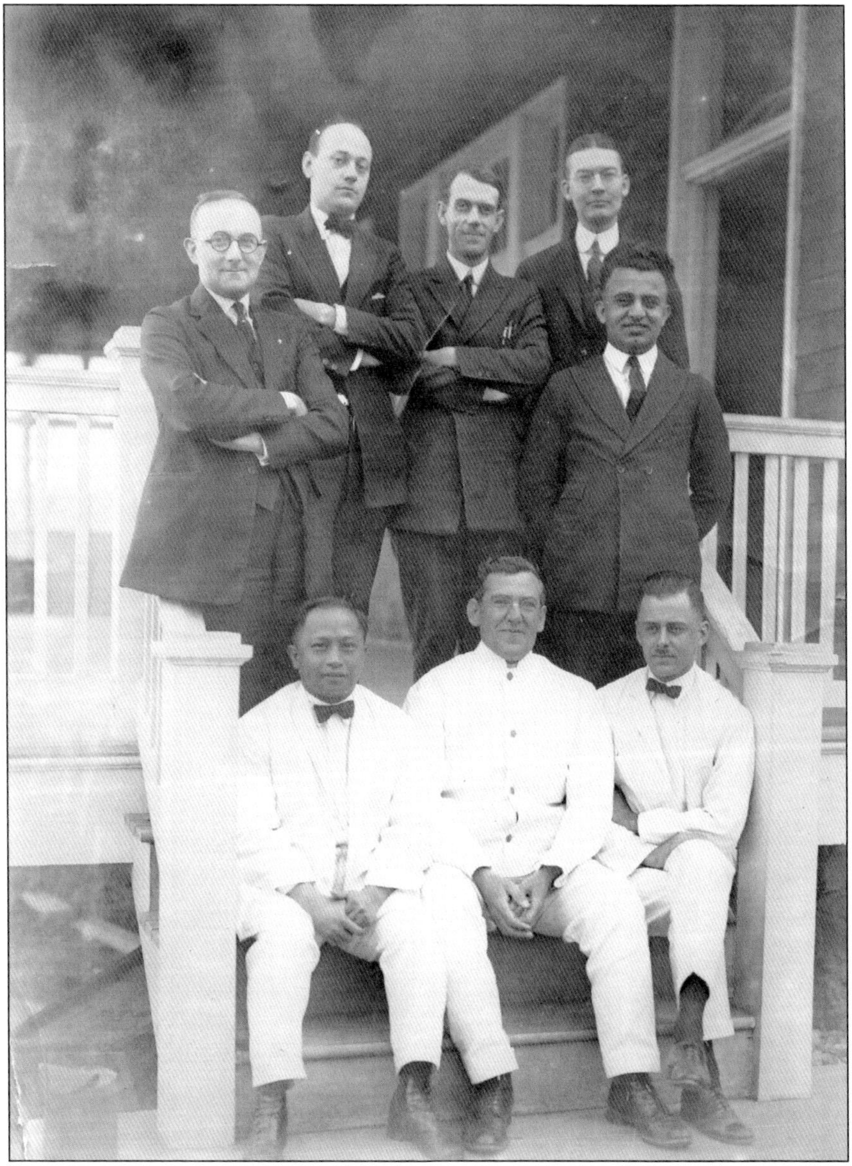

Dr. Victor F. Cullen, at left in the second row in this *c.* 1925 photograph, worked for about 40 years as superintendent of the Maryland State Sanatorium, established in 1906 near Sabillasville. While suffering from tuberculosis, he visited the state sanatorium and found it to be a primitive cluster of patient shacks and an administration building on a 198-acre tract of land. He offered his services and was appointed superintendent in 1909. Under his leadership, the hospital complex grew to include patient cottages and wards, staff residences, a railroad stop and post office, a store, an entertainment pavilion, a school, a working farm, and other facilities needed to make the hospital a nearly self-sufficient village. The hospital's patient population peaked at 510 in the late 1930s. Cullen opened a nursing school at the hospital to train young women as nurses specifically educated to care for tuberculosis sufferers. After his death in 1949, the hospital was renamed in his honor. The hospital closed in 1965, but his name was retained when the Maryland State Department of Juvenile Services reopened the facility as the Victor Cullen Center, a home for delinquent boys.

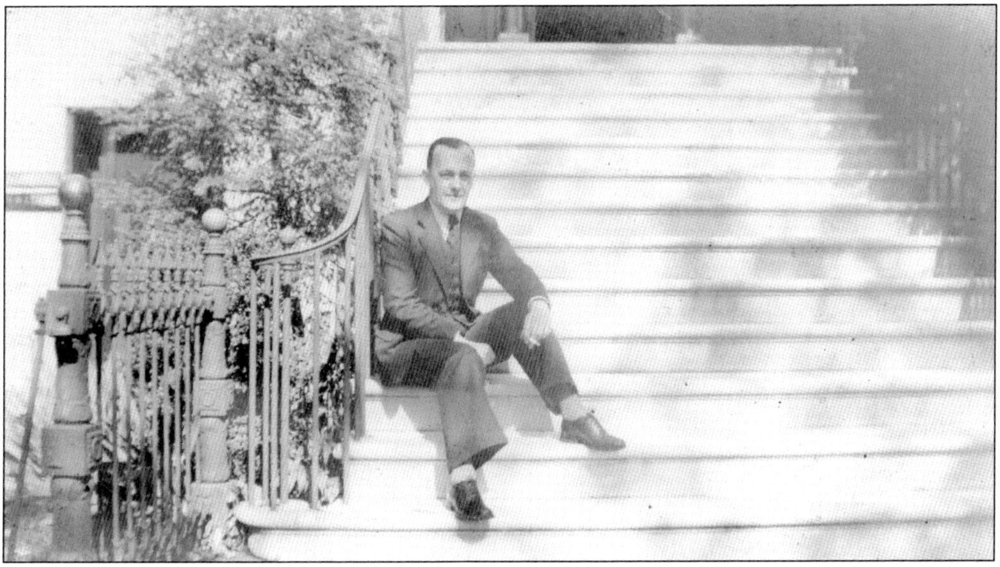

Marshall Lingan Etchison was often described as a "connoisseur of everything," and he may have been. Etchison taught piano at his studio on Church Street in Frederick for 34 years. He also began collecting antiques in earnest as a young man. Though he traveled the world in search of treasures, he had a keen interest in local history and served as president of the Historical Society of Frederick County from 1944 to 1946. Following his death in 1960, much of his eclectic collection was donated to the society.

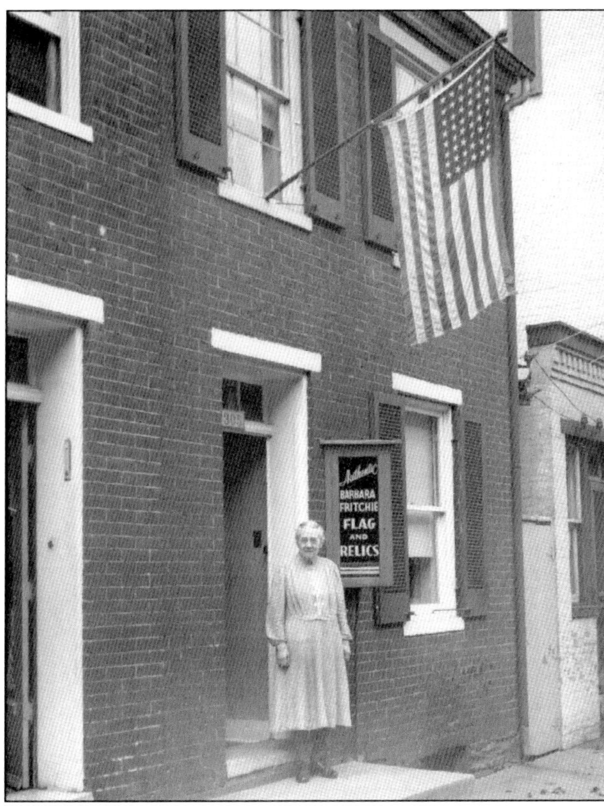

Posed at her home on South Market Street in Frederick, Eleanor Abbott proudly invites the public to see her collection of Barbara Fritchie memorabilia. Born in 1870, Abbott was great-grandniece of John Greenleaf Whittier's Civil War heroine and was happy to perpetuate her aunt's notoriety. Abbott was first engaged as hostess of the newly reconstructed Barbara Fritchie House in 1927, but in 1933, she left the popular tourist attraction and took her family relics with her.

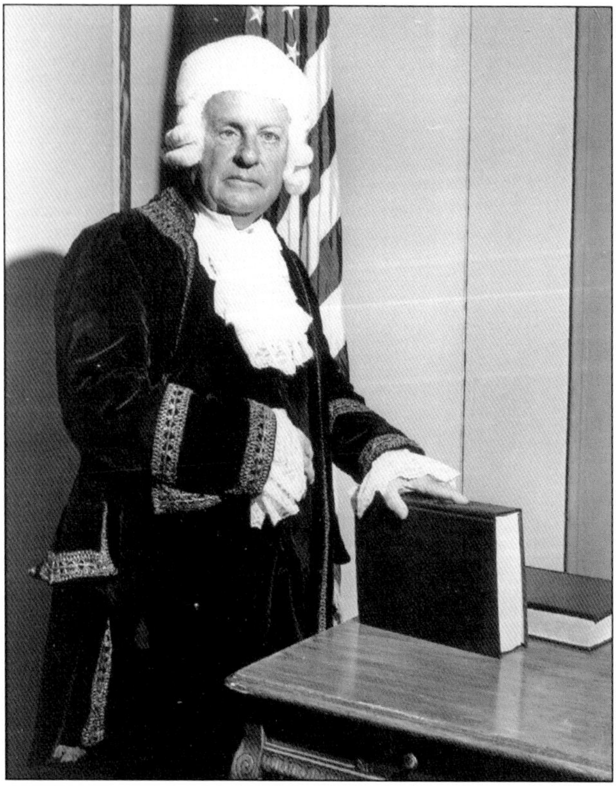

Harry L. Decker portrayed Pres. James Madison in *The Treason Trial of General Wilkinson*, a play he wrote, in 1976. Decker was employed for 45 years by the Potomac Edison Company, but his passion was local history. Also involved with theater, he married his hobbies in this play, performed as part of Frederick's U.S. bicentennial celebration. The Historical Society of Frederick County sponsors an annual essay contest for fourth graders named in his honor.

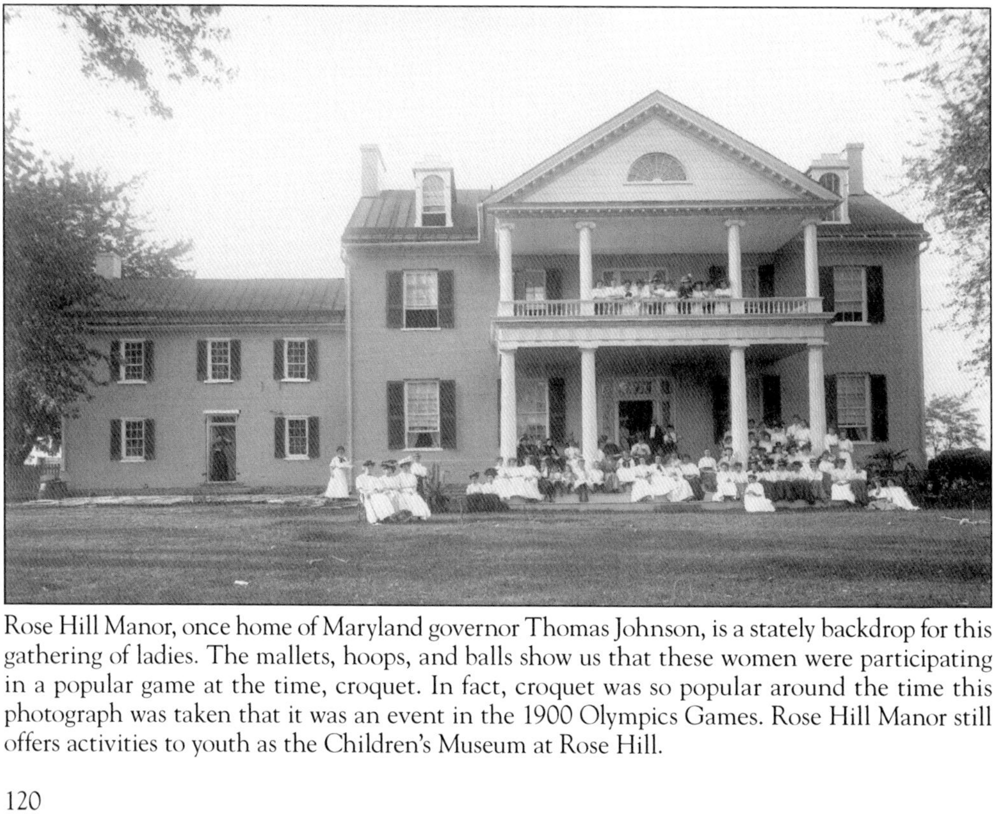

Rose Hill Manor, once home of Maryland governor Thomas Johnson, is a stately backdrop for this gathering of ladies. The mallets, hoops, and balls show us that these women were participating in a popular game at the time, croquet. In fact, croquet was so popular around the time this photograph was taken that it was an event in the 1900 Olympics Games. Rose Hill Manor still offers activities to youth as the Children's Museum at Rose Hill.

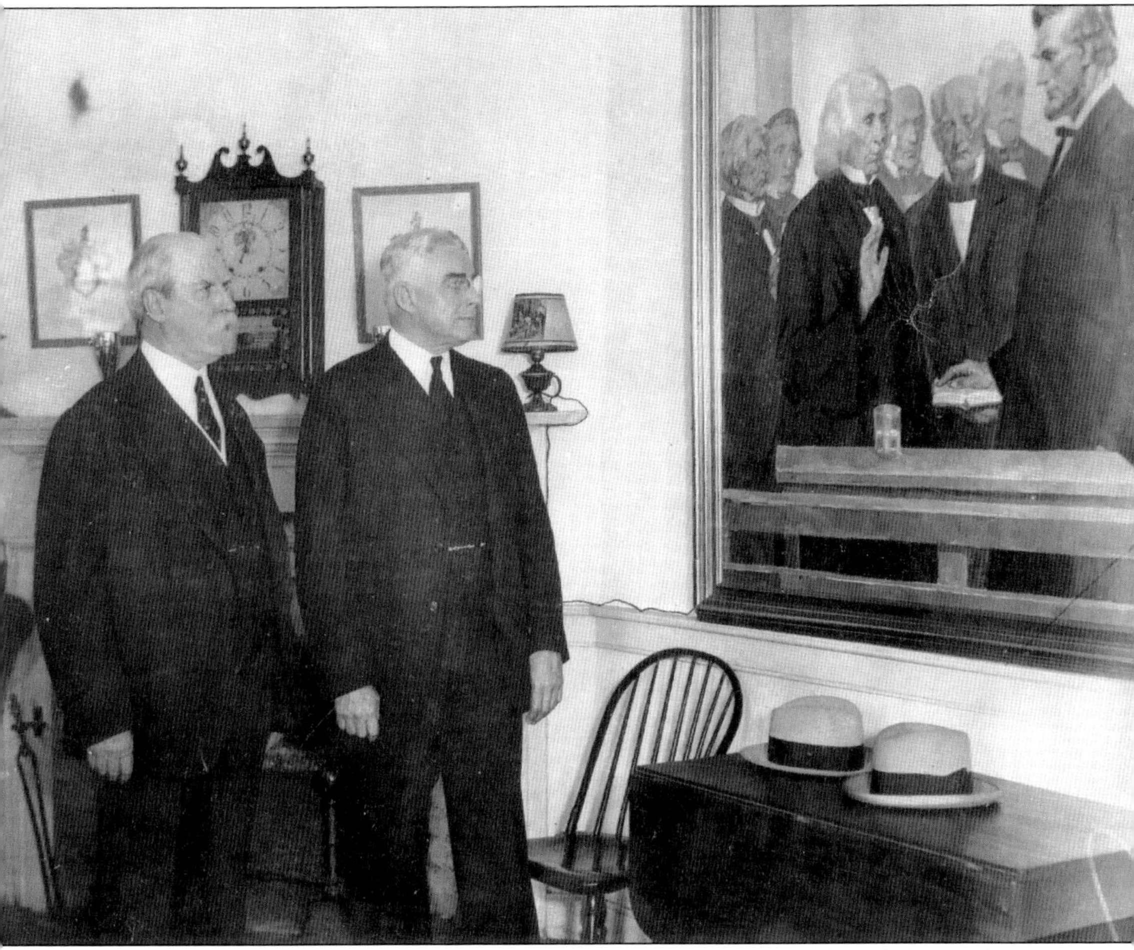

On September 26, 1931, Chief Justice Charles Evans Hughes visited Frederick to dedicate a bust of former chief justice Roger Brooke Taney at the Frederick County Courthouse. The ceremony, broadcast live on national radio, was followed by a visit to Taney's grave site at St. John's Cemetery. Chief Justice Hughes, at left, also was given a tour of the Roger Brooke Taney Home on Bentz Street by Maryland governor Albert C. Ritchie. The two men are pictured gazing at Henry Roben's painting of Justice Taney administering the oath of office to Abraham Lincoln. Chief Justice Hughes was one of a number of Supreme Court justices who have visited the historic site since it opened in 1930, including, most recently, the late Chief Justice William H. Rehnquist and Justice Sandra Day O'Connor. The Taney House now is operated as a museum by the Historical Society of Frederick County.

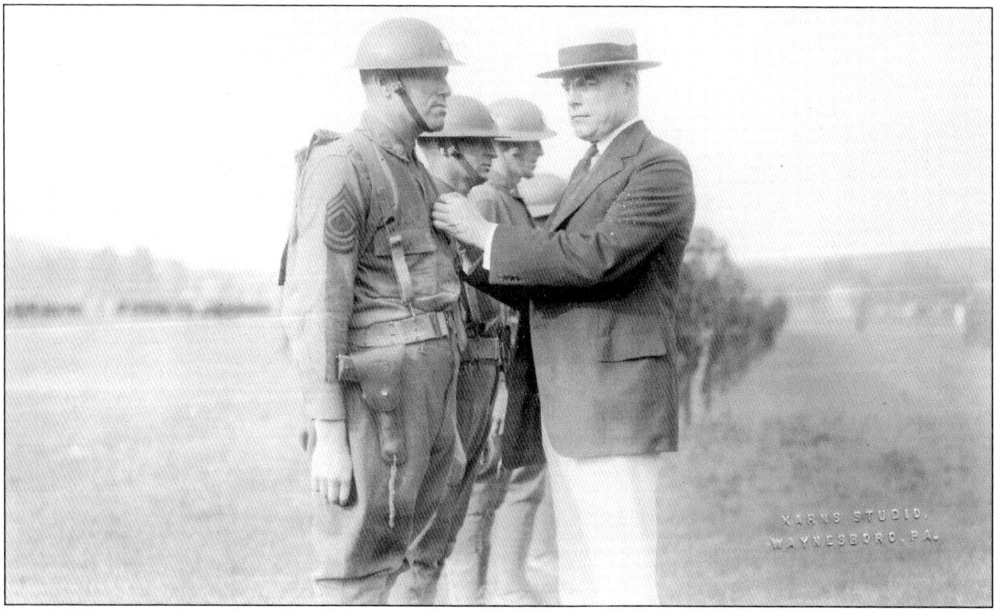

Gov. Albert Ritchie awarded ribbons for marksmanship during his August 10, 1928, visit to Camp Ritchie, a National Guard installation in northern Frederick County named in his honor. He was there to observe 1,200 guardsmen who were engaged in a 15-day training exercise. Governor Ritchie was greeted with a 19-gun salute, a reception, and a luncheon and, like any savvy politician, enjoyed a photo opportunity.

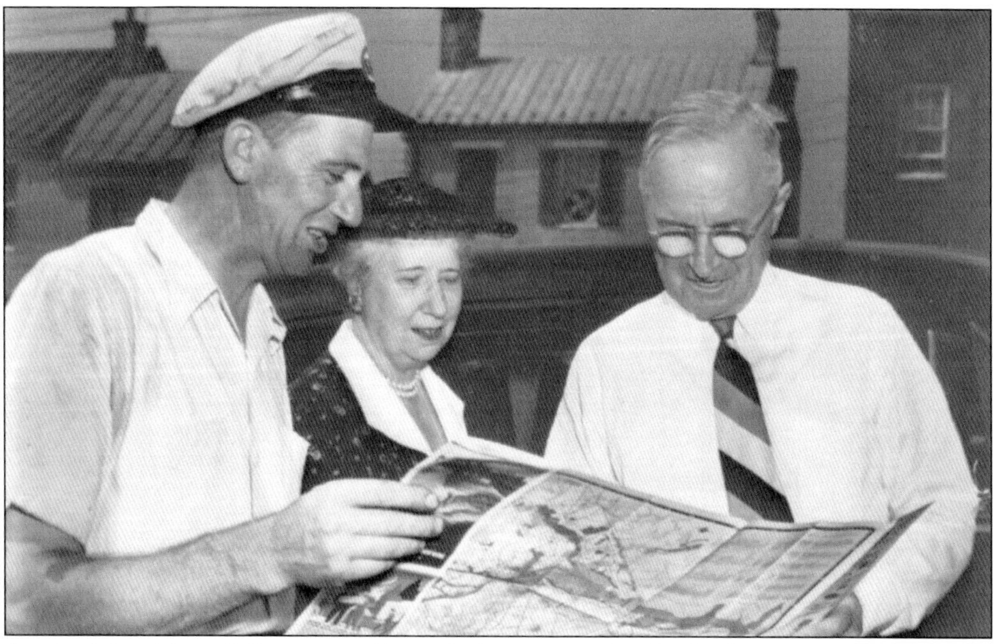

A retired Pres. Harry S. Truman and his wife, Bess, stopped at the Gulf service station of Carroll Kehne (at left) on West Patrick Street in Frederick on a sweltering July 21, 1953. The president filled up his Chrysler, cooled down with a Coke, and posed for the herd of press that had caught up with him. Truman, no stranger to Frederick County, was motoring from his home in Missouri to Washington, D.C. The station was torn down in 1975.

C. Clifton Virts, blind for most of his life, did not let this fact limit him. He served in the Maryland Legislature for 32 years and then worked as a Frederick County court examiner until his death in 1985. He and his service dog, Omar, were a common sight around Frederick. Omar was a celebrity in his own right and has a street named in his honor. This image was taken in Baker Park for the 1946 political campaign.

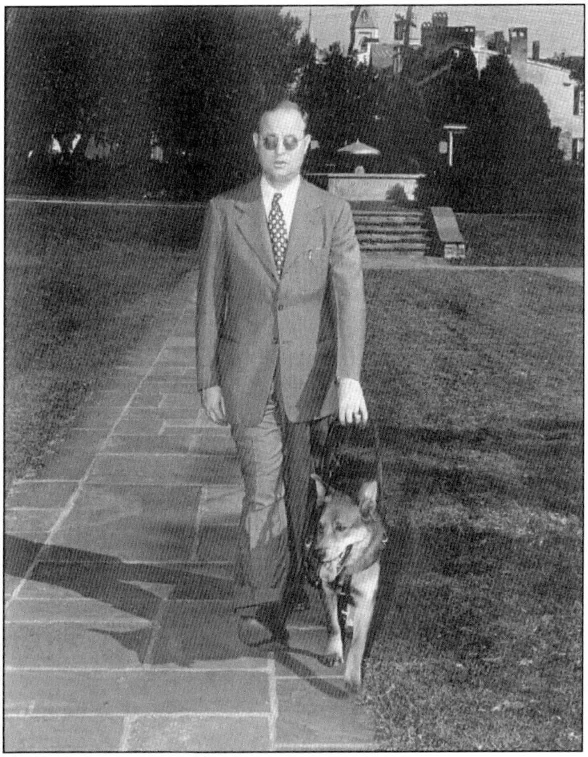

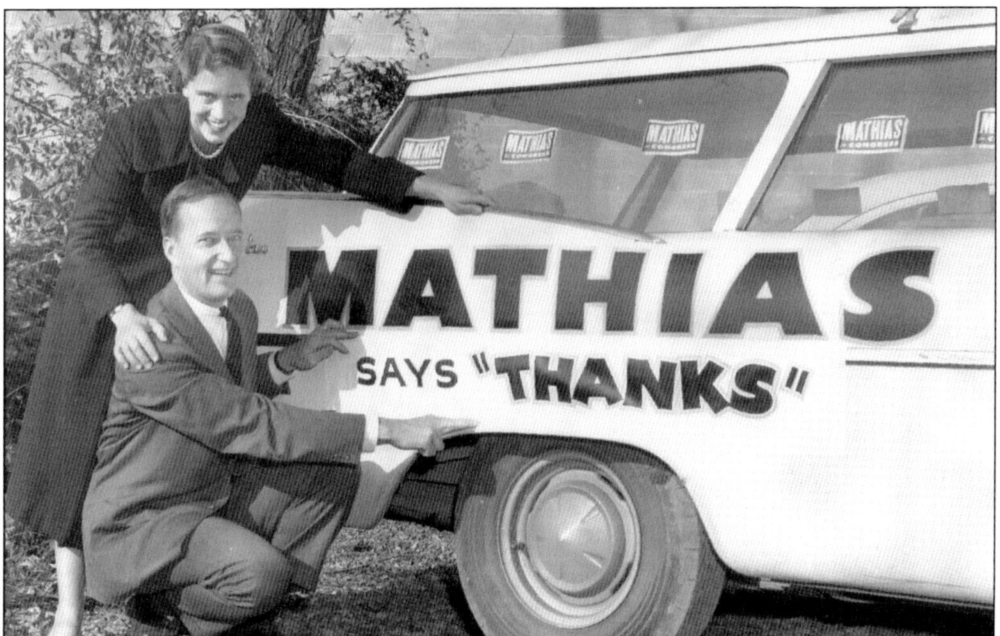

Charles "Mac" and Ann Mathias celebrated Mac's election to Congress from Maryland's Sixth District with a "thank you" tour of the district in the days following the election. Mathias, a Frederick County native, served as the Sixth District Representative from 1961 to 1969. He then served three terms as U.S. senator from Maryland from 1969 to 1987.

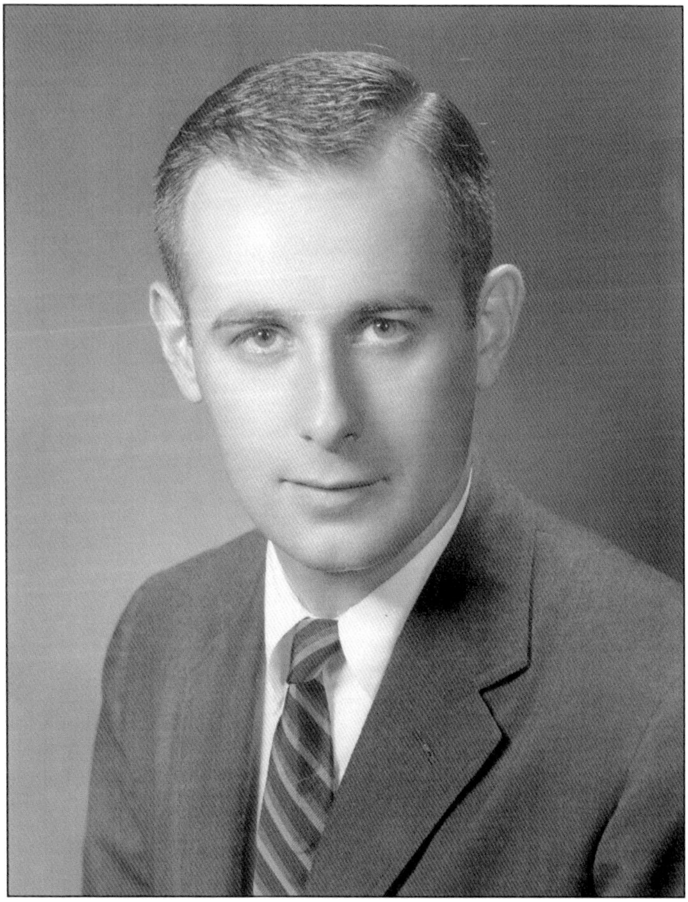

Goodloe E. Byron represented Frederick County in the U.S. Congress from 1971 until his untimely death at age 49 in 1978. Byron was born into a political family; both his father and his mother had occupied the Congressional seat he later held. After Goodloe Byron's death during the 1978 campaign, his widow, Beverly, was chosen by the Democratic Party to run for his seat, which she won and held until 1993.

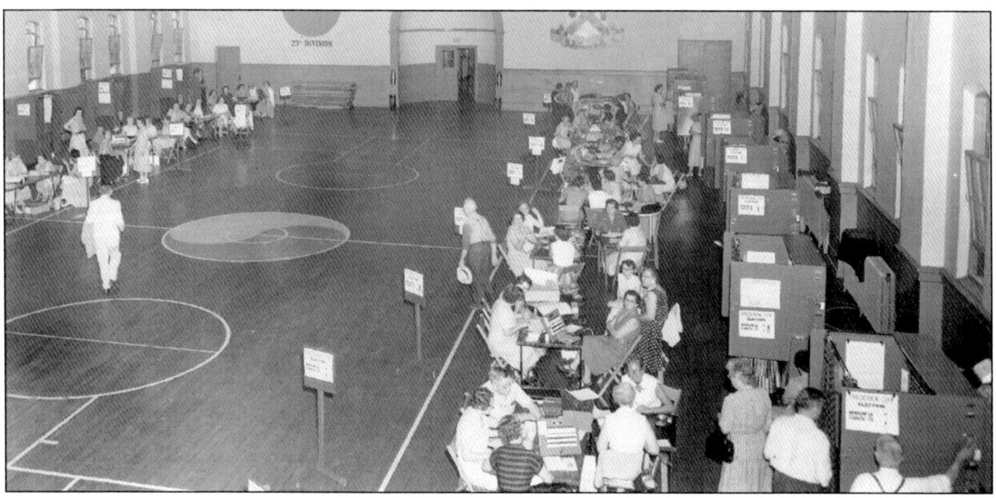

This bird's-eye view of the polls set up for the Frederick city election in the Armory, now Talley Recreation Center, was probably taken in 1966. That year, it was particularly hot on the second Tuesday in June, as evidenced by the women's sleeveless dresses and men in shirtsleeves. It turned out to be the last city election held in June. In 1969, Election Day was changed to the first Tuesday in November to avoid conflicts with state and national election cycles.

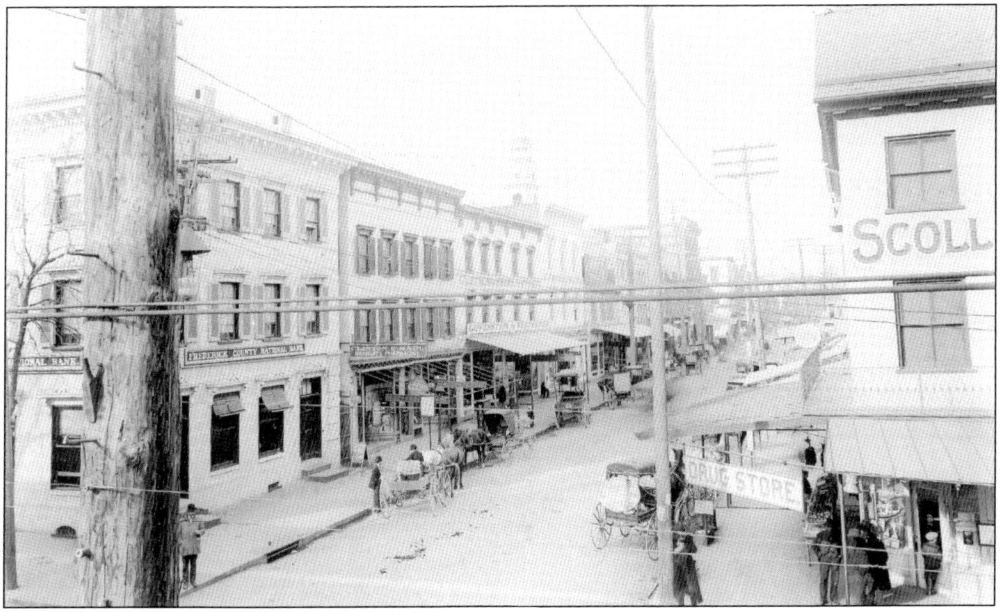

This view of North Market Street in Frederick was taken *c.* 1895. The hustle and bustle of "Square Corner" was as evident then as it is now, even if parking looks less of a problem. While businesses and some buildings have changed over the years, the busy cross street of today would be recognizable to these locals. Of particular note in this image is the boy in the bottom right who appears to be staring intently into Scoll Brothers store. One wonders what the object of his desire might be.

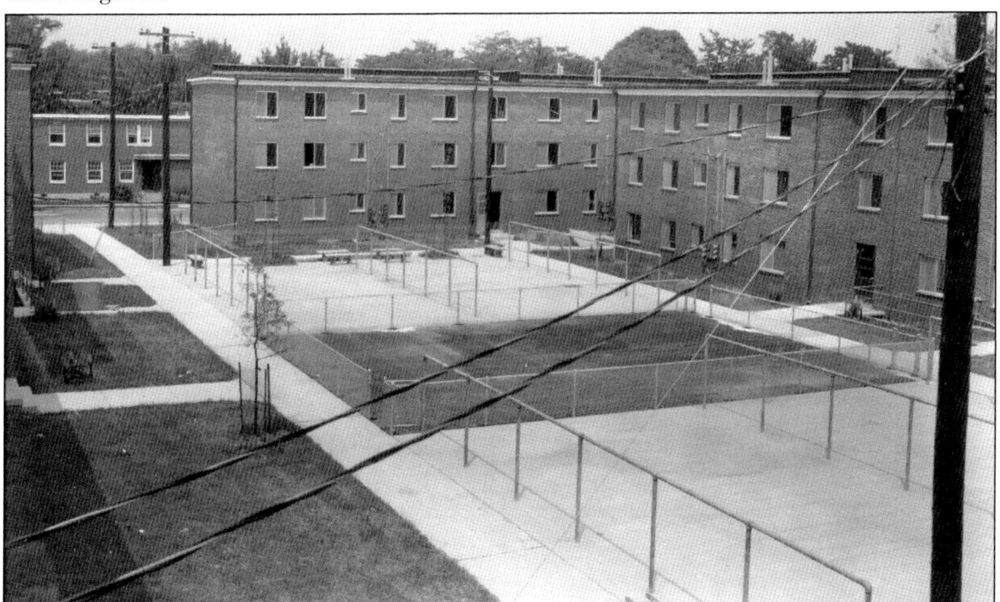

Frederick's Roger Brooke Taney Homes complex was built on North Bentz Street in 1943 as low-rent housing for white families. The Lincoln Apartments had been built previously on the southern end of town to serve the black community. The John Hanson public housing complex was built adjacent to the Taney complex in 1959, visible in the foreground. That 78-unit complex was open to all families. Both complexes were demolished in 2006 as part of a revitalization project.

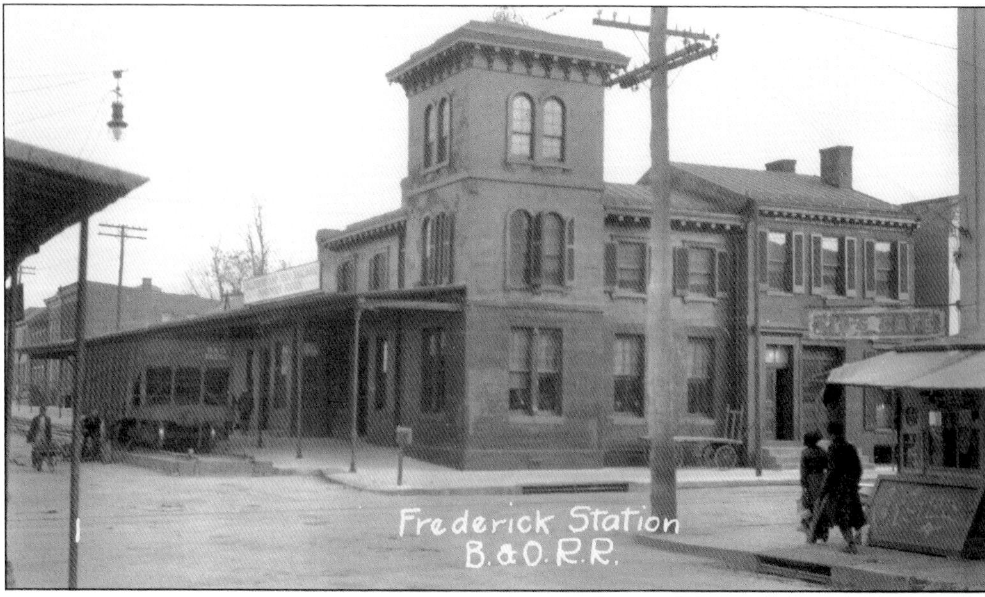

Travelers could enjoy fresh oysters at Kid's Café across from the Baltimore and Ohio Railroad Passenger Depot at the intersection of Market and All Saints Streets in Frederick. Opened in 1855, the station remained in operation for nearly 100 years, finally closing in 1948. However, travelers can still enjoy victuals at Kid's successor, Canal Bar and Grill, though its location has changed to farther down the street.

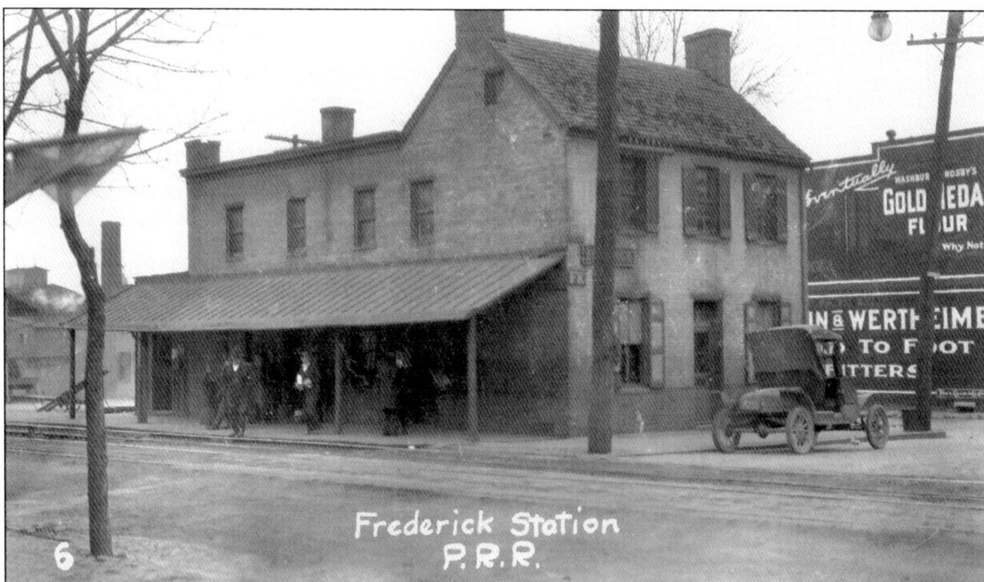

In 1925, G. M. Smith of the Pennsylvania Railroad (PRR) Company addressed members of the Frederick Rotary Club. He assured them that although the railroad had recently run losses on its passenger service, "motor trucks will never be able to successfully compete with the transportation lines on the long hauls" and "for this reason stockholders can always be assured of an investment in rail properties." The last 99 PRR passengers traveled through Frederick on August 14, 1948.

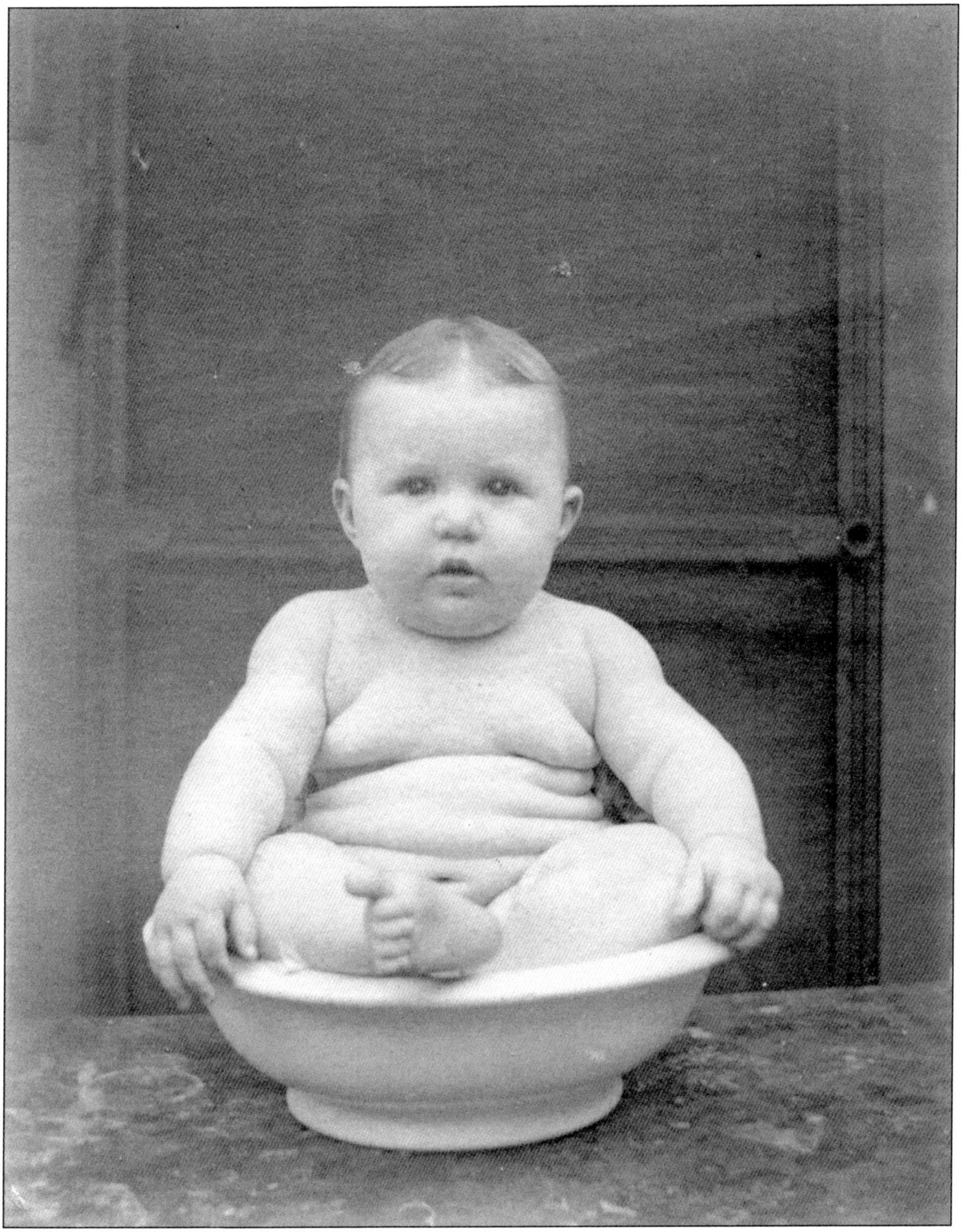

All we know about this amusing image is that it was taken around the beginning of the 20th century in Emmitsburg, and that is likely from where this little fellow hailed. While the picture may be worth 1,000 words, we sadly do not know the story of this boy-in-a-bowl. So this photograph is included to bring a smile to the reader's face and provide a cautionary tale. We kindly remind you to ensure that the stories of your precious moments—important parts of our community's history—are not lost; please include identification and notes with your own family photographs. You never know where they might turn up in 100 years' time. For more information about caring for your family photographs or arranging for their permanent preservation, contact the Historical Society of Frederick County.

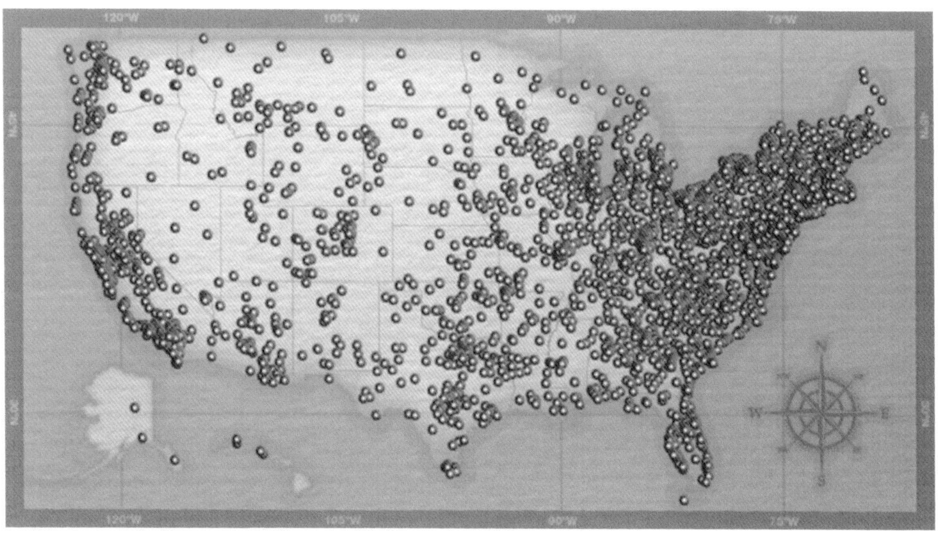